EuroWordNet:
A multilingual database with lexical semantic networks

Edited by

Piek Vossen
Faculty of Humanities,
University of Amsterdam

Reprinted from *Computers and the Humanities*, Volume 32, Nos. 2–3, 1998

Kluwer Academic Publishers
Dordrecht / Boston / London

A C.I.P. Catalogue for this book is available from the Library of Congress

ISBN 978-90-481-5120-2

Published by Kluwer Academic Publishers,
P.O. Box 17, 3300 AA Dordrecht, The Netherlands

Sold and distributed in North, Central and Latin America
by Kluwer Academic Publishers,
101 Philip Drive, Norwell, MA 02061, U.S.A.

In all other countries, sold and distributed
by Kluwer Academic Publishers Group,
P.O. Box 322, 3300 AH Dordrecht, The Netherlands

Printed on acid-free paper

TABLE OF CONTENTS

Computers and the Humanities **32:** 73–89, 1998.

Introduction to EuroWordNet

PIEK VOSSEN

*Universiteit van Amsterdam, Faculteit Geesteswetenschappen, Spuistraat 134, 1012 VB,
Amsterdam, The Netherlands E-mail: piek.vossen@hum.uva.nl*

Key words: multilingual lexical semantic database

Abstract. This paper gives a global introduction to the aims and objectives of the EuroWordNet
project, and it provides a general framework for the other papers in this volume. EuroWordNet is
an EC project that develops a multilingual database with wordnets in several European languages,
structured along the same lines as the Princeton WordNet. Each wordnet represents an autonomous
structure of language-specific lexicalizations, which are interconnected via an Inter-Lingual-Index.
The wordnets are built at different sites from existing resources, starting from a shared level of
basic concepts and extended top-down. The results will be publicly available and will be tested in
cross-language information retrieval applications.

1. General Information and Background

The goal of EuroWordNet[1] is to build a multilingual lexical database with wordnets
for several European languages, which are structured along the same lines as the
Princeton WordNet (Miller et al., 1990; Fellbaum, 1998; Fellbaum, this volume).
WordNet contains information about nouns, verbs, adjectives and adverbs in English and is organized around the notion of a *synset*. A synset is a set of words with
the same part-of-speech that can be interchanged in a certain context. For example,
{car; auto; automobile; machine; motorcar} form a synset because they can be
used to refer to the same concept. A synset is often further described by a gloss:
"4-wheeled; usually propelled by an internal combustion engine". Finally, synsets
can be related to each other by semantic relations, such as hyponymy (between
specific and more general concepts), meronymy (between parts and wholes), cause,
etc. as is illustrated in Figure 1.

In this example, taken from WordNet1.5, the synset {car; auto; automobile;
machine; motorcar} is related to:

- more general concepts or the hyperonym synset: {motor vehicle; automotive
  vehicle},
- more specific concepts or hyponym synsets: e.g. {cruiser; squad car; patrol car;
  police car; prowl car} and {cab; taxi; hack; taxicab},
- parts it is composed of: e.g. {bumper}; {car door}, {car mirror} and {car
  window}.

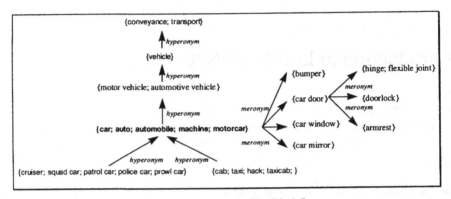

Figure 1. Synsets related to *car* in its first sense in WordNet1.5.

Each of these synsets is again related to other synsets as is illustrated for {motor vehicle; automotive vehicle} that is related to {vehicle}, and {car door} that is related to other parts: {hinge; flexible joint}, {armrest}, {doorlock}. In Fellbaum (1998) and Fellbaum (this volume) a further description is given of the history, background and characteristics of the Princeton WordNet. Fellbaum (this volume) and Alonge et al. (this volume) also further discuss the notion of a synset.

By means of these and other semantic/conceptual relations, all meanings can be interconnected, constituting a huge network or wordnet. Such a wordnet can be used for making semantic inferences about the meanings of words (what meanings can be interpreted as *vehicles*), for finding alternative expressions or wordings, or for simply expanding words to sets of semantically related or close words in information retrieval. Furthermore, semantic networks give information on the lexicalization patterns of languages, on the conceptual density of areas of the vocabulary and on the distribution of semantic distinctions or relations over different areas of the vocabulary. Fellbaum (this volume) and Gonzalo et al. (this volume) further discuss some of the uses of both WordNet and EuroWordNet.

The European wordnets will be stored in a central lexical database system and each meaning will be linked to the closest synset in the Princeton WordNet1.5, thus creating a multilingual database. In such a database it will be possible to go from one meaning in a wordnet to a meaning in another wordnet, which is linked to the same WordNet1.5 concept. Such a multilingual database is useful for cross-language information retrieval, for transfer of information from one resource to another or for simply comparing the different wordnets. A comparison may tell us something about the consistency of the relations across wordnets, where differences may point to inconsistencies or to language-specific properties of the resources, or also to properties of the language itself. In this way, the database can also be seen as a powerful tool for studying lexical semantic resources and their language-specificity. The first results of such comparison are described in Peters et al. (this volume).

In EuroWordNet, we initially have been working on 4 languages: Dutch, Italian, Spanish and English. The size of each of these wordnets, except for English, will be about 30,000 comparable synsets, roughly corresponding to 50,000 word meanings. For comparison, the size of WordNet1.5 is 91,591 synsets and 168,217 word meanings.[2] In an extension to the project, the database is extended with German, French, Estonian and Czech: the size of these wordnets will be between 7,500–15,000 synsets.

The wordnets are limited to nouns and verbs, although adjectives and adverbs are included in so far they are related to nouns and verbs (see Alonge et al. (this volume) for the relations that may hold across parts-of-speech). The vocabulary will comprise all the generic and basic words of the languages: i.e. it will include all the meanings and concepts that are needed to relate more specific meanings, and all the words that occur most frequently in general corpora. For one domain, sub-vocabulary will be added to illustrate the possibility of integrating terminology in such a general-purpose lexicon.

The results of EuroWordNet will be publicly available (world-wide) and can be obtained by means of a license. The following institutes are responsible for building the separate wordnets:

Dutch: the University of Amsterdam (co-ordinator of EuroWordNet).

Spanish: the 'Fundacíon Universidad Empresa' (a co-operation of UNED Madrid, Politecnica de Catalunya in Barcelona, and the University of Barcelona).

Italian: Istituto di Linguistica Computazionale, C.N.R., Pisa.

English: University of Sheffield (adapting the English wordnet).

French: Université d' Avignon and Memodata at Avignon.

German: Universität Tübingen.

Czech: University of Masaryk at Brno in Czech.

Estonian: University of Tartu in Estonia.

Each of these institutes is responsible for the construction of their national wordnet, where most of them bring in material and resources developed outside the project (among which lexical resources from the publishers Van Dale for Dutch and Bibliograf for Spanish). The task of Sheffield is different because of the existence of WordNet for English. Their role consists of adapting the Princeton WordNet for the changes made in EuroWordNet and controlling the interlingua that connects the wordnets.

In addition to the builders there are 3 industrial users in the project:

- Bertin & Cie, Plaisir, France
- Xerox Research Centre, Meylan, France
- Novell Linguistic Development, Antwerp, Belgium

They will demonstrate the use of the database in their (multilingual) information-retrieval applications. Novell also has an additional role as the developer of the shared EuroWordNet database.

In this introductory paper, we will give an outline of the project and provide a framework for the other papers of this volume, which give specific details on different aspects. The work described in all these papers is the result of joined work by the 5 institutes that make up the first EuroWordNet consortium: the University of Amsterdam, the Istituto di Linguistica Computazionale del CNR (Pisa), the 'Fundacíon Universidad Empresa' (UNED Madrid, Politecnica de Catalunya, and the University of Barcelona), the University of Sheffield and Novell Linguistic Development (Antwerp). In the next section we will give an overview of the database with the different modules representing the project results we are aiming at. In Section 3 we will outline the general approaches and phases for building the wordnets. Section 4 gives an overview of the results and their availability. Finally, in Section 5 we give a global overview on the possible ways in which the database could be used or further developed. In addition, a glossary of the terminology is given. Where necessary we will refer to the other papers in this volume, in which further details are discussed.

2. The Overall Design of the EuroWordNet Database

The construction of a generic semantic resource is not a trivial task. Meaning and interpretation is studied by a variety of disciplines and paradigms, with different viewpoints and requirements. There is a widely held feeling that the role of general semantics or common knowledge in the processes of language understanding is still too complex to be adequately described with the current technology. The aim of EuroWordNet is therefore not to develop full semantic lexicons that make use of complex representation languages and inferencing mechanisms but to limit the information and mechanisms to those basic semantic relations between words that are well understood. The semantic relations incorporated in the Princeton Word-Net1.5 (Miller et al., 1990; Fellbaum, 1990; Beckwith and Miller, 1990; Gross and Miller, 1990) are acknowledged in a wide range of scientific areas: formal semantics, AI, cognitive linguistics, lexicology, information science, mathematics. Fellbaum (this volume) gives a further specification of WordNet.

Furthermore, the relations do not rely on any specific knowledge representation formalism and are expected to form the backbone of any knowledge system of the future. Even though the relational approach to meaning in WordNet and EuroWordNet cannot be seen as a complete specification of a word's meaning, it is nevertheless possible to extend this basic information with more comprehensive specifications, partly using corpus-based techniques. Even stronger, both McCarthy (1997) and Sanfilippo (1997) demonstrate that the availability of wordnet structures is very useful for automatically extracting this information from corpora.

The design of the EuroWordNet-database is thus first of all based on the structure of the Princeton WordNet and specifically version WordNet1.5. The notion of a synset and the main semantic relations have been taken over in EuroWordNet. However, some specific changes have been made to the design of the database, which are mainly motivated by the following objectives:

1) to create a multilingual database;
2) to maintain language-specific relations in the wordnets;
3) to achieve maximal compatibility across the different resources;
4) to build the wordnets relatively independently (re)-using existing resources;

The most important difference of EuroWordNet with respect to WordNet is its multilinguality, which however also raises some fundamental questions with respect to the status of the monolingual information in the wordnets. In principle, multilinguality is achieved by adding an equivalence relation for each synset in a language to the closest synset in WordNet1.5. Synsets linked to the same WordNet1.5 synset are supposed to be equivalent or close in meaning and can then be compared. However, what should be done with differences across the wordnets? If 'equivalent' words are related in different ways in the different resources, we have to make a decision about the legitimacy of these differences. For example, in the Dutch wordnet we see that *hond* (dog) is both classified as *huisdier* (pet) and *zoogdier* (mammal). However, there is no equivalent for *pet* in Italian, and the Italian *cane*, which is linked to the same synset *dog*, is only classified as a *mammal* in the Italian wordnet.

In EuroWordNet, we take the position that it must be possible to reflect such differences in lexical semantic relations. The wordnets are seen as linguistic ontologies rather than ontologies for making inferences only. In an inference-based ontology it may be the case that a particular level or structuring is required to achieve a better control or performance, or a more compact and coherent structure. For this purpose it may be necessary to introduce artificial levels for concepts which are not lexicalized in a language (e.g. *natural object, external body parts*), or it may be necessary to neglect levels (e.g. *watchdog*) that are lexicalized but not relevant for the purpose of the ontology. A linguistic ontology, on the other hand, exactly reflects the lexicalization and the relations between the words in a language. It is a "wordnet" in the true sense of the word and therefore captures valuable information about conceptualizations that are lexicalized in a language: what is the available fund of words and expressions in a language.

The difference is illustrated in Figure 2, where the hyponymic structure of WordNet1.5 reflects a combination of lexicalized and non-lexicalized categories and the Dutch Wordnet only contains categories lexicalized in the language. In WordNet1.5 we see that the synset for *object* is first subdivided into two subclasses *artifact* and *natural object*, of which the latter is not a lexicalized expression in English (which you would expect to find as a headword in a dictionary) but rather a regularly composed expression.

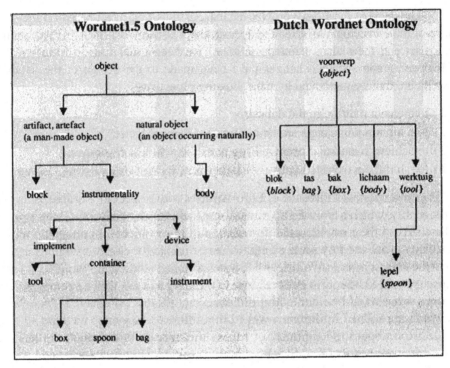

Figure 2. Lexicalized and Non-lexicalized levels in wordnets.

The class *artifact* has an important subclass *instrumentality*, which is used to group related synsets such as *implement*, *device*, *tool* and *instrument* below a common denominator. Such a grouping seems helpful to organize the hierarchy and predict the functionality of the subclasses. However, it does not give correct predictions about the substitutability of the nouns: you cannot refer to *containers*, *boxes*, *spoons*, and *bags* using the noun *instrumentality* in English.

In the Dutch hierarchy, we see that artificial levels such as *natural object* and *instrumentality* have not been used. Furthermore, there are no exact equivalents for *artifact* and *container* in Dutch.[3] As a result of this, we get a much flatter hierarchy in which particular properties such as *natural*, *artificial* and *functionality* cannot be derived from the hyponymy relations.[4] On the other hand, the network correctly predicts the expressive capacity of the Dutch lexicon because it only includes the legitimate words (and multiword-expressions) of the language. We could invent new classes and expressions in Dutch to capture different generalizations, we could even take over the WordNet1.5 classes, but there are no a priori criteria to decide what are useful classes and what are not. We may end up by adding any conceivable semantic property as a class to create very rich inheritance structures, or we may take over all possible classifications from all the other wordnets. However, this would destroy the wordnet as a network of legitimate expressions in a language and it would still not automatically give us a good conceptual ontology for inheriting properties.

Furthermore, it is possible to extend the database with a separate language-neutral or application-specific ontology which takes care of the inferences and is well designed for that purpose. When this ontology is linked to the EuroWordNet database, all the wordnets can access these classifications to find the correct inferences for their synsets. The wordnets then provide the precise mapping of the language-specific vocabulary on this ontology. To obtain such an ontology, we are co-operating with the ANSI Group on Standardizing Ontologies, which is developing a standardized Reference Ontology.

In addition to the theoretical motivation there is also a practical motivation for considering the wordnets as autonomous networks. To be more cost-effective, they will be (as far as possible) derived from existing resources, databases and tools. This gives each of the sites a different starting point for building their local wordnet. It is therefore important that we allow for a maximum of flexibility in producing the wordnets and structures.

To be able to maintain the language-specific structures and to allow for the separate development of independent resources, we make a distinction between the language-specific modules and a separate language-independent module. Each language module represents an autonomous and unique language-specific system of language-internal relations between synsets. Equivalence relations between the synsets in different languages and WordNet1.5 will be made explicit in the so-called Inter-Lingual-Index (ILI). Each synset in the monolingual wordnets will have at least one equivalence relation with a record in this ILI. Language-specific synsets linked to the same ILI-record should thus be equivalent across the languages, as is illustrated in Figure 3 for the language-specific synsets linked to the ILI-record *drive*.

Figure 3 further gives a schematic presentation of the different modules and their inter-relations. In the middle, the language-external modules are given: the ILI, a Domain Ontology and a Top Concept Ontology. The ILI consists of a list of so-called ILI-records (ILIRs) which are related to word-meanings in the language-internal modules, (possibly) to one or more Top Concepts and (possibly) to domains. The language-internal modules then consist of a lexical-item-table indexed to a set of synsets, between which the language-internal relations are expressed.

The ILI is an unstructured list of meanings, mainly taken from WordNet1.5, where each ILI-record consists of a synset, an English gloss specifying the meaning and a reference to its source. The only purpose of the ILI is to mediate between the synsets of the language-specific wordnets. No relations are therefore maintained between the ILI-records as such. The development of a complete language-neutral ontology is considered to be too complex and time-consuming given the limitations of the project. As an unstructured list there is no need to discuss changes or updates to the index from a many-to-many perspective. Note that it will nevertheless be

[7]

Architecture of the EuroWordNet Data Structure

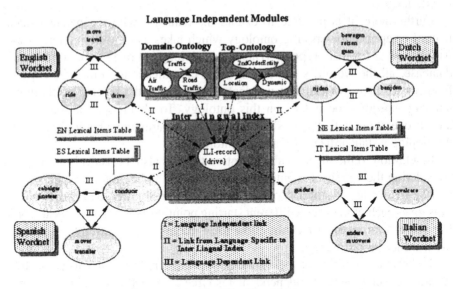

Figure 3. The global architecture of the EuroWordNet database.

possible to indirectly see a structuring of a set of ILI-records by viewing the language-internal relations of the language-specific concepts that are related to the set of ILI-records. Since WordNet1.5 is linked to the index in the same way as any of the other wordnets, it is still possible to recover the original internal organization of the synsets in terms of the semantic relations in WordNet1.5. A further discussion on the advantages and disadvantages of different multilingual designs and the ways of comparing the wordnets is given in Peters et al. (this volume).

Some language-independent structuring of the ILI is nevertheless provided by two separate ontologies, which may be linked to ILI records:

- the Top Concept ontology, which is a hierarchy of language-independent concepts, reflecting important semantic distinctions, e.g. Object and Substance, Location, Dynamic and Static;
- a hierarchy of domain labels, which are knowledge structures grouping meanings in terms of topics or scripts, e.g. Traffic, Road-Traffic, Air-Traffic, Sports, Hospital, Restaurant;

Both the Top Concepts and the domain labels can be transferred via the equivalence relations of the ILI-records to the language-specific meanings, as is illustrated in Figure 3. The Top Concepts *Location* and *Dynamic* are for example directly linked to the ILI-record *drive* and therefore indirectly also apply to all language-specific concepts related to this ILI-record. Via the language-internal relations the Top Concept can be further inherited by all other related language-specific concepts.

The main purpose of the Top Ontology is to provide a common framework for the most important concepts in all the wordnets (see Section 3 below). It consists of 63 basic semantic distinctions that classify a set of 1024 ILI-records representing the most important concepts in the different wordnets. The classification has been verified by the different sites, so that it holds for all the language-specific wordnets. Rodriquez et al. (this volume) describe the Top Ontology and its motivation in detail.

The domain-labels can be used directly in information retrieval (and also in language-learning tools and dictionary publishing) to group concepts in a different way, based on scripts rather than classification. Domains can also be used to separate the generic from the domain-specific vocabularies. This is important to control the ambiguity problem in Natural Language Processing. These issues are further discussed in Gonzalo et al. (this volume).

In EuroWordNet, the domain ontology will only be built for a small fragment of the vocabulary, for illustration purposes. However, users of the database can freely add domain labels to the ILI or adjust the top ontology without having to access or consider the language-internal relations of each wordnet. In the same way, it is possible to extend the database with other ontologies (as suggested above for the ANSI Reference ontology) provided that they are specified according to the EuroWordNet format and include a proper linking to the ILI.

The ILI starts off as a list of WordNet1.5 synsets, but will be adapted to provide a better matching across the wordnets. There are two types of changes to the ILI. First of all, there will be concepts in the local wordnets which are not present in WordNet1.5, e.g. *a female cashier*. To be able to still express equivalence relations between such a concept in other wordnets (*cajera* in Spanish, *cassière* in Dutch), the ILI has to be extended. The ultimate ILI will thus become the superset of all concepts occurring in the different wordnets. Another update of the ILI consists of globalizing other meaning distinctions present in WordNet1.5. In the case of extreme sense-differentiation, e.g. *clean* having 19 senses, it is difficult to match equivalent synsets to exactly the same WordNet senses. By extending the ILI with global senses that group multiple specific meanings, different matches to these specific meanings can still be recovered. Such updates can be made relatively easy because the ILI lacks any further structure.

Once the wordnets are properly linked to the ILI, the EuroWordNet database makes it possible to compare wordnet fragments via the ILI and to track down differences in lexicalization and in the language-internal relations, for example as described above for *containers* in the Dutch wordnet and WordNet1.5. Peters et al. (this volume) discuss in detail the motivation of the ILI as the unstructured superset of concepts, its adaptation and the possible ways of comparing the wordnets.

Summarizing, the modular multilingual design of the EWN-database has the following advantages:

- it will be possible to use the database for multilingual information retrieval, by expanding words in one language to related words in another language via the ILI;
- the different wordnets can be compared and checked cross-linguistically which will make them more compatible;
- language-dependent differences can be maintained in the individual wordnets;
- it will be possible to develop the wordnets at different sites relatively independently;
- language-independent information such as the glosses, the domain-knowledge and the analytic Top Concepts can be stored only once and can be made available to all the language-specific modules via the inter-lingual relations;
- the database can be tailored to a user's needs by modifying the Top Concepts, the domain labels or instances, (e.g. by adding semantic features) without having to access the language-specific wordnets.

In addition to the multilingual design of the database, there have been some changes to the language-internal relations with respect to WordNet1.5. The major innovations are:

1. the use of labels to the relations that make the semantic entailments more explicit and precise;
2. the introduction of cross part-of-speech relations, so that different surface realizations of similar concepts within and across languages can still be matched;
3. the addition of some extra relations to differentiate certain shallow hierarchies.

Conjunction and *disjunction* are examples of relation labels that can be assigned to multiple relations of the same kind. Conjunction of relations is typical for meronymy: i.e. multiple parts that together make up a single whole (e.g. *wings, nose, tail, door* are parts that make up an *airplane* conjunctively). However, it may also apply to other relations such as hyponymy: a *knife* is both a *weapon* and a *piece of cutlery* at the same time. In other cases, multiple parts or hyperonyms are clearly disjunctive: an *albino* is either an *animal, human* or a *plant*, a *threat* may be a *person, idea* or *thing*, an *airplane* either has *propellers* or *jets*.

Whereas in WordNet, the parts-of-speech represent distinct networks, in EuroWordNet they are interconnected in various ways. A typical cross-part-speech relations is xpos-synonymy between words with different part-of-speech that can be used to describe the same concept, e.g. between the verb *adorn* and the noun *adornment* or the noun *death* and the adjective *dead*. However, also other relations across parts-of-speech are allowed such as: causation relations between *die* and *dead*, *redden* and *red*, or semantic role relations between nouns and verbs, such as agent (*teacher*), patient (*student*), location (*school*) related to *teach*. The latter relations also differentiate shallow hierarchies, such as *persons* or *physical changes*, where many hyponyms only differ in the associated role or result.

These changes directly improve the use of the database for Language Engineering applications, but also create a more elaborate network, which is useful for research in general on important semantic relations in languages. All the language-internal relations have been defined using explicit tests in all the four languages. These tests ensure minimal consensus on the interpretation of the relations across the sites. A further discussion on the specific semantic relations and the above changes is given in Alonge et al. (this volume) on the Linguistic Design of the database.

3. General Approach for Building the Wordnets

As suggested above, the EuroWordNet database is built (as much as possible) from available existing resources and databases with semantic information developed in various projects. This will not only be more cost-effective given the limited time and budget of the project, but will also make it possible to combine information from independently created wordnets. Redundancy of information can be used to fill gaps for other wordnets or as evidence for language-specificity of deviating patterns.

In general, the wordnets are built in two major cycles as indicated by I and II in Figure 4 below. Each cycle consists of a building phase and a comparison phase:

1. Building a wordnet fragment
    1.1. Specification of an initial vocabulary
    1.2. Encoding of the language-internal relations
    1.3. Encoding of the equivalence relations
2. Comparing the wordnet fragments
    2.1. Loading of the wordnets in the EuroWordNet database
    2.2. Comparing and restructuring the fragments
    2.3. Measuring the overlap across the fragments

The building of a fragment is done using local tools and databases that are tailored to the specific nature and possibilities of the available resources. The available resources differ considerably in quality and explicitness of the data. Whereas some sites have the availability of partially structured networks between word senses, others start from genus words extracted from definitions that still have to be disambiguated in meaning.

After the specification of a fragment of the vocabulary, where each site uses similar criteria (there may again be differences due to the different starting points), globally, two approaches are followed for encoding the semantic relations:

Merge Model: the selection is done in a local resource and the synsets and their language-internal relations are first developed separately, after which the equivalence relations to WordNet1.5 are generated.

Expand Model: the selection is done in WordNet1.5 and the WordNet.1.5 synsets are translated (using bilingual dictionaries) into equivalent synsets in the other language. The wordnet relations are taken over and where necessary

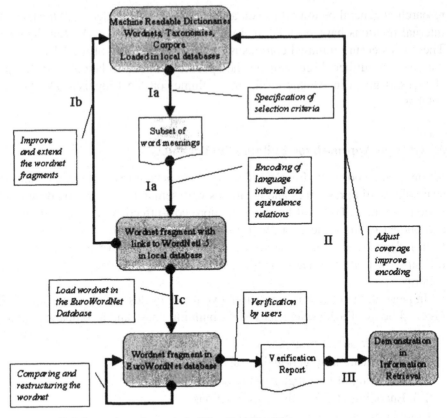

Figure 4. Global overview of steps in building EuroWordNet.

adapted to EuroWordNet. Possibly, monolingual resources are used to verify the wordnet relations imposed on non-English synsets.

The Merge Model, which is followed for most languages, results in a wordnet that is independent of WordNet1.5, possibly maintaining the language-specific properties. The Expand model, which is followed for Spanish, will result in a wordnet that is very close to WordNet1.5 but which will also be biased by it. Whatever approach is followed also depends on the quality of the available resources.[5]

After the first production phase (steps Ia and Ib in Figure 4) the results are converted to the EuroWordNet import format and loaded into the common database (step Ic). At that point various consistency checks are carried out, both formally and conceptually. By using the specific options in the EuroWordNet database it is then possible to further inspect and compare the data, to restructure relations where necessary and to measure the overlap in the fragments developed at the separate sites. Those meanings not covered by a site may be included in the extension of the vocabulary in the next building phase.

After each cycle, there will be a verification phase by the users in the project. Feedback from the users can be incorporated in the next building cycle. At the end of the project the results will be used in a (cross-language) information retrieval application (phase III).

The overall design of the EuroWordNet database makes it possible to develop the individual language-specific wordnets relatively independently while guaranteeing a minimal level of compatibility. Nevertheless, some specific measures have been taken to enlarge the compatibility of the different resources:

1. The definition of a common set of so-called Base Concepts that is used as a starting point by all the sites to develop the cores of the wordnets. Base Concepts[6] are meanings that play a major role in the wordnets.
2. The classification of the Base Concepts in terms of the Top Ontology.
3. The exchange of problems and possible solutions for encoding the relations for the Base Concepts.

The work and the rationale behind the Base Concepts and the Top Ontology are further described in Rodriquez et al. (this volume). Vossen et al. (this volume) give a detailed account of the typical problems and solutions that are encountered when dealing with these crucial but complex concepts.

4. Results and Availability

The EuroWordNet results will be available as separate modules, both in Ascii format and integrated in the EuroWordNet database:

1. the Top Concepts and the Top Ontology.
2. the classification of Base Concepts in terms of the Top Ontology.
3. the Inter-Lingual-Index, consisting of synsets, English glosses, and (optionally) Top Concepts and/or domain-labels.
4. the first vocabulary subset for each language, containing the local Base Concepts and their direct semantic environment.
5. the second vocabulary subset for each language, containing further extensions of the Base Concepts.
6. for each language some sub-vocabulary on a specific domain.
7. the EuroWordNet database in which the different modules can be accessed and compared, and from which fragments can be exported.

A license will have to be obtained to either use individual modules or the full package. Different licenses will be available for commercial and non-commercial usage. A fee may be requested for commercial usage, depending on the amount of background information that is included in a module. The distribution and licensing will be handled by ELRA (the European Language Resources Association, http://www.icp.inpg.fr/ELRA).

In addition to the consignment of the actual data, the methodologies, tools and results will be fully documented. The most important documents will be:

1. Definition of the semantic relations.
2. The Architecture of the EuroWordNet database.
3. Description of the actual wordnets in terms of coverage, richness and quality.
4. Description of the tools, resources and methods used to build the wordnets.
5. A specification of the EuroWordNet database import format.
6. Manual for operating the EuroWordNet Multilingual viewer.

Using these documents it will be possible for external groups to decide on the approach which fits their situation best and to build wordnets compatible to EuroWordNet. The documents are public and can be obtained from the EuroWord-Net home-page (http://www.hum.uva.nl/~ewn) as soon as they become available. In addition to general information on the project, the home-page also contains data-samples, the top-ontology, the selection of the Base Concepts, a specification of the EuroWordNet import format and the public viewer Periscope that provides a multilingual graphical interface to the data samples.

5. Usage and Exploitation of the Results

The wordnets are not intended for a single specific use. However, the budget of the project does not allow for an extensive study and demonstration of the different possible uses. We have therefore limited the actual demonstration to the usage in information retrieval systems (IRS). This choice is mainly based on the fact that a module using EuroWordNet is relatively easy to build for IRS. Other systems, such as Machine Translation Systems, Authoring Tools and Language Learning Tools, also depend on other complex modules and require more detailed lexical data, in which for example semantic and syntactic information is integrated.

The development and testing of an IRS as such, however, goes beyond the scope of this project. The user-requirements of such a full system include aspects such as flexibility, on-line help, visual representation of the results, allowing for different retrieval techniques. The aim of this project is not to develop such a system but to provide a generic basic resource that could be included in such a broader IRS.

Given the current state of the art in IRSs the availability of general, generic resources such as a wordnet is typically expected to help non-expert users when retrieval by indexing is problematic because:

1) the indexing system does not cover the desired aspect or facet that a user is looking for,
2) the words chosen by the user are not included in the indexing key-word list,
3) the user speaks another language.

Various IR systems already use WordNet1.5 to enhance a user's query by expand-ing it to all related terms. In Gonzalo et al. (this volume) a more detailed discussion is given of the use of wordnets in both monolingual and cross-language information retrieval.

In addition to the direct scope of the project, we have also set up a EuroWordNet User-Group of wordnet-builders and users that covers a wider range of languages and applications:

- publishers, providing the initial resources or interested in the development of similar products.
- research institutes and R&D departments of universities and companies working in the field of knowledge engineering or linguistic databases.
- research institutes and R&D departments of universities and companies interested in using or applying similar resources or developing services or products.
- end-users interested in products helping them to deal with information.

The User-Group currently consists of 40 members. The role of the User-Group is to give feed-back to early releases of the project results (including samples, the EuroWordNet database, documentation, definition of standards and data formats) which will be taken into account in the incremental building of the resources. By directly disseminating the results to the User-Group, we also hope to create a wider awareness of the project results and to pave the way for the extension of the resources to other languages, larger vocabularies and other types of applications.

On a longer term we expect that EuroWordNet will open up a whole range of new applications and services in Europe at a trans-national and trans-cultural level. It will give information on the typical lexicalization patterns across languages, which will be crucial for machine translation and language learning systems. It will give non-native users and non-skilled writers the possibility to navigate or browse through the vocabulary of a language in new ways, giving them an overview of expression which is not feasible in traditional alphabetically-organized resources. Finally, it will stimulate the development of sophisticated lexical knowledge bases that are crucial for a whole gamut of future applications, ranging from basic infor-mation retrieval to question/answering systems, language understanding and expert systems, from summarizers to automatic translation tools and resources.

6. Glossary

Base Concept, BC	A basic (language-specific) concept in terms of which other word meanings can be defined.
Concept	A conceptual unit either in the form of a Synset, Word Meaning, Top Concept, Domain Concept, or an ILI-record.
Definition	A natural language description of a word meaning in a lexical resource.
Domain Concept	A concept restricting a word meaning to a certain topic or domain.
Domain Ontology	A set of hierarchically related Domain Concepts.

Entry	A record in a lexical resource as a unit of information.
Equivalence relation	A relation from a synset in a language-specific wordnet to an ILI-record in the ILI.
EuroWordNet database	The multilingual database (Polaris), in which the indexed wordnets can be created, accessed, compared and edited.
EuroWordNet viewer	The public database, Periscope, for viewing the wordnets from a multilingual perspective.
EWN	EuroWordNet
Gloss	A semantic indicator of a word meaning, either in the form of a definition or an example.
Hyperonym/ Hypernym	The synset that classifies or subsumes a more specific synset
Hyponym	A synset that is classified or is subsumed by a more general synset
Hyponymy/Hypernymy	A relation between a more specific synset and a more general synset that classifies it.
ILI	The Inter-Lingual-Index: an unstructured fund of synsets inter-linking language-specific synsets from different word-nets in EuroWordnet.
ILI-record	A single synset in the ILI, minimally consisting of a set of synonyms, a gloss and a reference to its source.
Language-internal relation	A relation between synsets in a language-specific wordnet.
Lemma, headword	A conventional key for a lexical entry.
Synset	A set of synonymous word meanings
Synset member, Synset variant	A word meaning which is a member of a synset
Top Concept, TC	A language-independent concept representing a fundamental semantic distinction.
Top Ontology	A set of hierarchically related Top Concepts.
Word form	A unique form of a word, irrespective of its occurrence as different word tokens.
Word meaning, Word sense, Sense	A specific meaning of a word.
Word token	The occurrence of a word form in text.
Word type	A word stem, irrespective of the word forms.
Wordnet	A semantic network of synsets with semantic relations between them.
WordNet	WordNet as conceived by Princeton University
WordNet1.5, WN1.5	The database version WordNet1.5 as it has been published by Princeton University

Acknowledgements

This project is funded by the European Commission. Furthermore, we are indebted to the publishers (Van Dale and Bibliograf) that kindly provided their resources for the creation of the database.

[16]

Notes

[1] EuroWordNet (LE2-4003 and LE-8328) is funded by the European Community within the Telematics Application Programme of the 4th Framework (DG-XIII, Luxembourg).

[2] Note that each meaning of a word (e.g. *car* in sense 1 and *car* in sense 2) belongs to a different synset, and each synset may contain several word senses.

[3] The word "container" does exist in Dutch but is only used for big containers on ships or for big garbage cans.

[4] Other relations may still express these properties. In Dutch for example, the *containers* could have a instrument-role relations with *bevatten* (to contain). These relations are further discussed in Alonge et al. (this volume).

[5] The specific tools, resources and databases for building the wordnets as such are not deliverables of the project. Most of these tools and databases have been developed outside the scope of EuroWordNet. We will nevertheless produce a document describing all of them together with the approaches used to build the different wordnets. For each of these tools and methods we will specify the performance, the requirements and the availability.

[6] The notion of Base Concepts should not be confused with Basic-Level Concepts as defined by Rosch (1977). According to Rosch, the Basic Level is the level at which two conflicting principles of classification are in balance: 1) to predict features for as many instances as possible, 2) to predict as many features as possible. Typically, this balance occurs at an average level of specificity (where the level can vary due to interest and experience). Base Concepts are technically defined as the concepts with most relations. This more strongly correlates with the first principle, and they are therefore in most cases more general than the Basic Level Concepts.

References

Beckwith, R. and G. A. Miller. "Implementing a Lexical Network". *International Journal of Lexicography*, 3(4) (1990), 302–312.

Fellbaum, C. "English Verbs as a Semantic Net". *International Journal of Lexicography*, 3(4) (1990), 278–301.

Fellbaum, C. (ed.) *WordNet: An Electronic Lexical Database*. Cambridge, MA: MIT Press, 1998.

Gross, D. and K. J. Miller. "Adjectives in Wordnet". *International Journal of Lexicography*, 3(4) (1990), 265–277.

McCarthy, D. "Word Sense Disambiguation for Acquisition of Selectional Preferences". In *Proceedings of the ACL/EACL'97 Workshop on Automatic Information Extraction and Building of Lexical Semantic Resources*. Ed. P. Vossen, G. Adriaens, N. Calzolari, A. Sanfilippo and Y. Wilks, 1997.

Miller G., R. Beckwith, C. Fellbaum, D. Gross, K. J. Miller. "Introduction to WordNet: An On-line Lexical Database". *International Journal of Lexicography*, 3(4) (1990), 235–244.

Rosch, E. "Human Categorisation". In *Cross-Cultural Psychology*, Vol. I. Ed. N. Warren, London: Academic Press, 1977, pp. 1–49.

Sanfilippo, A. "Using Semantic Similarity to Acquire Co-occurrence Restrictions from Corpora". In *Proceedings of the ACL/EACL'97 Workshop on Automatic Information Extraction and Building of Lexical Semantic Resources*. Ed. P. Vossen, G. Adriaens, N. Calzolari, A. Sanfilippo, and Y. Wilks, 1997.

Computers and the Humanities **32**: 91–115, 1998.
© 1998 *Kluwer Academic Publishers.*

The Linguistic Design of the EuroWordNet Database

ANTONIETTA ALONGE[1,2], NICOLETTA CALZOLARI[1,3], PIEK VOSSEN[4,5], LAURA BLOKSMA[4,6], IRENE CASTELLON[7,8], MARIA ANTONIA MARTI[7,9] and WIM PETERS[10]

[1]*istituto di Linguistica Computazionale, CNR, Via della Faggiola 32, 56126 Pisa, Italy; E-mail:* [2]*aalonge@pg.tecnonet.it,* [3]*glottolo@ilc.pi.cnr.it;* [4]*Universiteit van Amsterdam, Faculteit Geesteswetenschappen, Spuistraat 134, 1012 VB Amsterdam, The Netherlands; E-mail:*[5]*Piek.Vossen@let.uva.nl,* [6]*lbloks@let.uva.nl;* [7]*University of Barcelona, Computational Linguistics Research Group, Gran Via 585, 08007 Barcelona, Spain; E-mail:* [8]*castel, amarti@lingua.fil.ub.es,* [9]*amarti@lingua.fil.ub.es;* [10]*University of Sheffield, Computer Science Department, Portobello Street 211, Regent Court, Sheffield, S1 4DT, Great Britain; E-mail: w.peters@dcs.sheffield.ac.uk*

Key words: equivalence relations, lexical-semantic relations, language-internal relations, synset

Abstract. In this paper the linguistic design of the database under construction within the EuroWordNet project is described. This is mainly structured along the same lines as the Princeton WordNet, although some changes have been made to the WordNet overall design due to both theoretical and practical reasons. The most important reasons for such changes are the multilinguality of the EuroWordNet database and the fact that it is intended to be used in Language Engineering applications. Thus, i) some relations have been added to those identified in WordNet; ii) some labels have been identified which can be added to the relations in order to make their implications more explicit and precise; iii) some relations, already present in the WordNet design, have been modified in order to specify their role more clearly.

1. Introduction

The EuroWordNet (EWN) database is a 'relational' semantic database in which the meaning of each word is basically described by means of its relations to other word meanings. The linguistic design of the database is based on that of the Princeton WordNet 1.5 (WN1.5), i.e. it is organized around the notion of a 'synset' (a set of synonyms representing a concept) with basic semantic relations encoded between the synsets. Most of the WN relations, commonly accepted in various approaches to semantics, have been taken over in EWN. Nevertheless, some important changes have been made to the set of relations to be encoded in EWN for the following reasons:

- the WN1.5 relations do not seem sufficient to describe all the meaning nuances which i) may be important from a theoretical point of view, e.g. to clarify the relation between semantics and syntax; ii) could be useful for Information Retrieval (IR) or other Language Engineering (LE) applications;
- the EWN database is a multilingual resource, thus it was necessary to add relations which clarify particular similarities/differences in the semantic constituency of words which have a close meaning across different languages;
- some important data can be (or have been) easily extracted from Machine Readable Dictionaries (MRDs), which are our main sources of data,[1] but cannot be encoded using the WN1.5 relations.

We have thus aimed at a more general *model* that incorporates different types of important semantic relations which are extractable from dictionaries (and other sources) and of usage for LE applications. The definition of such a broad model does not, however, imply that we are also going to provide all possible relations for all meanings. Given the project's limitations in time and budget, the encoding of additional semantic relations is restricted to those meanings which can be (semi-)automatically derived from our MRDs or to those meanings which cannot be related properly by means of the more basic relations only.

A fundamental difference between EWN and the Princeton WordNet is the multilinguality of the former. The language-specific wordnets are therefore stored in a central lexical database system in which we specify *equivalence relations* between each language-specific synset and synsets in the Inter-Lingual-Index[2] (ILI), which will be mostly based on synsets taken from WN1.5. In this paper, we shall explain the kinds of choices made mainly with respect to the *Language-Internal Relations* (LIRs). Only a brief description of the *Equivalence Relations* (ERs) will be given. More practical issues connected with the actual encoding of the relations are provided by Vossen et al. (this volume). The paper is further organized as follows: in section 2 we illustrate the kind of criteria we are using to verify a relation between synsets and state some principles on the basis of which these criteria should be used. Section 3 is devoted to the discussion of the status and (theoretical/practical) relevance of the main LIRs we are encoding within EWN. In section 4, an overview of all the relations is provided together with a brief discussion of the ERs. Some concluding remarks are presented in section 5.

2. Criteria for the Identification of Relations between Synsets

As the work in EWN is being carried out at different sites by groups with different backgrounds and cultural traditions, it is very important to have clear and explicit sets of criteria and definitions to determine the existence of semantic relations between synsets. Thus, substition tests or diagnostic frames based on normality judgements (cf. Cruse, 1986) have been created to verify relations. Inserting two words in the test sentences built for each relation will mostly evoke a strong 'normality'/'abnormality' judgement (generally indicated by means of a '*yes/no*' score, although, in some cases, also other values are allowed: *probably, unclear, unlikely*), on the basis of which the relation can be determined. For instance, synsets are identified on the basis of the possibility of a word being replaced by another in a specific context (cf. Vossen, this volume), and word senses are therefore defined by all the possible uses of a word in contexts. The general test used to determine whether two words are synonymous is the following:

$Word_1$ in *context$_c$* entails and is entailed by $Word_2$ in *context$_c$*

This corresponds to the possibility of two nouns being mutually substitutable in sentence (a) below and of two verbs being mutually substitutable in sentence (b):[3]

a. X is a *Noun$_1$* therefore X is a *Noun$_2$*

b. Y *Verb(-phrase)$_1$* therefore Y *Verb(-phrase)$_2$*

For instance, *fiddle* and *violin* are synonyms on the basis of the 'normality' of (1a) and (1b), while *dog* and *animal* are not, due to the 'abnormality' of (2b); in a similar way, *enter* and *go into* are synonyms, while *walk* and *move* are not:

1a. It is a *fiddle* therefore it is a *violin*.

2a. It is a *violin* therefore it is a *fiddle*.

3a. It is a *dog* therefore it is an *animal*.

4a. *It is an *animal* therefore it is a *dog*.[4]

1b. John *entered* the room therefore John *went into* the room.

2b. John *went into* the room therefore John *entered* the room.

3b. The dog *walked* therefore the dog *moved*.

4b. *The dog *moved* therefore the dog *walked*.

We have built tests like the ones above for every relation in EWN, in each of the different languages. Note that these tests are devised to detect only semantic relations and are not intended to cover differences in register, style or dialect between words. The tests not only provide us with a common definition for carrying out the work independently but can also be used by external people to verify the quality of our work (see Alonge, 1996; Climent et al., 1996 for a detailed discussion of all the tests elaborated).

In addition to the tests there are some other principles which can be used for encoding the relations. One of them is the *Economy principle* (Dik, 1978) which states that a word should not be defined in terms of more general words when there are more specific words that can do the job. If we apply this to hyperonymy/hyponymy[5] the principle can be formalized as follows:

If a word W_1 is the hyperonym of W_2 and W_2 is the hyperonym of W_3 then W_3 should not be directly linked to W_1 but to W_2.[6]

This principle should prevent intermediate levels from being skipped, i.e. senses from being (directly) linked too high up in the hierarchy. A second principle used is the *Compatibility principle* which can be formulated as:

If a word W_1 is related to W_2 via relation R_1, W_1 and W_2 cannot be related via relation R_n, where R_n is defined as a relation distinct from R_1.

In other words, if two word senses are linked by a particular type of relation (e.g. as synonyms), then they cannot be linked by means of any other relation (e.g. as antonyms). Although this general rule directly follows from the way in which the relations are defined, there are cases in which it is somehow difficult to maintain it. For instance, group nouns or collectives, such as *cutlery* and *furniture*, can easily be linked by *hyponymy* and *meronymy* to the terms representing individual items included in the groups, such as *fork* and *table* respectively (cf. Vossen et al., this volume, for a more detailed discussion).

3. The EWN Language-Internal Relations

As said above, the language-internal relations in EWN are mostly based on WN1.5. The most important relation in WN1.5 is synonymy, which is implicit in the notion of a synset. As in WN1.5, the notion of synonymy adopted in EWN is not the strongest one, which maintains that two expressions are synonymous if the substitution of one for the other *never* changes the truth value of a sentence in which the substitution is made. Instead, a weaker definition is adopted stating that "two expressions are synonymous in a linguistic context C if the substitution of one for the other in C does not alter the truth value" (Miller et al., 1990). One such context is thus sufficient to allow a synonymy relation.

Table I. WordNet1.5 Relations that are taken over in EuroWordNet

Relation	*PoS linked*	*Example*
ANTONYMY	noun/noun; verb/verb; adjective/adjective	man/woman; enter/exit; beautiful/ugly
HYPONYMY	noun/noun; verb/verb	slicer/knife; walk/move
MERONYMY	noun/noun	head/nose
ENTAILMENT	verb/verb	buy/pay
CAUSE	verb/verb	kill/die

The other important relations encoded in WN1.5 between synsets are given in Table I together with examples for the various parts-of-speech (PoSs) linked. The following types of changes have been made in EWN:

- the possibility of adding features to relations;
- new relations, also occurring across PoSs;
- new interpretations of some relations.

These changes will be described in more detail below. However, for a more complete discussion of issues connected with the changes made see Alonge (1996) and Climent et al. (1996).

3.1. RELATION FEATURES

A major difference between the EWN database and the structure of WN1.5 is the possibility of adding features to the relations. These features are needed to differentiate the precise semantic implications that follow from the defined relations. The following types of features have been distinguished:

- conjunction or disjunction of multiple relations of the same type related to a synset;
- non-factivity and intention of causal relations;
- reversal of relations;
- negation of relations.

3.1.1. *Conjunction/Disjunction*

The *conjunction* and *disjunction* labels are used to explicitly mark the status of multiple relations of the same type displayed by a synset. In WN1.5 the interpretation is not explicit. It is a matter of practice that e.g. multiple meronyms linked to the same synset are automatically taken as conjunctives: "all the parts together constitute the holonym *car*". Furthermore, we see that different senses are distinguished for words referring to parts belonging to different kinds of holonyms (e.g. *door*):

door1 – (a swinging or sliding barrier that will close the entrance to a room or building; "he knocked on the door"; "he slammed the door as he left") PART OF: doorway, door, entree, entry, portal, room access

door6 – (a swinging or sliding barrier that will close off access into a car; "she forgot to lock the doors of her car") PART OF: car, auto, automobile, machine, motorcar.

In more traditional resources, similar relations are often expressed by explicit disjunction or conjunction of words in the same definition. Note that this is also done in the definition of the first sense of *door* in WN1.5 where *room* and *building* are coordinated. In EWN, disjunction and conjunction can also explicitly be indicated by a label added to the relations:

{airplane}		{door}	
HAS_MERONYM: c1	{door}	HAS_HOLONYM: d1	{car}
HAS_MERONYM: c2d1	{jet engine}	HAS_HOLONYM: d2	{room}
HAS_MERONYM: c2d2	{propeller}	HAS_HOLONYM: d3	{airplane}

Here c1, c2 and d1, d2, d3 represent conjunction and disjunction respectively, where the index keeps track of the scope of nested combinations. For example, in the case of *airplane* we see that either a *propeller* or a *jet engine* constitutes a part that is combined as the second constituent with *door*. Note that one direction of a relationship can have a conjunctive index, while the reverse can have a disjunctive one. Finally, when conjunction and disjunction labels are absent, multiple relations of the same type are interpreted as non-exclusive disjunction (and/or).

3.1.2. *Non-factive and Intention*

As will be discussed in more detail below, we have identified a whole 'family' of so-called 'CAUSE' relations, for which various subtypes have been distinguished. Since, however, some sub-distinctions are still being discussed, and/or cannot easily be encoded within the limited time of the present project, we also have the possibility of encoding an underspecified CAUSE relation together with some labels which determine different kinds of implications.

The label *non-factive* can be added to a causal relation to indicate that the relation does not necessarily hold. Following Lyons (1977), different types of causality can be distinguished, reflecting the factivity of the effect:

- factive: event E_1 implies the causation of E_2
  "to kill causes to die"
- non-factive: E_1 probably or likely causes event E_2 or E_1 is intended to cause some event E_2
  "to search may cause to find".

Thus, in our database a causal relation is taken as factive unless we add the label *non-factive*. Furthermore, the label *intention* can be encoded to indicate a clear intention to cause a certain result by an involved agent. By adding the labels *non-factive* and *intention*, we can distinguish between different kinds of implications of causal relations:

to sadden	CAUSES	sad	
to decapitate	CAUSES	to die	*intention*
to search	CAUSES	to find	*non-factive*; *intention*

The addition of this information may, for instance, be very useful for applied systems that make inferences.

3.1.3. *Reversed*

It is a requirement of the database that every relation has a reverse counter-part. However, there are relations that are conceptually bi-directional, and others that are not. In the case of hyperonymy/hyponymy, the relation holds in both directions: e.g. since *hammer* is a hyponym of *hand tool*, *hand tool* is a hyperonym of *hammer*. In the case of, for example, a meronymy relation the implicational direction may, instead, vary:

hand	HAS_MERONYM	finger	
finger	HAS_HOLONYM	hand	
car	HAS_MERONYM	door	
door	HAS_HOLONYM	car	*reversed*

computer	HAS_MERONYM	disk drive	*reversed*
disk drive	HAS_HOLONYM	computer	

Here we see that in the case of *finger* and *hand* the dependency or implication holds in both directions. On the contrary, *car* always implies the meronym *door* but *door* does not necessarily imply the holonym *car*. For *computer* and *disk drive*, we see the opposite dependency: a *disk drive* is a part of a *computer* but not every *computer* has a *disk drive*. Since relations that are stated in one direction are automatically reversed in the database, it could not be possible to distinguish these different directions of implication. Therefore, the label *reversed* is added to those relations that are not necessarily implied or not conceptually salient but are only the result of the automatic reversal.

3.1.4. *Negation*

The negation label *negative* explicitly expresses that a relation does not hold:

macaque	HAS_MERONYM	tail	
finger	HAS_MERONYM	tail	*negative*

Such a label can be used to explicitly block certain implications. For instance, a *macaque* has a tail. Normally, parts are inherited along a taxonomy, thus, being a kind of macaque, the *Barbary ape* should have a tail. However, a *Barbary ape* does not have a tail, and by using the label *negative* this inference can be blocked.

In the following subsections, more examples will be given of the use of these labels when discussing relations.

3.2. NEW RELATIONS IDENTIFIED

The most important change with respect to WN1.5 is that we have added various links which apply across parts of speech in EWN. This, on the one hand, allows the interlinking of the noun and verb wordnets; on the other it is useful to encode data on word meanings 'strongly' implied within the meaning of other words (e.g. arguments incorporated within a verb root). This has led to the definition of several new relations which are listed in Table II together with examples. In the next subsections we shall discuss the most relevant new relations and the motivations for distinguishing them. (For a more complete discussion of all the LIRs being encoded see Alonge, 1996; Climent et al., 1996.)

3.2.1. *Interlinking Different PoSs*

The first fundamental difference between EWN relations and WN1.5 is the possibility of having hierarchical relations applying across parts of speech. In WN1.5 each PoS forms a separate system of language-internal relations. As a result, conceptually close concepts are totally separated only because they differ in PoS. For

Table II. New relations in EuroWordNet

Relation	PoS linked	Example
XPOS_NEAR_SYNONYMY	noun/verb	arrival/to arrive
XPOS_ANTONYMY	noun/verb	arrival/to leave
XPOS_HYPERONYMY	noun/verb	to go/arrival
INVOLVED/ROLE	verb or noun/noun or adverb	to hammer/hammer; enter/inside
BE_IN_STATE/STATE_OF	noun/adjective	poor/poor

instance, the noun *adornment* and the verb *to adorn* refer to the same process ("the act of decorating oneself with something"), but this is not displayed in WN1.5. Moreover, *adornment* is ultimately connected with the nominal hyperonym *change of state* and *to adorn* with the verbal hyperonym *to change* (which refers to a change of state). These fundamental tops are not related in any way either.

To avoid this rigid distinction between nouns and verbs, it is possible in EWN to explicitly express synonymy, hyponymy and antonymy relations across PoSs. Instead of separating the networks on the basis of their PoSs, traditionally identified by using a mixture of morphological, syntactic and semantic criteria, we make a distinction among the semantic orders of the entities to which word meanings can refer (cf. Lyons, 1977):

- first-order entities (1oes): concrete, physical things (referred to by concrete nouns);
- second-order entities (2oes): properties, acts, processes, states, events (referred to by nouns, verbs and also adjectives);
- third-order entities (3oes): propositions which exist independently of time and space (referred to by abstract nouns) (cf. Rodriguez et al., this volume, for a more detailed discussion of these distinctions).

For instance in the Italian wordnet, a synonymy relation is encoded between *morire* (to die) and the second-order noun *morte* (death) and both the verb and the noun are linked by a hyponymy relation to the verb *annegare* (to drown). Therefore, 1oes, 2oes and 3oes do form distinct networks, which are ontologically separate as well.

This approach does not seem merely more appropriate from a theoretical point of view, given that the distinction we have drawn is clearly based on semantic grounds, but will also yield some remarkable advantages with respect to the use of the database both for IR purposes and for other LE applications:

- it avoids problems which may originate from the fact that the traditional PoS distinctions are not applicable to all languages (Lyons, 1977);
- it makes it possible to match expressions with very different syntactic structures, but comparable content, by means of the unification of second-order nouns and verbs in the same ontology (Vossen and Bon, 1996);

- it allows the linking of mismatches across languages that involve a PoS shift (cf. e.g. the Dutch nouns *afsluiting* and *gehuil* which are translated into English as *to close* and *to cry* respectively).

The cross-PoS relations are explicitly encoded using different relations. The most important relation is XPOS_NEAR_SYNONYMY. The following substitution test is used to verify this relation in English:

Comment:	Synonymy between verbs and nouns denoting events or processes
Test sentences:	
a)	If something/someone/it Xs then (a/an) Y takes place
Score:	yes
b)	If (a/an) Y takes place then something/someone/it Xs
Score:	yes
Conditions:	– X is a verb in the third person singular form
	– Y is a noun in the singular
	– preferably there is a morphological link between the noun and the verb
Example (1):	
a)	If something/someone/it dies then death takes place
b)	If death takes place then something/someone/it dies
Effect:	to die XPOS_NEAR_SYNONYM death
	death XPOS_NEAR_SYNONYM to die
Example (2):	
a)	If something/someone/it moves then a movement takes place
b)	If a movement takes place then something/someone/it moves
Effect:	to move XPOS_NEAR_SYNONYM movement
	movement XPOS_NEAR_SYNONYM to move

(Alonge, 1996; Climent et al., 1996 list similar tests for the other languages.)

In addition to synonymy it is also possible to express hyponymy relations across PoSs. For instance, the Italian noun *arrivo* (arrival) is connected within the dictionary to the verb *arrivare* (to arrive) and has been encoded as its near-synonym in our database. Consequently, it will also be a hyponym of *andare* (to go), given that the same relation holds for *arrivare*:

arrivo (N)	XPOS_NEAR_SYNONYM	*arrivare* (V)
arrivare (V)	HAS_HYPERONYM	*andare* (V)
andare (V)	HAS_HYPONYM	*arrivare* (V)

| *arrivo* (N) | HAS_XPOS_HYPERONYM | *andare* (V) |
| *andare* (V) | HAS_XPOS_HYPONYM | *arrivo* (N) |

Moreover, XPOS_HYPONYMY is typically used when there is a close relation to a more general word with a different PoS, and there is no hyperonym of the kind within the same PoS, e.g. *to love* and *emotion*.

Finally, we can explicitly create cross-PoS antonymy relations between 2oes with different PoSs. This type of relation is only used rarely.

3.2.2. *Encoding Information on Various Semantic Components: the* INVOLVED/ROLE *Relation*

Besides linking the second-order noun and verb wordnets, we identified other relations that specifically relate second-order nouns and verbs with first-order/third-order nouns (but also adverbs).[7] These relations are needed for both practical and theoretical reasons. They are necessary to differentiate shallow hier-archies occurring in the networks derived from our sources. For instance, we see that many classes of verbs are defined by means of a phrase whose syntactic head (the hyperonym) is not very significant. It refers to a general concept, such as *become*, *get*, *make*, which also applies to many other verbs which, however, display significant meaning differences. What follows the definition head (be it a noun, a NP, a PP, etc.) often provides a much better characterization of the verb's meaning but this information cannot be captured by stating only a hyponymy relation. In the next example we see some hyponyms of the Italian verb *andare* derived from the Italian Lexical Database:

pattinare	=	"andare sui pattini"
to skate		to go *on skates*
navigare	=	"andare (detto di navi)"
to sail		to go (*said of ships*)
coricarsi	=	"andare a letto"
		to go *to bed*
uscire	=	"andare fuori"
to go out		to go *out*
camminare	=	"andare a piedi"
to walk		to go *on foot*

While *andare* (to go) simply indicates motion along a path, its hyponyms refer to very different 'kinds of motion':

[28]

- the first one indicates *motion by means of a vehicle*;
- the second one refers to *motion performed (only) by specific vehicles*;
- the third one indicates *motion to a specific place* (incorporated within the meaning of the verb itself);
- the fourth one refers to *motion from and to partially-specified locations* (from inside to outside);
- the last one is an *undirected/manner-of-motion* verb.

If we only coded a hyponymy relation with *andare* for these verbs, we would lose much important semantic information provided for them within our source. This phenomenon occurs in all the languages and resources covered in EuroWordNet. Hyponymy classification is thus not so informative for many verbal hierarchies. Moreover, also in hierarchies of concrete nouns we see that many nouns are grouped into large undifferentiated classes: *anything, something, object, thing, person*. Again, these shallow classes can only be differentiated by considering other elements from the definitions. For instance, in one of its senses, *threat* is a hyponym of *person* in WN1.5, defined as "a person who inspires fear or dread". Together with it, hundreds of other nouns (among which we find, e.g., *engineer, inhabitant, religionist, Elizabethan*, etc.) are linked to *person* by means of a hyponymy relation. Obviously, this relation by itself does not provide much significant information. We thus use the INVOLVED/ROLE relation for encoding data which better characterize a word meaning.

The INVOLVED relation is used to encode data on arguments or adjuncts lexicalized within the meaning of a 2oe. I.e., it indicates a relation between a second-order verb or noun and a first-order/third-order noun (or also an adverb) whose meaning is incorporated in (or 'strongly' connected with) the 2oe. ROLE is used for the opposite relation (from 1oes/3oes, to 2oes). In addition to the general relation the specific subtype relations listed in Table III have been distinguished. A general test for the INVOLVED/ROLE relation has been created (given below), however, more specific tests have been formulated for each subtype.

Comment:	Involvement/role relation in general
Test sentence:	(A/an) X is the one/that who/which is directly involved in Y
Score:	yes
Conditions:	– X is a first-order/third-order noun (or adverb)
	– Y is a verb in the gerundive form or a second-order noun
Example:	A hammer is that which is directly involved in hammering
Effect:	to hammer INVOLVED hammer
	hammer ROLE to hammer

This relation is only being used to encode data on arguments/adjuncts that are *strongly* implied in the meaning of a verb/noun. This is not the same as encoding the

Table III. Subtypes of INVOLVED/ROLE relations

Relation	Examples
INVOLVED_AGENT ROLE_AGENT	sgambettare/neonato (to kick one's (small) legs about)/(baby)
INVOLVED_PATIENT ROLE_PATIENT	to teach/learner
INVOLVED_INSTRUMENT ROLE_INSTRUMENT	to paint/paint-brush
INVOLVED_LOCATION ROLE_LOCATION	to swim/water
INVOLVED_SOURCE_DIRECTION ROLE_SOURCE_DIRECTION	to disembark/ship
INVOLVED_TARGET_DIRECTION ROLE_TARGET_DIRECTION	rincasare/casa (to go back home)/(home)
INVOLVED_RESULT ROLE_RESULT	freeze/ice
INVOLVED_MANNER ROLE_MANNER	shout/loudly

arguments or adjuncts co-occurring with a verb/noun in a sentence. In the relational approach we follow, we only encode the semantic features *incorporated* in the meaning of a word. These certainly also determine the kind of syntactic contexts in which that word may occur, but do not necessarily coincide with them. For instance, whereas a verb like *to move* allows agent arguments, there is no inherent reference to a particular 'involved-agent' in its meaning (because, in fact, many kinds of 'agents' can move). No INVOLVED_AGENT relation is therefore encoded for *move*. However, the Italian verb *sgambettare*, meaning *to kick one's (small) legs about* and referring to a movement typically performed by babies, clearly incorporates the 'agent-protagonist' *baby*. Therefore, this information can be encoded by means of the relation INVOLVED_AGENT. Thus, the various relations are only being encoded when there is a *clear* and *strong* association with another word in the meaning of a verb/noun, generally indicated in dictionary definitions.

The use of the INVOLVED/ROLE relation to differentiate shallow hierarchies is in line with the view of the meaning of a word as proposed by Cruse (1986) (and before by Haas, 1964). In this view the meaning of a word is conceived of as a kind of 'semantic field', containing all of the possible (grammatical) sentential contexts of the word and all of the possible (grammatical) substitutes within those contexts. Thus, the meaning of a word is made up, at least in part, of (the meanings of) other words which therefore correspond to 'semantic traits' (semantic components) of the first word. Following Cruse, such semantic traits should carry the lightest possible burden of theory. In fact, no claim is made that they are primitive, functionally discrete, universal, or drawn from a finite inventory. Furthermore, in Cruse's view there is no claim that the meaning of any word can be exhaustively characterized by any finite set of such semantic traits.

The adoption of the 'relational' approach to word meaning has, however, some consequences already pointed out by Cruse (1986, p. 19):

> One is that any attempt to draw a line between the meaning of a word and 'ency-clopaedic' facts concerning the extra-linguistic referents of the word would be quite arbitrary; another is that there is no motivation for isolating 'pragmatic meaning' as a separate domain of lexical meaning.

Indeed, we are trying to capture (language-dependent) lexicalization patterns and lexical expressive power, wherever this is possible, without claiming that we are comprehensively encoding all possible implicatures, but also without drawing a sharp distinction between what is strictly speaking 'semantic' and what could be described as 'pragmatic meaning'.[8]

The relevance of encoding this type of information is apparent in the most recent theoretical developments in lexical semantics. Research in this field has demonstrated that there is often a direct connection among the arguments/adjuncts lexicalized within a verb root (corresponding to some of its semantic components) and the verb's syntactic properties (cf. e.g. Levin, 1993). Furthermore, (groups of) languages display different 'preferences' for patterns of lexicalization of semantic components in verb roots (Talmy, 1985). This information is thus crucial for the development of LE systems.

As we have seen above, the various lexical relations carry different 'degrees' of implications. Whereas hyponymy always implies a strong and necessary link from one word meaning to another word meaning (since it corresponds to the logical notion of class inclusion), the INVOLVED/ROLE relation may have various degrees of 'necessity'. This can be indicated by means of the label *reversed* (as has been shown above for meronymy):

spaniel	HAS_HYPERONYM	dog
dog	HAS_HYPONYM	spaniel
dog	ROLE_AGENT	to bark
to bark	INVOLVED_AGENT	dog
guard-dog	ROLE_AGENT	to guard
to guard	INVOLVED_AGENT	guard-dog *reversed.*

In many cases, we see how the use of multiple labels, together with this relation, can provide useful information which would otherwise be lost. One of the senses of the Italian verb *volare* (to fly) is defined in our source as "to move in the air, said of winged animals or of airplanes and similar means and of the people inside them". Thus, we can use the *disjunction* label to explicitly express that the verb may have different *involved_agents*:

volare   INVOLVED_AGENT d1   winged animal
          INVOLVED_AGENT d2   means of transport (i.e. airplanes)
          INVOLVED_AGENT d3   people (inside means of transport).

One of the hyponyms of *volare* is the verb *svolazzare* (to fly about, to flit, to flutter), which is typically said of animals. By using the label *negative* we may block wrong inferences which could follow from the hyponymy relation between this verb and *volare*:

svolazzare   INVOLVED_AGENT   means of transport (i.e. airplanes)   *negative*
              INVOLVED_AGENT   people (inside means of transport)   *negative*.

3.3. DIFFERENT INTERPRETATIONS OF WN1.5 RELATIONS

The status of some of the relations encoded within WN1.5 was reconsidered in EWN and different interpretations of them were formulated.

3.3.1. NEAR_SYNONYMY *and* NEAR_ANTONYMY

As already mentioned, synsets are based on a *weakened* notion of synonymy. Still, there are cases in which it is difficult to state that two words displaying a 'similar' meaning should be put in the same synset. There can be various types of problems: sometimes the synonymy test gives unclear results, the hyponyms of the two words cannot be interchanged and there are no other relations that can be applied (see Vossen et al., this volume, for a more detailed discussion). A typical example in English is formed by *tool, instrument, machine, device, apparatus,* which have very close meanings but represent different clusters of hyponyms and are not really synonymous. Instead of weakening the notion of synonymy even further, we have introduced the NEAR_SYNONYMY relation, by means of which we can express that these words are more similar than other co-hyponyms at the same level, but not similar enough to be joined in a synset.

A similar broadening of the relation has been applied to the notion of antonymy. Intuitively, antonymy relates lexical opposites, such as *to ascend* and *to descend, good* and *bad* or *justice* and *injustice*. Except for the fact that antonymy is a symmetric relation, it is still unclear what is exactly meant by 'opposition' which may cover a large range of phenomena (Cruse, 1986). In WN1.5 (Miller et al., 1990), antonymy is only globally defined as follows: 'the antonym of a word X is sometimes not-X, but not always', and it is limited to the opposition relation between specific words or synset variants and not between synsets as a whole. For instance, *appearance* and *arrival* are, in the appropriate senses, synonyms; but the antonyms are different for each word (*disappearance* and *departure*). In EWN we maintained this strict notion of antonymy for opposing synset variants. However, when there is no clear word-based opposition or when there is doubt about the kind of opposition, we use the NEAR_ANTONYMY relation which holds between synsets.

In practice, the NEAR_SYNONYMY and NEAR_ANTONYMY relations are often derived as an intermediate stage. They can then be further elaborated into synset-membership or antonymy at a later moment, using additional evidence or data.

3.3.2. *PART-WHOLE Relations*

Part-whole (or meronymy) relations form a complex family of relations (Winston et al., 1987; Vossen and Copestake, 1993; Vossen, 1995). Whereas in the WN1.5 database three kinds of meronymy relations are distinguished (part/whole, member/group and component/substance), in EWN we have distinguished five subtypes:

- a relation indicating a whole and its constituent parts:
  hand   HAS_MERO_PART   finger

- a relation indicating a set and its members:
  fleet   HAS_MERO_MEMBER   ship

- a relation indicating an object and the substance it is made of:
  book   HAS_MERO_MADEOF   paper

- a relation indicating a whole and a portion of it:
  bread   HAS_MERO_PORTION   slice

- a relation indicating a place and location included within it:
  desert   HAS_MERO_LOCATION   oasis.

In EWN all these different kinds of part-whole relations can thus be encoded, together with a HAS_MERONYM/HAS_HOLONYM underspecified relation, generally used for unclear cases. A practical reason for making these distinctions is that the resources (in all the languages), from which the data are derived, contain many specific patterns and structures, such as *amount of, member of, group of, place where, made of, which contains*, which can be converted directly into these relations. Furthermore, the type of meronymy is important to predict semantic implications that can be inferred (Vossen and Copestake, 1993). On the other hand, we find patterns, such as *part of, piece of* or PPs, which are ambiguous with respect to the specific subtype of meronymy. In these cases we still want to derive the underspecified meronymy relation.

Finally, as we have seen above, the implications of meronymy relation can be further differentiated using labels:

- parts which belong to one type of a whole (unique):
  finger   HAS_HOLO_PART   hand

- parts which can belong to a specific range of wholes (non-unique but specific):

window	HAS_HOLO_PART d1	building
	HAS_HOLO_PART d2	vehicle

- substances which can make up a wide range of wholes (unrestricted):

book	HAS_MERO_MADEOF	paper	
paper	HAS_HOLO_MADEOF	book	*reversed.*

The different wholes in which *window* can be contained are tagged with a disjunction label: d1, d2. The explicit disjunction suggests that it can be connected to a specific (and limited) range of concepts. In the case of *book/paper* we see that there is no specific conceptual dependency from *paper* to *book* (only the other way around), and therefore the label *reversed* is added. Thus, it does not make any sense to list all the different wholes that can be made of *paper* as a disjunctive list.

3.3.3. CAUSES *and* IS_CAUSED_BY

The causal relation is used in WN1.5 to indicate a relation between two verbs: where one refers to an event causing a resulting event, process or state referred to by the second verb (like in the case of *show/see*, *give/have*). In WN1.5 the causal relation only holds between verbs and, furthermore, only should hold (according to Fellbaum, 1990) between verbs referring to temporally disjoint situations. In our database the cause relation cuts across the different PoSs and can therefore be used to link verbs and second-order nouns denoting events or processes (henceforth *dynamic situations* or *dSs*) to verbs, second-order nouns or adjectives. In addition, we distinguish three possible cases of temporal relationship between (dynamic/non-dynamic) situations with a causal relation:

- a cause relation between two situations which are temporally disjoint: there is no time point when dS_1 takes place and also S_2 (which is caused by dS_1) takes place and vice versa (e.g., in the case of *to shoot/to hit*);
- a cause relation between two situations which are temporally overlapping: there is at least one time point when both dS_1 and S_2 take place, and there is at least one time point when dS_1 takes place and S_2 (which is caused by dS_1) does not yet take place (e.g., in the case of *to teach/to learn*);
- a cause relation between two situations which are temporally co-extensive: whenever dS_1 takes place also S_2 (which is caused by dS_1) takes place and there is no time point when dS_1 takes place and S_2 does not take place, and vice versa (e.g., in the case of *to feed/to eat*).

As a matter of fact, we have identified a whole family of 'causal' relations. Various relations have been distinguished through the analysis of our data:

a) RESULTS_IN:

to kill	RESULTS_IN	to die
to redden	RESULTS_IN	red

b) FOR_PURPOSE_OF:

to search	FOR_PURPOSE_OF	to find
to butcher	FOR_PURPOSE_OF	to feed
to graft	FOR_PURPOSE_OF	to improve

c) ENABLES_TO:

| vision | ENABLES_TO | to see |

d) IS_MEANS_FOR:

| to heat | IS_MEANS_FOR | to distill |
| procedure | IS_MEANS_FOR | result |

However, given the granularity of such distinctions, we do not know whether the encoding of them will be possible within the limits of the present project. Thus, for the time being we are using an underspecified cause relation, together with some of the labels discussed above, to encode all these links.

The general test used to detect a (factive/without explicit intention) cause relation is the following:

Comment:	Causation relation (general)
Test sentences:	
a)	(A/an) X causes (a/an) Y
	(A/an) X has (a/an) Y as a consequence
	(A/an) X leads to (a/an) Y
Score:	yes
b)	the converse of (a)
Score:	no
Conditions:	– X is a verb in the infinitive form or X is a noun in the singular
	– Y is a verb in the infinitive form or Y is a noun in the singular or Y is an adjective
Example:	
a)	to sadden causes (to be) sad
	to sadden has (to be) sad as a consequence
	to sadden leads (someone) (to be) sad
b)	*(to be) sad causes to sadden
	*(to be) sad has to sadden as a consequence
	*(to be) sad leads (someone) to sadden
Effect:	to sadden CAUSES sad
	sad IS_CAUSED_BY to sadden

Note that by using this relation together with some of the the features identified we may clarify some sense distinctions related to a same entry. For instance, *to teach* may be used to refer either to an intentional or to a non-intentional causing of learning:

5. He taught him to read.
6. The experience taught me to keep my fingers to myself.[9]

Thus, the two different implications would be indicated as follows:

$$\text{teach}_1 \quad \text{CAUSES} \quad \text{learn} \quad \textit{intention}$$
$$\text{teach}_2 \quad \text{CAUSES} \quad \text{learn}$$

The CAUSE relation may, in certain cases, overcome the problems of shallow hierarchy structures in our sources. Consider the case of some hyponyms of the Italian verb *rendere* (make, cause to become):

| *arrossare* | = | "rendere rosso" |
| to redden | | to make *red* |

| *imbiancare* | = | "rendere bianco" |
| to whiten | | to make *white* |

| *rattristare* | = | "rendere triste" |
| to sadden | | to make *sad* |

| *ingrassare* | = | "rendere grasso" |
| to fatten | | to make *fat* |

Here we see that the first two verbs refer to causing change in colour, the third one refers to causing change in mood and the last one to causing change in weight. These differences in the results produced do not follow in any way from the relation to the superordinate verb. However, we are still dealing with very different situations which may be very important to know from the point of view of applications which have to do with content understanding. In EWN it is possible to differentiate these caused results by using the general CAUSE relation.

3.3.4. HAS_SUBEVENT *and* IS_SUBEVENT_OF

According to Fellbaum (1990), "the different relations that organize the verbs can be cast in terms of one overarching principle, lexical entailment." Two basic kinds of lexical entailment can be distinguished: one involves 'temporal inclusion' (the two situations referred to by the verbs in the relation partially or totally overlap); the other involves 'temporal exclusion' (the two situations are variously temporally disjoint). These temporal relationships between verbs are taken as the basis for a further distinction of four kinds of entailment:

a. + Temporal Inclusion
    a1. co-extensiveness (e. g., *to limp/to walk*)
    a2. proper inclusion (e.g., *to snore/to sleep*)
b. – Temporal Inclusion
    b1. backward presupposition (e.g., *to succeed/to try*)
    b2. cause (e.g., *to give/to have*)

Thus, within WN1.5, class (a1) verbs are linked by means of the hyponymy (called *troponymy* for verbs) relation, (b2) verbs are linked by means of a causal relation and both (a2) and (b1) verbs are linked by means of a generic *Entailment* relation. That is, the latter relation is applied to those cases that do not fall within the more specific classes of verbs linked by means of hyponymy or cause relations. Entailment is thus used to minimally capture the direction of the entailment implication when all the rest fails.

Within our project we decided to encode data related to the WN1.5 entailment relation in a different way. In fact, it seems to us that the 'backward presupposition' – entailment can be expressed by using the causal relation in conjunction with the *non-factivity* label. The above examples can be represented as follows:

| to succeed | IS_CAUSED_BY | to try | |
| to try | CAUSES | to succeed | *non-factive, intention* |

In the case of 'proper-inclusion' Fellbaum suggests that a meronymy relation may hold but that the difference in the entailment direction cannot be captured in a uniform way: *buy* entails *pay* and *snore* entails *sleep*. However, in EuroWordNet, both the meronymy relation and the entailment direction can be captured using the *reversed* label in combination with a HAS_SUBEVENT/IS_SUBEVENT_OF relation:

| to snore | IS_SUBEVENT_OF | to sleep | |
| to sleep | HAS_SUBEVENT | to snore | *reversed* |

| to buy | HAS_SUBEVENT | to pay | |
| to pay | IS_SUBEVENT_OF | to buy | *reversed* |

Whereas the same SUBEVENT relation holds between *sleep* versus *snore* and *buy* versus *pay*, *buy* necessarily entails *pay*, whereas *sleep* only optionally entails *snore*. The latter case is expressed by the label *reversed*.

4. Overview of the Relations

So far we have only taken the LIRs into consideration. The ERs between each language and WN1.5 synsets (which are mainly used as the interlingual connection) are to a large extent equivalent to the LIRs. Thus, for instance, SYN-ONYMY and EQ_SYNONYMY can be defined in a similar way, the only difference being that the latter holds between words of different languages. Therefore, an EQ_SYNONYMY relation can be identified between the Italian verb *diventare* and *to become*, while *arrossire* (to blush) will be linked to *to become* by means of an EQ_HAS_HYPERONYM relation.

In Table IV, the complete list of relations is given for quick reference.[10] For each relation the following information is given:

  i) its name,
 ii) the parts of speech linked (with the indication of the 'direction' of the linking),
iii) further labels which eventually apply to the relation itself,
 iv) the type of data linked (i.e., Word Meanings or synset Variants).

5. Conclusion

The identification and definition of the relations to be encoded in the EWN database have represented an important and fundamental phase of the work carried out so far in EWN. Aiming at a cost-effective multilingual resource, useful for various LE applications, we had to deal with both theoretical and practical issues which resulted in the development of a quite rich framework. Given the aforementioned budget/time limitations of the project, we will not express all possible relations for the full vocabulary in each language. Moreover, the more sophisticated relations will be applied to those cases where they are easily extractable and/or really necessary to precisely locate a word meaning in the semantic network as a whole (especially when the traditionally accepted relations such as hyponymy and synonymy are not very helpful). In this respect, the broader linguistic model is also needed to adequately deal with all the different problems and phenomena that we will encounter.

More specifically, we think that the model and the samples of encoded data can be very useful for various tasks. The possibility of stating connections among different PoSs referring to the same concepts, both language-internally and across languages, may be of great utility especially for IR systems (Vossen and Bon, 1996). Secondly, the relations that display argument incorporation within word meanings make it possible to identify differences in lexicalisation patterns across languages. This will again be crucial for applications like e.g. machine translation and language learning systems. Furthermore, these and other non-hierarchical relations (i.e. cause, subevent, etc.) may be very useful to clarify both differences across wordnets (e.g. apparently 'equivalent' words across languages displaying different language-internal relations) and gaps or mismatches across languages. Finally, we think that the relations we are encoding on a large scale in relation to a

Table IV. Semantic relations and relation features in EuroWordNet

Relation type	Parts of speech	Labels	Data types
NEAR_SYNONYM	N<>N, V<>V		WM<>WM
XPOS_NEAR_SYNONYM	N<>V, N<>AdjAdv, V<>AdjAdv		WM<>WM
HAS_HYPERONYM	N>N, V>V	dis, con	WM<>WM
HAS_HYPONYM	N>N, V>V	dis	WM<>WM
HAS_XPOS_HYPERONYM	N>V, N>AdjAdv, V>AdjAdv, V>N, AdjAdv>N, AdjAdv>V	dis, con	WM<>WM
HAS_XPOS_HYPONYM	N>V, N>AdjAdv, V>AdjAdv, V>N, AdjAdv>N, AdjAdv>V	dis	WM<>WM
HAS_HOLONYM	N>N	dis, con, rev, neg	WM<>WM
HAS_HOLO_PART	N>N	dis, con, rev, neg	WM<>WM
HAS_HOLO_MEMBER	N>N	dis, con, rev, neg	WM<>WM
HAS_HOLO_PORTION	N>N	dis, con, rev, neg	WM<>WM
HAS_HOLO_MADEOF	N>N	dis, con, rev, neg	WM<>WM
HAS_HOLO_LOCATION	N>N	dis, con, rev, neg	WM<>WM
HAS_MERONYM	N>N	dis, con, rev, neg	WM<>WM
HAS_MERO_PART	N>N	dis, con, rev, neg	WM<>WM
HAS_MERO_MEMBER	N>N	dis, con, rev, neg	WM<>WM
HAS_MERO_MADEOF	N>N	dis, con, rev, neg	WM<>WM
HAS_MERO_LOCATION	N>N	dis, con, rev, neg	WM<>WM
ANTONYM	N<>N, V<>V		VA<>VA
NEAR_ANTONYM	N<>N, V<>V		WM<>WM
XPOS_NEAR_ANTONYM	N<>V, N<>AdjAdv, V<>AdjAdv		WM<>WM
CAUSES	V>V, N>V, N>N, V>N, V>AdjAdv, N>AdjAdv	dis, con, non-f, int, rev, neg	WM<>WM
IS_CAUSED_BY	V>V, N>V, N>N, V>N, AdjAdv>V, AdjAdv>N	dis, con, non-f, int, rev, neg	WM<>WM
HAS_SUBEVENT	V>V, N>V, N>N, V>N	dis, con, rev, neg	WM<>WM
IS_SUBEVENT_OF	V>V, N>V, N>N, V>N	dis, con, rev, neg	WM<>WM
ROLE	N>V, N>N, AdjAdv>N, AdjAdv>V	dis, con, rev, neg	WM<>WM
ROLE_AGENT	N>V, N>N	dis, con, rev, neg	WM<>WM
ROLE_INSTRUMENT	N>V, N>N	dis, con, rev, neg	WM<>WM

Table IV. Continued

Relation type	Parts of speech	Labels	Data types
ROLE_PATIENT	N>V, N>N	dis, con, rev, neg	WM<>WM
ROLE_LOCATION	N>V, N>N, AdjAdv>N, AdjAdv>V	dis, con, rev, neg	WM<>WM
ROLE_DIRECTION	N>V, N>N, AdjAdv>N, AdjAdv>V	dis, con, rev, neg	WM<>WM
ROLE_SOURCE_DIRECTION	N>V, N>N, AdjAdv>N, AdjAdv>V	dis, con, rev, neg	WM<>WM
ROLE_TARGET_DIRECTION	N>V, N>N, AdjAdv>N, AdjAdv>V	dis, con, rev, neg	WM<>WM
ROLE_RESULT	N>V, N>N	dis, con, rev, neg	WM<>WM
ROLE_MANNER	AdjAdv>N, AdjAdv>V	dis, con, rev, neg	WM<>WM
INVOLVED	V>N, N>N, V>AdjAdv, N>AdjAdv	dis, con, rev, neg	WM<>WM
INVOLVED_AGENT	V>N, N>N	dis, con, rev, neg	WM<>WM
INVOLVED_PATIENT	V>N, N>N	dis, con, rev, neg	WM<>WM
INVOLVED_INSTRUMENT	V>N, N>N	dis, con, rev, neg	WM<>WM
INVOLVED_LOCATION	V>N, N>N, V>AdjAdv, N>AdjAdv	dis, con, rev, neg	WM<>WM
INVOLVED_DIRECTION	V>N, N>N, V>AdjAdv, N>AdjAdv	dis, con, rev, neg	WM<>WM
INVOLVED_SOURCE_DIRECTION	V>N, N>N, V>AdjAdv, N>AdjAdv	dis, con, rev, neg	WM<>WM
INVOLVED_TARGET_DIRECTION	V>N, N>N, V>AdjAdv, N>AdjAdv	dis, con, rev, neg	WM<>WM
INVOLVED_RESULT	V>N, N>N	dis, con, rev, neg	WM<>WM
INVOLVED_MANNER	V>AdjAdv, N>AdjAdv	dis, con, rev, neg	WM<>WM
BE_IN_STATE	N>AdjAdv, V>AdjAdv	dis, con, rev, neg	WM<>WM
STATE_OF	AdjAdv>N, AdjAdv>V	dis, con, rev, neg	WM<>WM
FUZZYNYM	N<>N, V<>V		WM<>WM
XPOS_FUZZYNYM	N<>V, V<>AdjAdv, N<>AdjAdv		WM<>WM
EQ_SYNONYM	N<>N, V<>V		WM<>ILIR
EQ_NEAR_SYNONYM	N<>N, V<>V, N<>AdjAdv, V<>AdjAdv		WM<>ILIR
EQ_HAS_HYPERONYM	N>N, N>V, N>AdjAdv, V>V, V>N, V>AdjAdv, AdjAdv>N, AdjAdv>V		WM<>ILIR
EQ_HAS_HYPONYM	N>N, N>V, N>AdjAdv, V>V, V>N, V>AdjAdv, AdjAdv>N, AdjAdv>V		WM<>ILIR

Table IV. Continued

Relation type	Parts of speech	Labels	Data types
EQ_HAS_HOLONYM	N>N		WM<>ILIR
EQ_HAS_MERONYM	N>N		WM<>ILIR
EQ_INVOLVED	N>N, V>N		WM<>ILIR
EQ_ROLE	N>N, N>V		WM<>ILIR
EQ_CAUSES	N>N, V>V, N>V, V>N, V>AdjAdv, N>AdjAdv		WM<>ILIR
EQ_IS_CAUSED_BY	N>N, V>V, N>V, V>N, AdjAdv>V, AdjAdvV>N		WM<>ILIR
EQ_HAS_SUBEVENT	N>N, V>V, N>V, V>N		WM<>ILIR
EQ_IS_SUBEVENT_OF	N>N, V>V, N>V, V>N		WM<>ILIR
EQ_BE_IN_STATE	V>AdjAdv, N>AdjAdv		WM<>ILIR
EQ_IS_STATE_OF	AdjAdv>V, AdjAdv>N,		WM<>ILIR
HAS_INSTANCE	N>PN		WM>I
BELONGS_TO_CLASS	PN>N		I>WM

Parts of Speech:
N = noun
V = verb
AdjAdv = Adjective or Adverb
PN = pronoun or name
Features:
dis = disjunctive
con = conjunctive
rev = reversed
non-f = non-factive
int = intention
neg = negative
Data types:
WM = word meaning or synset
I = instance
ILIR = ILI record
VA = synset variant

substantial portion of the lexicon for different languages may also offer useful data for theoretical semantic/linguistic research.

Notes

[1] Although MRDs are being used as main sources of data, also textual corpora are in some cases being exploited, to individuate information missing within dictionaries. Furthermore, we are re-using data which were acquired within previous European research projects (e.g. *Acquilex* (http://www.cl.cam. ac.uk/Research/NL/acquilex/acqhome.html) and *Delis* (http://www2.echo.lu/ langeng/en/re1/delis.html)) by analysing both MRDs and corpora.

[2] See both Vossen (this volume) and Peters et al. (this volume) for more details on the ILI and on the multilingual design of the database.

[3] Since a verb may require a complement obligatorily, in certain cases we have to insert whole verb phrases into the test sentence. In such cases, either the same complement has to be used with the two verbs for them to be considered synonyms, or whole verb-phrases are encoded as (semantically indivisible) multiword expressions in which the same meaning of another verb is lexicalized. For instance, one of the senses of the Italian verb *iniziare* (to start) has been encoded as a synonym of *dare inizio* ('give-start') (i.e., the verb and the verb-phrase have been included in the same synset), given that in *dare inizio* the verb *dare* is rather semantically 'empty' (it only indicates 'causation') while the object contributes the fundamental meaning to the phrase, and within the phrase as a whole the same semantic reference of *iniziare* is lexicalized.

[4] '*' is used, here and in the following examples, to indicate 'semantic abnormality'.

[5] What we indicate here as *hyperonymy* is sometimes spelled as *hypernymy* (e.g., in WN). Moreover, in WN a distinction is drawn between hyperonymy (the relation occurring between nouns) and *troponymy* (occurring between verbs), because of the different nature of the relation linking verbs to their superordinates discussed in Fellbaum (1990) (but cf. also Cruse, 1986). Although we generally agree with Fellbaum's remarks on this issue, we have decided to use the traditional label *hyperonymy* also for the relation linking verbs, adopting, however, a more elaborated test to detect it with respect to the one used for nouns (cf. Alonge, 1996).

[6] Of course, since the hyponymy (or IS-A) relation is a *transitive* relation, W_3 will also be a hyponym of W_1.

[7] Although some links to adjectives and adverbs are being encoded, we are not building wordnets for them within this project.

[8] The information we are encoding is not, of course, *all* the semantic (in the more comprehensive sense of *semantic* referred to here) information which could be encoded for lexical items. We believe that the database we are building could be further filled in and enriched in the future with data coming from other sources and, in particular, from textual corpora. This will be partly performed, for the Italian wordnet, within a national research project (starting in 1999), in which the results obtained in EWN will be extended by encoding further data in connection with both the same lexical subsets already taken into consideration within EWN and additional subsets.

[9] Example provided by an anonymous reviewer.

[10] Some relations listed here have not been discussed in the present work, mainly because they are rarely encoded. For details on these relations see Alonge, 1996 and Climent et al., 1996.

References

Alonge, A. *Definition of the Links and Subsets for Verbs*. Deliverable D006, *EuroWordNet*, LE2-4003, Computer Centrum Letteren, University of Amsterdam, 1996.

Climent, S., H. Rodriguez and J. Gonzalo. *Definition of the Links and Subsets for Nouns of the EuroWordNet Project*. Deliverable D005, EuroWordNet, LE2-4003, Computer Centrum Letteren, University of Amsterdam, 1996.

Cruse, D. A. *Lexical Semantics*. Cambridge: Cambridge University Press, 1986.

Dik, S. *Stepwise Lexical Decomposition*. Lisse: Peter de Ridder Press, 1978.

Fellbaum, C. "English Verbs as a Semantic Net". *International Journal of Lexicography*, 3(4) (1990), 302–312. (A revised version of the paper will appear in Fellbaum, C. (ed.), *Wordnet: a Lexical Reference System and its Applications*. Cambridge: Mass., The MIT Press, 1998.)

Gruber, J. *Lexical Structures in Syntax and Semantics*. Amsterdam: North-Holland, 1976.

Haas, W. "Semantic Value". In *Proceedings of the IXth International Congress of Linguists*, The Hague, Mouton, 1964.

Levin, B. *English Verb Classes and Alternations: a Preliminary Investigation*. Chicago: The University of Chicago Press, 1993.

Lyons, J. *Semantics*. London: Cambridge University Press, 1977.

Miller, G., R. Beckwith, C. Fellbaum, D Gross and K. Miller. "Introduction to WordNet: An On-Line Lexical Database". *International Journal of Lexicography*, 3(4) (1990), 302–312. (A revised version of the paper will appear in Fellbaum, C. (ed.), *Wordnet: a Lexical Reference System and its Applications*. Cambridge: Mass., The MIT Press, 1998.)

Sanfilippo, A., T. Briscoe, A. Copestake, M. A. Martì-Antonin and A. Alonge. "Translation Equivalence and Lexicalization in the ACQUILEX LKB". *Proceedings of the 4th International Conference on Theoretical and Methodological Issues in Machine Translation*, Montreal, Canada, 1992.

Talmy, L. "Lexicalization Patterns: Semantic Structure in Lexical Form". In *Language Typology and Syntactic Description: Grammatical Categories and the Lexicon*. Ed. T. Shopen, Cambridge: Cambridge University Press, 1985.

Vossen P. *Conceptual and Grammatical Individuation in the Lexicon*. PhD. Thesis, University of Amsterdam, Studies in Language and Language Use, No. 15. IFOTT, Amsterdam, 1995.

Vossen P. and A. Bon. *Building a Semantic Hierarchy for the Sift Project*. Sift LRE 62030, Deliverable D20b, University of Amsterdam, Amsterdam, 1996.

Vossen P. and A. Copestake. "Untangling Definition Structure into Knowledge Representation". In *Default Inheritance in Unification-Based Approaches to the Lexicon*. Eds. E. J. Briscoe, A. Copestake and V. de Paiva, Cambridge: Cambridge University Press, 1993.

Winston M., R. Chaffin and D. Herrmann. "A Taxonomy of Part-Whole Relations". *Cognitive Science* 11 (1987), 417–444.

Computers and the Humanities **32**: 117–152, 1998.
© 1998 *Kluwer Academic Publishers.*

The Top-Down Strategy for Building EuroWordNet: Vocabulary Coverage, Base Concepts and Top Ontology

HORACIO RODRÍGUEZ[1], SALVADOR CLIMENT[2], PIEK VOSSEN[3,4],
LAURA BLOKSMA[3,5], WIM PETERS[6], ANTONIETTA ALONGE[7,8],
FRANCESCA BERTAGNA[7,9] and ADRIANA ROVENTINI[7,10]

[1]*Universitat Politècnica de Catalunya. Jordi Girona Salgado, 1-3, 08034 Barcelona Spain; E-mail:*
horacio@lsi.upc.es; [2]*Universitat de Barcelona, Gran Via de les Corts Catalanes, 585, 08007*
Barcelona Spain; E-mail: climent@lingua.fil.ub.es; [3]*Universiteit van Amsterdam, Faculteit*
Geesteswetenschappen, Spuistraat 134, 1012 VB Amsterdam, The Netherlands; E-mail:
[4]*Piek.Vossen@let.uva.nl,* [5]*lbloks@let.uva.nl;* [6]*University of Sheffield, Computer Science*
Department, Portobello Street 211, Sheffield, S1 4DT, UK; E-mail: w.peters@dcs.sheffield.ac.uk;
[7]*Istituto di Linguistica Computazionale, CNR, Via della Faggiola 32, 56126 Pisa, Italy; E-mail:*
[8]*aalonge@pg.tecnonet.it;* [9]*f.bertagna@ilc.pi.cnr.it;* [10]*adriana@ilc.pi.cnr.it*

Key words: Base Concepts, ontology building, Top Ontology

Abstract. This paper describes two fundamental aspects in the process of building of the EuroWord-Net database. In EuroWordNet we have chosen for a flexible design in which local wordnets are built relatively independently as language-specific structures, which are linked to an Inter-Lingual-Index (ILI). To ensure compatibility between the wordnets, a core set of common concepts has been defined that has to be covered by every language. Furthermore, these concepts have been classified via the ILI in terms of a Top Ontology of 63 fundamental semantic distinctions used in various semantic theories and paradigms. This paper first discusses the process leading to the definition of the set of Base Concepts, and the structure and the rationale of the Top Ontology.

1. Introduction

The general approach of EuroWordNet is to build a multilingual database with wordnets for several languages, mainly from existing resources. Each site in the project is responsible for its language-specific wordnet using their tools and resources built up in previous national and international projects (Acquilex, Sift, Delis, Parole, Novell-ConceptNet, Van Dale, Biblograf). This is not only more cost-effective but also gives us the possibility to combine and compare information from multiple independently-created resources. A comparison may tell us something about the vocabularies of the languages (typical lexicalisation patterns) or about the consistency and quality of the resources (how much coherence is there across the resources, how rich are the resources compared to each other). Creating an overall overview and classification is a crucial step to get to grips with the area of semantics where large-scale resources are hardly available and solid criteria are hard to find.

The separate construction of wordnets at different sites provides a lot of flexibility but it also creates a major disadvantage. Because each site has a different starting point in terms of the quality and quantity of available lexical resources, tools and databases, the interpretations and coverage of the different wordnets may easily drift apart. Obviously, comparison and transfer as described above is an option only when the information in each wordnet is coded in a more-or-less compatible way. To some extent, compatibility is established by loading the results in a common database, which requires the same data structuring. Furthermore, a minimal level of consensus is established by using explicit tests to verify the relations across words (as detailed in (Alonge et al., this volume)). However, this is not sufficient.

Still there are two specific compatibility issues at stake:

- the coverage of the vocabulary: the wordnets should globally deal with the same conceptual areas or domains
- the interpretation of the relations should be the same for all the sites.

Despite the definitions and tests created to identify the relations it is still possible to apply them in different ways. The way we deal with these interpretation issues for the more problematic cases is described in (Vossen et al., this volume). In this paper we will further describe the general approach for building that we have followed and the conceptual definition of the vocabulary that will be covered. As we will see in section 2, this approach deals with several conflicting requirements. To satisfy these requirements we have agreed on a top-down approach, starting with a shared set of so-called common Base Concepts for all sites and extending it in more specific directions, where the sites are free to encode the wider contexts for these shared meanings. These Base Concepts are the most important meanings prevailing in the local wordnets and making up the core of the multilingual database. In section 3 we briefly describe the resources and methodologies of each site to clarify the different backgrounds and starting points. In section 4 we describe the technical procedure by which the set of common Base Concepts (BCs) has been established. Section 5 then describes a Top-Ontology of basic semantic distinctions, which has been developed to get to grips with these BCs. All BCs have been clustered in terms of these Top-Ontology Concepts providing a shared descriptive framework for the covered vocabulary. At the end of the paper an overview is given in Figure 3 of the vocabularies that are discussed.

2. The General Approach for Building the Wordnets

When defining the vocabulary to be covered we are faced with several conflicting requirements:

1. The vocabulary has to be generic: include all general word meanings on which more specific concepts depend and those meanings that are used most frequently.
2. The conceptual coverage across the different wordnets has to be the same: that is they should roughly contain the same areas of concepts.
3. The vocabularies should nevertheless reflect or at least respect language-specific lexicalisation patterns.
4. There should be maximum freedom and flexibility for building the wordnets at the different sites: due to the different nature of the resources and tools there may not be one unified approach to build the wordnets which is best for all sites.

To achieve 2 we could simply take a particular set of synsets from WordNet1.5 as a starting point and make sure that these concepts are translated into the other languages and that language-internal relations are provided in these languages. However, this would endanger requirement 1 and 3, and perhaps also 4, for several reasons. First of all, the selection will be strongly biased by English and by the specific features of WordNet1.5 (including imbalances in the vocabulary of WordNet1.5). What is more important is that we may miss typical lexicalisations and important meanings which are relevant to the other languages but which do not follow from the structure of WordNet1.5.

The assessment of the above requirements implies control at two levels: within each individual language and cross-linguistically. For these reasons we adopted a more complicated approach which will however establish a better common ground applicable to all the wordnets:

1. Each group separately defines a fragment of the vocabulary in the different local resources using the same criteria.
2. The local selections are then translated to equivalent WordNet1.5 synsets.
3. The sets of translations are compared to see how much overlap there is across the sites.
4. From this comparison a common set will be determined.
5. Each site adapts its selection to include the common set.

After such a cycle the vocabulary will then be extended and the steps 1 through 5 are repeated.

What should then be the criteria for making these local definitions? The major conceptual criterion given above is that it should include all the word meanings that play a major role in the different wordnets and those meanings that are used most frequently. The latter is difficult to verify because there are still no data on frequency of meanings. Instead of word meaning frequency, the selections can only be verified for word frequency. Fortunately, the former criterion can be satisfied by taking those meanings that exhibit most relations with other meanings and/or that occupy high positions in the hierarchies. There are several reasons for focusing on this group:

- These word meanings and their direct semantic neighbourhood form the core of the wordnets, on which the meanings of the other words depend.
- It is easier to extend the wordnets with more specific concepts when all the basic building blocks are present and well-defined.

Furthermore, early experiments in building some wordnet fragments showed that many problems in encoding relations are concentrated in a relatively small set of complex word meanings that strongly correlates with this set. Typically, words at the higher, more abstract levels of hierarchies, such as *object*, *place* or *change*, tend to be polysemous, have vaguely-distinguishable meanings and cannot easily be linked to other more general meanings. Furthermore, the available resources are often not very helpful either for these words (see (Vossen et al., this volume) for an extensive discussion of these problems). On the other hand, at the more specific levels (e.g. *tennis shoes*) meanings can be easily linked to a more general concept (*shoes*), also making the resources from which this information can be extracted more reliable.

To summarize, we see that the most important areas to create a generic semantic lexicon are also the most complex areas where resources are of little help. We therefore divided the building of the wordnets into two major phases:

- (mostly) manual construction of core-wordnets for a set of common Base Concepts and its direct semantic context.
- top-down extension of these core-wordnets, using (semi-)automatic techniques and relying on the information from the adopted resources.

In this way we can more effectively focus our manual effort on the more difficult and more important cases (also exchanging problems and solutions to achieve a maximum of consensus) and apply the automatic techniques to the areas of the resources which are more reliable. By starting off with a common set of Base Concepts we furthermore ensure that the cores of the wordnets are richly encoded and at least comparable: having the same conceptual coverage. On the other hand, there is sufficient freedom to fill in language-specific lexicalisations and extensions in addition to this core. The rest of this paper is then devoted to a further definition and characterization of the Base Concept Vocabulary. First, we will briefly specify the different backgrounds and, next, the local selections of Base Concept by each site and the common set of Base Concepts derived from these. This set is then further characterized using a Top-Ontology of basic semantic distinctions. The second phase, the Extension of the Base Concepts will not be discussed in detail in this paper. We will just acknowledge that the extensions will be based on the following general criteria:

- In general, the Common Base Concepts will be extended with their hyponyms. In a first phase of extension the most relevant hyponyms will be included. Relevance is based on their potential of further extensibility – i.e., hyponyms that have hyponyms themselves. The output will then be re-considered in order to add hyponyms of those Base Concepts which appear to be badly represented using such criterion – i.e., BCs which give raise to shallow hierarchies.

- A degree of common coverage of vocabulary across languages has to be ensured. We therefore compare and adapt the local coverage to achieve a reasonable level of overlap across the wordnets. This will be carried out in a similar way as is described for the Base Concepts in section 4.2 below.
- To further ensure that the wordnets include the generic parts of the vocabulary we will compare the selection of entries in EuroWordNet (EWN) with the vocabulary covered in the EC-project *Parole*. In the Parole project morpho-syntactic lexicons for the most frequent words are built, where the frequency is derived from comparable corpora in several European languages.
- Finally, some specific vocabulary will be added for the domain of computers and software. The domain-terminology is necessary to test the EWN database for Information Retrieval tasks. See Figure 3 at the end of this paper for an overview of the vocabularies.

3. Local Resources and Methods

All the partners involved in EWN have a variety of lexical resources and tools at their disposal and had developed methodologies for performing their specific tasks. In (Vossen (ed.), 1997) a detailed account of such resources is presented. In the following paragraphs a summary of the main lexical resources is presented.

3.1. RESOURCES

The University of Amsterdam (henceforth AMS) uses an object-oriented lexical database system (Boersma, 1996) developed for the Sift-project (LRE 62030). The object-oriented treatment of the data makes it possible to efficiently manipulate lexicons, collections of entries, collections of senses or single entries and/or senses. Within the AMS LDB the following resources have been loaded for EuroWordNet:

- Celex Dutch lemma lexicon with basic syntactic information and corpus frequency information.
- WordNet 1.5.
- The content of a lexical database VLIS (Van Dale Lexical Information System) provided by Van Dale.
- The Van Dale Dutch-English dictionary (Martin and Tops, 1986).

The data from the Van Dale Lexical Information System (VLIS) has been used as input for developing the Dutch wordnet. The database contains the merge of several contemporary Dutch dictionaries published by Van Dale in recent years. The coverage of VLIS is as in Table I. The Van Dale database is sense-oriented and contains, in addition to traditional information (such as definitions and usage codes), explicit semantic relations between word senses. Important semantic relations in VLIS

Table I. Entries and senses in the Dutch Resource

	nouns	verbs
entries	63,962	8,822
senses	74,678	14,268

Table II. Entries and senses in the Italian Resource

	nouns	verbs
entries	24,635	5,546
senses	45,608	14,091

are hyp(er)onymy, synonymy, antonymy, partitive and associative. The hyponymy-relations result in 1727 tops (1429 noun tops and 298 verb tops). As such it can be seen as a partially-structured semantic network similar to WordNet1.5.

At the Istituto di Linguistica Computazionale del CNR, in Pisa (PSA), three main sources for the Italian data are used:

- The Italian Monolingual Lexical Database (constructed from a number of sources).
- Italian/English Bilingual Lexical Database (constructed on the basis of the Collins-Giunti Italian-English dictionary).
- An Electronic Dictionary of Synonyms available at ILC-CNR.

Main figures for the Italian lexical database in Table II. This database is enriched with a number of semantic relations between senses: hyperonymy, meronymy, causation, verb_to_noun, adjective_to_noun. This monolingual LDB has been used as the main source of data for the Italian wordnet; the semantic relations, with the exception of the synonym and antonym relations, are extracted (when present) from this source. The size of the bilingual database is approximately 30,000 senses on each side (Italian-English, English-Italian).

The main sources used by Spanish group (FUE) are:

- Spanish Monolingual: DGILE, Diccionario General Ilustrado de la Lengua Española (Alvar (ed.), 1987).
- English/Spanish and Spanish/English Bilinguals: VOX-HARRAP'S Esencial (VOX, 1992) and VOX Advanced.
- PIRAPIDES Verbal Database. Developed within the PIRAPIDES Project at the University of Barcelona.
- Several (partial) semantic (sense-based) taxonomies developed within the Acquilex project.

Table III. Entries and senses in the Spanish Resource

	nouns	verbs
entries	65,000	11,000
senses	105,000	24,000

Table IV. Entries and senses in the English Resources

	nouns	verbs	adjectives
Monolinguals			
LDOCE[1]	21,400	7,361	7,333
COBUILD[2]	6,566	6,566	3,490
Other Data			
CELEX	29,494	8,504	9,185
COMLEX	21,871	5,660	8,170

The figures for the monolingual dictionary in Table III. The Pirapides database consists of 3600 English verb forms organized around Levin's Semantic Classes (Levin 1993) connected to WN1.5 senses. The database contains the theta-Grids specifications for each verb (its semantic structure in terms of cases or thematic roles), translation to Spanish forms and diathesis information.

The resources in Table IV are used by the University of Sheffield (SHE) for English.

3.2. CONSTRUCTION METHODOLOGIES

Given the available resources, each group developed different methodologies for selecting candidate nodes, extracting the relations (both internal and external) and linking each entry to the appropriate WN1.5 synsets. All methodologies combine automatic procedures with manual work.

In the case of AMS, the main source for both the entries and relations is the VLIS database. The relations that match the EWN relations have been copied to the EWN structure. The building of the Dutch wordnet then mainly consists of:

• verifying the copied relations and information, which can be confirmed, edited or removed.
• adding missing relations.

For this manual process a special editor, so-called Surf-Editor, has been developed in the AMS LDB, that makes use of the fact that entries and senses are linked as hyper-text windows. Using this editor relations between multiple windows with activated senses can be edited, added or removed, while going from link to link (possibly in parallel for multiple resources). Only after the relations for the BCs have been coded, automatic techniques will be used to extract additional information from the definitions in monolingual dictionaries or translations in bilinguals. This information is compared with the information given or directly added when such information is missing.

At Pisa (PSA), it was decided to construct the Italian wordnet from a number of sources (at least, at the upper level of the taxonomies) to overcome, to some extent, the idiosyncracies of a single dictionary and to provide a more objective perspective on the data. The starting point was the creation of the BCs using data from the 3 different sources mentioned above. However, an integration of different sources has also highlighted the differences between them and the inconsistencies found in dictionary data: e.g. word senses and synonyms vary from source to source. So a considerable manual effort was devoted to guarantee the quality of the selection.

For Spanish, an approach more closely related to WN1.5 was followed. The starting point was to take the two highest levels in WN1.5 hierarchy. First the WN1.5 synsets have been translated (using bilingual resources) and the basic semantic relations have been established (only hyperonymy-hyponymy, synonymy, antonymy and causation in the first phase). This result has been used to extract the BCs for Spanish. In a second phase, additional taxonomies and monolingual resources are used to extract additional information and verify the results of the first phase.

Sheffield (SHE) takes a special position in the project because there is already a wordnet for English. The main task for SHE therefore consists of adapting WordNet1.5 by adding newly distinguished relations and improving the Word-Net1.5 synsets that are used in the Inter-Lingual-Index for interlinking the wordnets (see (Peters et al., this volume) for details).

4. The Base Concepts

The main characteristic of BCs is their importance in the wordnets. According to our pragmatic point of view, a concept is important if it is widely used, either directly or as a reference for other widely used concepts. Importance is thus reflected in the ability of a concept to function as an anchor to attach other concepts. This anchoring capability has been defined in terms of two operational criteria that can be automatically applied to the available resources:

- the number of relations (general or limited to hyponymy).
- high position of the concept in a hierarchy (in WN1.5 or in any local taxonomy).

It should be noted that these criteria can not be applied in an absolute sense. To precisely measure the number of relations and the position in the hierarchy, these relations have to be established and finalized in the first place. All sites however use partially structured data that will be changed considerably during the project. The selections below should therefore be seen as global approximations of the set of BCs. Only in the case of the selection for English it was possible to use more sophisticated measurements because WordNet1.5 was available as a stable resource. To establish a minimal level of cohesion in approach and results for the individual selections of BCs, each group used these criteria as the main basis in one form or another, where the exact working out may differ due to the different starting points. Additionally, some other criteria have been applied by some sites such as selecting all the members of the hyperonym chain of any already selected BC or general frequency in sources (MRDs, corpora). This process is described in 4.1 below.

Despite the relative uniformity of the criteria, this phase resulted on a low degree of overlap among the initial sets of (locally selected) BCs. This was not due to big differences on conceptualization across the languages involved in EWN, but more likely to the following reasons:

- Local selections were too small to be representative.
- Unclear translations into WordNet 1.5.

Therefore, to achieve the general compatibility of the wordnets, it was decided to follow an incremental process of merging and tuning of the BCs, which was carried out in two phases:

- definition of a more representative common set of BCs.
- a phase of re-selection of concepts as (common) BCs, to overcome differences in translation.

This general process is described in 4.2 below.

4.1. DEFINITION OF THE LOCAL BCS

Following the above criteria, an initial set of noun and verb senses, grouped in synsets, has been selected for each language given the available resources.

For AMS, the VLIS hierarchy was sufficiently structured to extract information on the importance of concepts. First, the meanings with most relations have been selected, summing up to 15% of the total amount of relations in the database. For nouns this comes down to all meanings with more than 15 relations, for verbs to all meanings with more than 12 relations. The resulting set was further limited by restricting it to meanings occurring at a hierarchical depth of 3. This initial set was extended with:

- excluded tops which nevertheless have a lot of descendants; where tops are defined as meanings without a hyperonym relation;
- excluded hyperonyms of the words selected so far; to make sure that all meanings needed to anchor the most frequent ones are present in the set.

The Dutch set of BCs has been manually translated into WordNet1.5 equivalences. In 6 cases there was no good equivalent in WordNet1.5 for Dutch BCs. In that case the Dutch BC was represented by the closest synset in WordNet1.5. In quit a few cases a single Dutch BC matched with several WordNet1.5 synsets. In that case, all the matching synsets have been generated. The reversed situation also occurred, although less frequently. In that case multiple Dutch BCs have been represented by a single WordNet1.5 synset.

In order to identify local Base Concepts, PSA used a semi-automatic procedure. A first list of lexical items was extracted automatically from the Italian monolingual LDB using as main criteria 1) the position (medium/high) in the taxonomy and 2) the number of relations with other lexical items (generally hyponyms). This set was then processed manually to meet the following objectives:

1. Overcome inconsistencies and lack of homogeneity of the data caused by nature of the sources and the automatic extraction techniques. For instance, if within the area of kinship terms the original extraction included 'husband' but not 'wife', the latter term was manually added.
2. Organize the data in terms of synonymy (i.e., grouping senses in synsets) and taxonomy.

The grouping of terms in synonyms was carried out semi-automatically. First, for each concept, information about potential synonymy was extracted automatically from the sources; then the resulting data were carefully evaluated and structured in synsets. The next step, namely the hierarchical organization of synsets, was performed manually after having realized that the application of automatic techniques to the existing sources was not useful to perform the task. This was due to several reasons, among them the following: (a) Many terms are defined in the dictionary by means of synonyms; (b) Many terms are defined by means of potential hyperonyms carrying a low semantic value – e.g. *atto*, *effetto*, *modo* (act, effect, manner). The list of BC synsets identified was then mapped to WN1.5 in order to establish cross-language lexical equivalences. A range of problems similar to those described for Dutch were identified at this stage.

For Spanish, two complementary main sources were used in the case of nouns: 1) An extended taxonomy of Spanish obtained from the monolingual dictionary DGILE (Alvar, 1987) and 2) A manual translation of the two highest levels of WN1.5. For verbs the main source was 3) the Pirapides database, already connected to WN1.5. Two additional sources were used as well: 4) Frequency counts of words in the definition (and examples) field of the monolingual DGILE and 5) Frequency counts of words in LEXESP (a 3 Mw balanced corpus of Spanish). The main criteria used in this case were:

1. A selected word is a translation of either a top concept or a direct hyponym of a top concept in WN1.5, and either (2) or (3):
   2. It occurs as genus word in the DGILE monolingual MRD 5 or more times.
   3. It shows a high frequency of occurrences in corpora: either (3.1) or (3.2):

    3.1. It occurs 50 times or more in the DGILE definition corpus.

    3.2. It occurs 100 times or more in LEXESP

SHE, for English, has used the notion of conceptual density (Agirre and Rigau, 1996), as the main criterion, for which three measures have been considered:

a) a node's total number of hyponymic descendants;
b) a node's mean branching factor (mean number of hyponyms in WN1.5);
c) a function of a) and the node's relative position in the hyponymic hierarchy.

After empirical investigation definition c) proved to be the most promising, and the result was computed in the following way:

$$\frac{\text{total num. of descendants}}{\text{level of concept / total num. of levels of the chain including the concept}}$$

Extracting the 20% topmost values for nouns yielded 1296 distinct noun synsets. For verbs the algorithm resulted in 236 distinct verb synsets.

4.2. DERIVING A COMMON SET OF BASE CONCEPTS

Once each group had selected its local set of BCs and linked it to WN1.5 synsets, we computed the different intersections (pairs, triples, etc.) of the local BCs. In the ideal case the selected sets of concepts should have coincided. In so far as they do not, we had to apply special measures to achieve a reasonable common set, to make the cores of the wordnets compatible.

    Only 30 BCs were part of all selections (24 noun synsets, 6 verb synsets). This is extremely low considering the uniformity of the criteria applied. There are several possible explanations for this:

1. There are major differences in the way meanings are classified, which have an effect on the frequency of the relations.
2. The resources cover very different vocabularies.
3. The individual selections are not representative enough.
4. The translations of the selection to WordNet1.5 synsets are not reliable.

The first explanation is acceptable and is inherent to our approach where each wordnet represents an autonomous language-internal network. Differences in the way meanings are classified will show up when the wordnets are compared. This may lead to a restructuring and to a more coherent set of important, classifying Base Concepts in the local wordnets. The second explanation is not likely to apply to general words and meanings. Since all sites use contemporary monolingual resources we do not expect that the core vocabularies differ a lot in coverage.

    With respect to the third and fourth explanations we took some specific measures, which are described below.

Table V. Intersections of local Base Concepts in terms of WordNet1.5 synsets

	Nouns				Verbs			
	AMS	**FUE**	**PSA**	**SHE**	**AMS**	**FUE**	**PSA**	**SHE**
AMS	1027	103	182	333	323	36	42	86
FUE	103	523	45	284	36	128	18	43
PSA	182	45	334	167	42	18	104	39
SHE	333	284	167	1296	86	43	39	236

Table VI. Proposed, selected and missing Base Concepts for each language

	Nouns				Verbs			
	Proposed	**Selected**	**Rejected**	**Missing**	**Proposed**	**Selected**	**Rejected**	**Missing**
AMS	1027	429	598	265	323	126	197	51
FUE	523	323	200	371	128	72	56	105
PSA	334	239	95	455	104	63	41	114
SHE	1296	594	702	100	236	132	104	45
Union	2287	694	1595		573	177	398	

4.2.1. *Merging of the local sets*

First of all, the individual sets may be too small to be representative but the merge of the sets may be sufficiently comprehensive. Instead of the total intersection of concepts we therefore took all synsets selected by two sites (Table V).

Merging these intersections resulted in a set of 871 WN1.5-synsets (694 nouns and 177 verbs) out of a total set of 2860 synsets. Given this set of common Base Concepts the local selections can be divided into:

- selected, i.e. synsets selected as CBC (Common Base Concept). This means that at least two sites considered this concept as basic.
- rejected, i.e. no other site has considered the concept as basic. The concept is not a common BC considered by the other sites but it can still be part of the local BCs that are being covered.

In addition, a third subset of BCs is assigned to each site:

- missing, i.e. this synset has been selected by at least two other sites, so it must be added as BC in the local selection

The results for each group are given in the Table VI. The table illustrates the fact that in the case of AMS nouns, for instance, from 1027 candidates (local BCs) 429 were selected (as being members of at least another selection) and 598 were

Table VII. The representation of Common Base Concepts as synsets in the local wordnets

1059	Local Synsets Related to CBCs	Direct Equivalence Relations[3]	CBCs Without Direct Equivalent
AMS	992	994	97
FUE	1012	1009	15
PSA	878	950	9

rejected. The last column says that 265 senses, belonging to the common BCs were missing in the local selection and thus have to be added to the AMS selection. The selection of the common BCs thus resulted in a set of missing nouns and verbs for every language. Each group tried to represent the missing BCs as far as possible. The result is maximal coverage of the 871 CBCs (694 nominal and 177 verbal) by all the sites in terms of local representatives. Table VII gives an overview of the representation of the CBCs in the local wordnets (see also Figure 3 at the end of this paper).

Eq_synonym relations have been assigned to local synsets that directly match a BC. Eq_near_synonyms have been assigned when multiple synsets match a BC or when there was a small difference. As is indicated in the last column, it may be the case that that there is no equivalent in the local language for a common BC. In that case it was linked to the closest meaning in the local wordnet via a so-called complex equivalence relation.[4] This is illustrated by the way in which the non-lexicalized BC "plant part" is represented in the Spanish wordnet by linking related Spanish synsets to it:

{cosa#1; objeto#1} (physical object)   Eq_has_hyponym   {plant part#1}

{organo#5; organo vegetal#1} (plant organ) Eq_has_hyperonym {plant part#1}

{flor#1, planta#1} (plant)   Eq_has_meronym   {plant part#1}

In total 105 CBCs could not be represented in all three wordnets, 13 of which not in two wordnets (Table VIII).

4.2.2. *Tuning of the initial Common Base Concepts*

One explanation for the low intersection given above was the unreliability of the translations. As described in (Vossen et al., this volume) and (Peters et al., this volume) the degree of polysemy of WordNet1.5 is much higher than in traditional resources. For example, a verb such as *clean* has 19 different senses in WordNet1.5, whereas traditional dictionaries only give one general sense. A danger of this extreme sense-differentiation is that a single sense in the traditional resources may match with several synsets in WordNet1.5. As a result of this, it is not unlikely

Table VIII. Common Base Concepts that are not lexicalized in at least two wordnets

body covering#1	mental object#1; cognitive content#1; content#2
body substance#1	natural object#1
social control#1	place of business#1; business establishment#1
change of magnitude#1	plant organ#1
contractile organ#1	plant part#1
material#3; matter#5	psychological feature#1
spatial property#1; spatiality#1	

Table IX. Senses overlap of Rejected Base Concepts

Nouns	Entries	Synsets[5]
RCs sharing one or more word forms with BCs	303	529
RCs sharing word form(s) between them, but not with any BC	87	194
Total	390	723

Verbs	Entries	Synsets
RCs sharing one or more word forms with BCs	158	285
RCs sharing word form(s) between them, but not with any BC	50	124
Total	208	409

that, in many cases, different WordNet1.5 synsets have been chosen as equivalent synonyms for language specific synsets, which are hardly distinguishable.

To measure the possible impact of this type of mismatching, we checked to what extent the rejected and selected BCs represent different senses of the same entries. Table IX gives an overview of the matches between Rejected Concepts (RCs) and BCs at the word level. From these we selected all RCs that represent different senses of the same entries (either RCs or RCs and BCs). This set has been further limited by the following constraints:

1. Only words shared by at least four synsets, RC or BC, have been included in the evaluation. In other words: at least four senses of a word must be involved. A check has been made to ensure that the rejected synsets belonging to these sense groups did not all originate from only one language specific wordnet, but have a more or less even distribution over the different language sites.
2. We have focussed on synsets that have more than average relations (19.49 for the BCs in WordNet1.5). This includes the relations for RCs as separate synsets, but also the merged relations of RCs that are very close.

Next we have carried out a manual check of all these cases to see whether they have been rejected because of a mismatching of translations from language specific concepts to WordNet1.5 senses. RCs have been reselected if:

a) Their meaning is more central or basic than a selected BC.
b) They have more than average number of relations.
c) They can be merged with another selected or rejected BC because they are very close in meaning.
d) They exhibit a regular polysemy relation with a selected or rejected BC: e.g. metonymy, diathesis alternations.

For instance, the RCs *position* (a place where or a way in which something is situated) and *disposition* (your usual mood) have been selected and then related to the BCs *position* (a job in an organization or hierarchy) and *disposition* (an attitude of mind esp. one that favors one alternative over others) respectively. For a further discussion on the identification of sense relations in terms of generalization and metonymy see (Peters et al., this volume).

To measure the closeness of senses of entries, a metric was applied to nominal RCs which had been developed by (Agirre and Rigau, 1996) for computing conceptual distance between RC and BC WordNet1.5 nodes. This measure takes into account the length of the shortest paths that connects the concepts involved, the depth of the hierarchy, and the density of the distribution of concepts in the hierarchy. If an RC-BC pair was found to be conceptually very close the RC synset was selected.

In some cases, RCs have not been re-selected:

a) In order to maximize the coverage of the BC set, direct RC hyponyms of existing BCs have principally not been selected unless they were judged strong enough candidates for inclusion – e.g. *airplane* has not been selected because of its BC direct hyperonym *aircraft*.
b) Noun basic-level concepts (Rosch, 1977; Lakoff, 1987) such as *bed*, *wheel*, *shoe*, *window*, *glass*, *eye* and *soup* represent a level of lexicalisation which is considered too specific for our selection purposes, and have not been selected.
c) Nominal taxonomic terms within the field of biology have not been selected as new BCs. They have very specific technical meanings, and are subsumed by the BC *group*.

The selection of RCs involving the methods described above resulted in an extension of the common BCs to a final set of 1024 synsets, representing 796 nominal CBCs and 228 verbal CBCs.

5. Top-Ontology Clustering of the Base Concepts

To get to grips with the set of Base Concepts we have constructed a Top-Ontology of basic semantic distinctions to classify them. There is no common, a priori agreement how to build an ontology. In fact there is no agreement on what an ontology is (collections of related objects so different as CYC (Lenat and Guha, 1990), Generalized Upper Model (Bateman et al., 1994) or WordNet1.5 (Miller et al., 1990) are considered ontologies). (Gruber, 1992) therefore uses a pragmatic definition of an ontology: "an explicit specification of a conceptualization", i.e. a description of the concepts and relationships that can exist for an agent or community of agents. He points out that what is important is what an ontology is used for. The purpose of an ontology is enabling knowledge sharing and reuse. In that context, an ontology is a specification used for making ontological commitments. This definition can, of course, include the frequent forms of a taxonomic hierarchy of classes or a thesaurus, but also structures including and using more sophisticated inference mechanisms and in-depth knowledge about the world (or about the involved domain).

Ontologies differ in their scope (general or domain specific), in the granularity of the units (just terminological labels or units owning more or less complex internal structure), in the kind of relations that can be defined between units, and in the more or less precise and well defined semantics of the units and relations (inheritance and other inference mechanisms). Further on, Gruber distinguishes between Representation Ontologies and Content Ontologies. The former provide a framework but do not offer guidance about how to represent the world (or the domain) while the latter make claims about how the world should be described.

Gangemi et al. (1996) discuss several approaches for building ontologies based on most of these distinctions. They pay attention, basically, to the order of selection of the candidate nodes: a top-down approach, starting from domain-independent top-nodes, that seems to be more adequate for general ontologies, a bottom-up approach that tries to induce more general behaviour from local (mostly terminological) nodes or an hybrid approach (the ONIONS methodology in their case) that tries to take profit of both previous ones.

However, not only the direction of selection is important for deciding the building strategy. Different approaches can be followed for filling information. One possibility is to follow a stepwise refinement approach, based on a cascade of enrichment processes: first selecting the candidate nodes to form a simple list of names, then establishing in successive cycles relations between them, and, finally, filling the information owned by each node. Of course, some of the refining cycles can be performed in not predefined order and sometimes in parallel. An alternative approach consists of starting with an initial node (or a small set of initial nodes), filling this node with all available information about it, establish all the relations involving this node and proceed recursively with each of the nodes related to it. The approach to be selected depends largely on the characteristics of the ontology to be built, i.e. domain, size, content, granularity, intended use, and so on.

Considering all these difficulties we decided to follow a new kind of approach, consisting basically of looking at the language-independent Top Ontology more as a lattice of classifying semantic features than as an ontology in the taxonomic sense. (see Guarino (1997) and Sowa (fc.) for a similar lattice approach to represent ontological notions From this point of view, multi-classification plays a major role in our approach: in EWN, interlingual concepts are not, in general, linked to a single node of the abstract ontology – but to a multiplicity of them. For instance, the interlinguistic representation of a car will be linked to three ontological nodes: Origin-Artifact, Form-Object, and Function-Vehicle. Such semantic information will spread to the lexicalisations of the concept in the local wordnets.

We consider this approach more flexible than usual ontologies since it shows several advantages, from which we can highlight the following:

- It provides different simultaneous ways of classifying concepts, which can be tailored according to the user's needs.
- Hierarchy is not necessary at this level since this information is already present in the language-specific wordnets.
- It allows to enrich the lexicalisations with linguistically-relevant semantic information (features).
- It provides a common framework for building and comparing the wordnets, e.g. to extend them in a systematic way or to detect gaps, allowing the encoding of language-specific lexicalisations in the hierarchies.

In the next sections we describe the basic principles of this approach in more detail.

5.1. STARTING POINTS FOR THE EUROWORDNET TOP-ONTOLOGY

As explained in the introduction to this volume and in (Peters et al., this volume), the EuroWordNet database consists of separate language-specific modules (as autonomous systems of language-internal relations), which are linked by an Inter-Lingual-Index. The Inter-Lingual-Index (ILI) is an unstructured fund of synsets (mainly taken from WorNet1.5), the so-called ILI-records. Language-specific synsets linked to the same ILI-record are assumed to be equivalent. The ILI-records further give access to all language-independent knowledge, among which a Top Ontology of fundamental semantic distinctions. This language-independent information can be transferred via the ILI-record, which is assigned to it, to all the language specific synsets that are linked to it. This is schematically represented in Figure 1.

In Figure 1 we see that the top-concept Object applies to the ILI-record *object*, which is linked to the Dutch and Italian concepts *voorwerp* and *oggetto* respectively. Likewise, the ontological distinction not only applies to the ILI-record but also to the language-specific meanings. The common BCs, described above, are all specified in the form of ILI-records, which are thus linked to fundamental concepts in the local wordnets.

The purpose of the EuroWordNet Top Ontology can then be detailed as follows:

a) It will enforce more uniformity and compatibility of the different wordnets. The classifications of the BCs in terms of the Top Ontology distinctions should apply

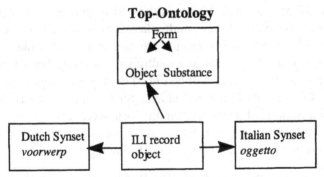

Figure 1. Overall structure of the EWN Database.

to all the involved languages. In practice this means that all sites verify the assignment of a Top Concept to an ILI-record for the synsets in their local word-nets that are linked to this ILI-record. For example, the features associated with the top-concept Object can only apply to the ILI-record *object*, when the features also apply to the Dutch and Italian concepts linked to this ILI-record as equiv-alences, as is illustrated in Figure 1 above. In addition the distinction should also hold for all other Dutch and Italian concepts that could possibly inherit this property from the language-internal relations (e.g. all the (sub)hyponyms linked to "voorwerp" in the Dutch wordnet and all the (sub)hyponyms linked to "oggetto" in the Italian wordnet). Note that the language internal distribution of such a feature can still differ from wordnet to wordnet, as long as no false implications are derived.

b) Using the Top Concepts (TCs) we can divide the Base Concepts (BCs) into coherent clusters. This is important to enable contrastive-analysis of the word meanings and it will stimulate a similar treatment. Furthermore, the clusters are used to monitor progress across the sites and to discuss problems and solutions per cluster.

c) The Top-Ontology provides users access and control of the database without having to understand each specific language in the wordnets. It is possible to customize the database by assigning features to the top-concepts, irrespective of the language-specific structures.

d) Although the wordnets in EWN are seen as autonomous language-specific struc-tures, it is in principle possible to extend the database with language-neutral ontologies, such as CYC, MikroKosmos or Sensus, by linking them to the cor-responding ILI-records. Such a linking will be facilitated by the top-concept ontology where similar concepts can be mapped directly.

From these purposes we can derive a few more specific principles for deciding on the relevant distinctions. The most important purpose of the Top Ontology is to provide a common starting point and high degree of compatibility across the wordnets for the BCs. As suggested before, the wordnets reflect language-specific dependencies between words. Likewise, the coding of the relations can be seen mainly as a linguistic operation, resulting in linguistically-motivated relations.[6] It is therefore important that the Top-Ontology incorporates semantic distinctions that play a role in linguistic approaches rather than purely cognitive or knowledge-engineering practices. We therefore have initially based the ontology on semantic classifications common in linguistic paradigms: Aktionsart models (Vendler, 1967; Verkuyl, 1972; Verkuyl, 1989; Pustejovsky, 1991), entity-orders (Lyons, 1977), Aristotle's Qualia-structure (Pustejovsky, 1995). Furthermore, we made use of ontological classifications developed in previous EC-projects, which had a similar basis and are well-known in the project consortium: Acquilex (BRA 3030, 7315), Sift (LE-62030), (Vossen and Bon, 1996).[7]

In addition to these theoretically-motivated distinctions there is also a practical requirement that the ontology should be capable of reflecting the diversity of the set of common BCs, across the 4 languages. In this sense the classification of the common BCs in terms of the top-concepts should result in:

- homogeneous Base Concept Clusters.
- average size of Base Concept Clusters.

Homogeneity has been verified by checking the clustering of the BCs with their classification in WordNet1.5. In this sense the ontology has also been adapted to fit the top-levels of WordNet1.5. Obviously, the clustering also has been verified with the other language-specific wordnets. The criterion of cluster-size implies that we should not get extremely large or small clusters. In the former case the ontology should be further differentiated, in the latter case distinctions have to be removed and the BCs have to be linked to a higher level. Finally, we can mention as important characteristics:

- the semantic distinctions should apply to both nouns, verbs and adjectives, because these can be related in the language-specific wordnets via a xpos_synonymy[8] relation, and the ILI-records can be related to any part-of-speech.
- the top-concepts are hierarchically ordered by means of a subsumption relation but there can only be one super-type linked to each top-concept: multiple inheritance between top-concepts is not allowed.
- in addition to the subsumption relation top-concepts can have an opposition-relation to indicate that certain distinctions are disjunct, whereas others may overlap.
- there may be multiple relations from ILI-records to top-concepts. This means that the BCs can be cross-classified in terms of multiple top-concepts (as long as these have no opposition-relation between them): i.e. multiple inheritance from Top-Concepts to Base Concepts is allowed.

It is important to realize that the Top Concepts are more like semantic features than like common conceptual classes. We typically find TCs for Living and for Part but we do not find a TC Bodypart, even though this may be more appealing to a non-expert. BCs representing *body parts* are now cross-classified by two feature-like TCs Living and Part. The reason for this is that the diversity of the BCs would require many cross-classifiying concepts where Living and Part are combined with many other TCs. These combined classes result in a much more complex system, which is not very flexible and difficult to maintain or adapt. Furthermore, it turned out that the BCs typically abstract from particular features but these abstractions do not show any redundancy: i.e. it is not the case that all things that are Living also always share other features.

An explanation for the diversity of the BCs is the way in which they have been selected. To be useful as a classifier or category for many concepts (one of the major criteria for selection) a concept must capture a particular generalization but abstract from (many) other properties. Likewise we find many classifying meanings which express only one or two TC-features but no others. In this respect the BCs typically abstract one or two levels from the cognitive Basic-Level as defined by (Rosch, 1977). So we more likely find BCs such as *furniture* and *vehicle* than *chair*, *table* and *car*.

5.2. THE EUROWORDNET TOP-ONTOLOGY

The current ontology (version 1) is the result of 4 cycles of updating where each proposal has been verified by the different sites. The ontology now consists of 63 higher-level concepts, excluding the top. Following (Lyons, 1977) we distinguish at the first level 3 types of entities:

1stOrderEntity

> Any concrete entity (publicly) perceivable by the senses and located at any point in time, in a three-dimensional space.

2ndOrderEntity

> Any Static Situation (property, relation) or Dynamic Situation, which cannot be grasped, heard, seen, felt as an independent physical thing. They can be located in time and occur or take place rather than exist; e.g. *continue, occur, apply*

3rdOrderEntity

> A proposition which exists independently of time and space. They can be true or false rather than real. They can be asserted or denied, remembered or forgotten. E.g. *idea, though, information, theory, plan.*

According to Lyons, 1stOrderEntities are publicly observable individual persons, animals and more or less discrete physical objects and physical substances. They can be located at any point in time and in, what is at least psychologically, a three-dimensional space. The 2ndOrderEntities are events, processes, states-of-affairs or situations which can be located in time. Whereas 1stOrderEntities **exist** in time and space 2ndOrderEntities **occur** or **take place**, rather than exist. The 3rdOrder-Entities are propositions, such as ideas, thoughts, theories, hypotheses, that exist outside space and time and which are unobservable. They function as objects of propositional attitudes, and they cannot be said to occur or be located either in space or time. Furthermore, they can be predicated as true or false rather than real, they can be asserted or denied, remembered or forgotten, they may be reasons but not causes.

The following tests are used to distinguish between 1st and 2nd order entities:

a   The same person was here again today
b   The same thing happened/occurred again today

The reference of 'the same person' is constrained by the assumption of spatiotemporal continuity and by the further assumption that the same person cannot be in two different places at the same time. The same event can occur in several different places, not only at different times but also at the same time. Third-order entities cannot occur, have no temporal duration and therefore fail on both tests:

*?   The idea, fact, expectation, etc ... was here/occurred/ took place

A positive test for a 3rdOrderEntity is based on the properties that can be predicated:

ok   The idea, fact, expectation, etc.. is true, is denied, forgotten

The first division of the ontology is disjoint: BCs cannot be classified as combinations of these TCs. As described in Alonge et al. (this volume) this distinction cuts across the different parts of speech in that:

- 1stOrderEntities are always expressed by (concrete) nouns.
- 2ndOrderEntities can be nouns, verbs and adjectives, where adjectives are always non-dynamic (refer to states and situations not involving a change of state).
- 3rdOrderEntities are always (abstract) nouns.

With respect to the BCs we therefore also see that all three parts-of-speech can be classified below 2ndOrderEntity. Note also that a BC may originally be a noun or verb in WordNet1.5 but may be associated with any part-of-speech in a local wordnet (Table X). Since the number of 3rdOrderEntities among the BCs was limited compared to the 1stOrder and 2ndOrder Entities we have not further subdivided them. The following BCs have been classified as 3rdOrderEntities:

Base Concepts classified as 3rdOrderEntities:
theory; idea; structure; evidence; procedure; doctrine; policy; data point; content; plan of action; concept; plan; communication; knowledge base; cognitive content; know-how; category; information; abstract.

Table X. Distribution of Part-of-Speech over the top-level

	Nouns	**Verbs**	**Total**
1stOrderEntities	491		491
2ndOrderEntities	272	228	500
3rdOrderEntities	33		33
Total	796	228	1024

The 1stOrderEntities and 2ndOrderEntities are then further subdivided according to the hierarchy which is shown in Figure 2 (where the indices indicate the number of assigned BCs). These subdivisions are further discussed in the next sections.

5.2.1. *Classification of 1st-Order-Entities*

The 1stOrderEntities are distinguished in terms of four main ways of conceptualizing or classifying a concrete entity:

a. Origin: the way in which an entity has come about.
b. Form: as an amorphous substance or as an object with a fixed shape, hence the subdivisions Substance and Object.
c. Composition: as a group of self-contained wholes or as a part of such a whole, hence the subdivisions Part and Group.
d. Function: the typical activity or action that is associated with an entity.

These classes are comparable with Aristotle's Qualia roles as described in Pustejovsky's Generative lexicon, (the Agentive Role, Formal Role, Constitutional Role and Telic Role respectively: (Pustejovsky, 1995) but are also based on our empirical findings to classify the BCs. BCs can be classified in terms of any combination of these four roles. As such the top-concepts function more as features than as ontological classes. Such a systematic cross-classification was necessary because the BCs represented such diverse combinations (e.g. it was not possible to limit Function or Living only to Object).

The main-classes are then further subdivided, where the subdivisions for Form and Composition are obvious given the above definition, except that Substance itself is further subdivided into Solid, Liquid and Gas. In the case of Function the subdivisions are based only on the frequency of BCs having such a function or role. In principle the number of roles is infinite but the above roles appear to occur more frequently in the set of common Base Concepts.

Finally, a more fine-grained subdivision has been made for Origin, first into Natural and Artifact. The category Natural covers both inanimate objects and substances, such as *stones*, *sand*, *water*, and all living things, among which *animals*, *plants* and *humans*. The latter are stored at a deeper level below Living. The intermediate level Living is necessary to create a separate cluster for natural objects and

Top[0]	
1stOrderEntity[1]	**2ndOrderEntity[0]**
Origin[0]	SituationType[6]
Natural[21]	Dynamic[134]
Living[30]	BoundedEvent[183]
Plant[18]	UnboundedEvent[48]
Human[106]	Static[28]
Creature[2]	Property[61]
Animal[123]	Relation[38]
Artifact[144]	**SituationComponent[0]**
Form[0]	Cause[67]
Substance[32]	Agentive[170]
Solid[63]	Phenomenal[17]
Liquid[13]	Stimulating[25]
Gas[1]	Communication[50]
Object1[62]	Condition[62]
Composition[0]	Existence[27]
Part[86]	Experience[43]
Group[63]	Location[76]
Function[55]	Manner[21]
Vehicle[8]	Mental[90]
Representation[12]	Modal[10]
MoneyRepresentation[10]	Physical[140]
LanguageRepresentation[34]	Possession[23]
ImageRepresentation[9]	Purpose[137]
Software[4]	Quantity[39]
Place[45]	Social[102]
Occupation[23]	Time[24]
Instrument[18]	Usage[8]
Garment[3]	
Furniture[6]	
Covering[8]	
Container[12]	
Comestible[32]	
Building[13]	
3rdOrderEntity[33]	

Figure 2. Structure of the EWN Top Ontology.

substances, which consist of Living material (e.g. *skin, cell*) but are not considered as *animate beings*. Non-living and Natural objects and substances, such as natural products like *milk, seeds, fruit*, are classified directly below Natural.

As suggested, each BC that is a 1stOrderEntity is classified in terms of these main classes. However, whereas the main-classes are intended for cross-classifications, most of the subdivisions are disjoint classes: a concept cannot be an Object and a Substance, or both Natural and Artifact. This means that within a main-class only one subdivision can be assigned. Consequently, each BC that is a 1stOrderEntity has at least one up to four classifications:

fruit:	Comestible (Function)
	Object (Form)
	Part (Composition)
	Plant (Natural, Origin)
skin:	Covering (Covering)
	Solid (Form)
	Part (Constituency)
	Living (Natural, Origin)
life 1:	Group (Composition)
	Living (Natural, Origin)
cell:	Part (Composition)
	Living (Natural, Origin)
reproductive structure 1:	Living (Natural, Origin)

The more classifications, the more informative the concept is. If a BC is classified by e.g. only one main-class it means that it can refer to things that vary in properties with respect to the other classes. This typically applies to words which we call Functionals and which occur relatively often as BCs. Functionals are words that can only be characterized in terms of some major activity-involvement and can vary with respect to their Form, Constituency, or Origin. Examples of Functionals are: *threat, belongings, product, cause, garbage*, which can refer to persons, animals, substances, objects, instruments, parts, groups, anything as long as it satisfies the described role. These nouns thus have an open denotation (although stereotypical constraints may hold) and fully rely on this relation.[9] Other classes below Function, e.g. Building, Vehicle are also linked to Artifact and therefore specified for Origin. Most of these are Objects, some are also specified for Group:

arms:	Instrument (Function)
	Group (Composition)
	Object (Form)
	Artifact (Origin)

In total, 124 different combinations of TCs have been used to classify all the 1stOrderEntities (491 BCs).

Finally, with respect to Composition it needs to be said that only concepts that essentially depend on some other concept, are classified as either Part or Group. It is not the case that all *persons* will be classified as Parts because they may be part of *group*. *Group*, on the other hand, typically depends on the elements as part of its meaning.

1stOrder Top Concept	Gloss
Origin	Considering the way concrete entities are created or come into existence.
Function	Considering the purpose, role or main activity of a concrete entity. Typically nouns that can refer to any substance, object which is involved in some event or process; e.g. *remains, product, threat*.
Form	Considering the shape of concrete entities, fixed as an object or amorphous substance
Composition	Considering the composition of concrete entities in terms of parts, groups and larger constructs
Part	Any concrete entity which is contained in an object, substance or a group; *head, juice, nose, limb, blood, finger, wheel, brick, door*
Group	Any concrete entity consisting of multiple discrete objects (either homogeneous or heterogeneous sets), e.g. *traffic, people, army, herd*
Substance	all stuff without boundary or fixed shape, considered from a conceptual point of view not from a linguistic point of view; e.g. *mass, material, water, sand, air*. Opposed to Object.
Object	Any conceptually-countable concrete entity with an outer limit; e.g. *book, car, person, brick*. Opposed to Substance.
Vehicle	e.g. *car, ship, boat*
Software	e.g. *computer programs* and *databases*
Representation	Any concrete entity used for conveying a message; e.g. *traffic sign, word, money*.
Place	Concrete entities functioning as the location for something else; e.g. *place, spot, centre, North, South*
Occupation	e.g. *doctor, researcher, journalist, manager*
Instrument	e.g. *tool, machine, weapon*
Garment	e.g. *jacket, trousers, shawl*
Furniture	e.g. *table, chair, lamp*
Covering	e.g. *skin, cloth, shield,*
Container	e.g. *bag, tube, box*
Comestible	food & drinks, including substances, liquids and objects.
Building	e.g. *house, hotel, church, office*
Plant	e.g. *plant, rice*; Opposed to Animal, Human, Creature.
Human	e.g. *person, someone*
Creature	Imaginary creatures; e.g. *God, Faust, E.T.*; Opposed to Animal, Human, Plant
Animal	e.g. *animal, dog;* Opposed to Plant, Human, Creature.
Living	Anything living and dying including objects, organic parts or tissue, bodily fluids; e.g. *cells; skin; hair, organism, organs*.
Natural	Anything produced by nature and physical forces; Opposed to Artifact.
Artifact	Anything manufactured by people; Opposed to Natural.

MoneyRepresentation	Physical Representations of value, or money; e.g. *share, coin*
LanguageRepresentation	Physical Representations conveyed in language (e.g. spoken, written or sign language); e.g. *text, word, utterance, sentence, poem*
ImageRepresentation	Physical Representations conveyed in a visual medium; e.g. *sign language, traffic sign, light signal*
Solid	Substance which can fall, does not feel wet and you cannot inhale it; e.g. *stone, dust, plastic, ice, metal*; Opposed to Liquid, Gas
Liquid	Substance that can fall, feels wet and can flow on the ground; e.g. *water, soup, rain*; Opposed to Gas, Solid.
Gas	Substance that cannot fall, you can inhale it and it floats above the ground; e.g. *air, ozon*; Opposed to Liquid, Solid.

5.2.2. *The classification of 2ndOrderEntities*

As explained above, 2ndOrderEntities can be referred to using nouns and verbs (and also adjectives or adverbs) denoting static or dynamic Situations, such as *birth, live, life, love, die* and *death*. All 2ndOrderEntities are classified using two different classification schemes, which represent the first division below 2ndOrderEntity:

- the SituationType: the event-structure in terms of which a situation can be characterized as a conceptual unit over time;
- the SituationComponent: the most salient semantic component(s) that characterize(s) a situation;

The SituationType reflects the way in which a situation can be quantified and distributed over time, and the dynamicity that is involved. It thus represents a basic classification in terms of the event-structure (in the formal tradition) or Aktionsart properties of nouns and verbs. The fundamental SituationTypes are Static and Dynamic. The SituationComponents represent a more conceptual classification, resulting in intuitively coherent clusters of word meanings. The SituationComponents reflect the most salient semantic components that apply to our selection of Base Concepts. Examples of SituationComponents are: Location, Existence, Cause.

Typically, SituationType represents disjoint features that cannot be combined, whereas it is possible to assign any range or combination of SituationComponents to a word meaning. Each 2ndOrder meaning can thus be classified in terms of an obligatory but unique SituationType and any number of SituationComponents.

5.2.2.1. *SituationTypes.* Following a traditional Aktionsart classification (Vendler, 1967; Verkuyl, 1972; Verkuyl, 1989), SituationType is first subdivided into Static and Dynamic, depending on the dynamicity of the Situation:

Dynamic

Situations implying either a specific transition from one state to another (Bounded in time) or a continuous transition perceived as an ongoing temporally unbounded process; e.g. *event, act, action, become, happen, take place, process, habit, change, activity*. Opposed to Static.

Static

Situations (properties, relations and states) in which there is no transition from one eventuality or situation to another: non-dynamic; e.g. *state, property, be*. Opposed to Dynamic.

In general words, Static Situations do not involve any change, Dynamic Situations involve some specific change or a continuous changing. The traditional test for making dynamicity explicit is to combine the noun or verb with a manner phrase that specifies the inherent properties of the Situation:

a.   ?he sits quickly.
b.   he sat down quickly.
      a quick, wild meeting.

The static verb *to sit* cannot be combined with quickly, but the dynamic verb *to sit down* and dynamic noun *meeting* can. Different aspectual modifications, such as (im)perfective, progressive, depend on this qualification.

Static Situations are further subdivided into Properties, such as *length, size*, which apply to single concrete entities or abstract situations, and Relations, such as *distance, space*, which only exist relative to and in between several entities (of the same order):

Property

Static Situation which applies to a single concrete entity or abstract Situation; e.g. *colour, speed, age, length, size, shape, weight*.

Relation

Static Situation which applies to a pair of concrete entities or abstract Situations, and which cannot exist by itself without either one of the involved entities; e.g. *relation, kinship, distance, space*.

Dynamic Situations are subdivided into events which express a specific transition and are bounded in time (BoundedEvent), and processes which are unbounded in time (UnboundedEvent) and do not imply a specific transition from one situation to another (although there can be many intermediate transitions):

BoundedEvent

Dynamic Situations in which a specific transition from one Situation to another is implied; Bounded in time and directed to a result; e.g. *to do, to cause to change, to make, to create*.

UnboundedEvent

Dynamic Situations occurring during a period of time and composed of a sequence of (micro-)changes of state, which are not perceived as relevant for characterizing the Situation as a whole; e.g. *grow, change, move around, live, breath, activity, hobby, sport, education, work, performance, fight, love, caring, management.*

We typically see that many verbs and nouns are under-classified for boundedness and sometimes even for dynamicity. This means that they can get a more specific interpretation in terms of a bounded change or an unbounded process when they are put in a particular context. A verb such as to walk names a bounded event when it is combined with a destination phrase, as in (a), but it is unbounded when it is combined with a location phrase as in (b):

a. He walked to the station (?for hours) (in 2 hours)
b. He walked in the park (for hours) (?in 2 hours)

The boundedness is made more explicit using duration phrases that imply the natural termination point of the change (*in 2 hours*) or explicitly do not (*for hours*).

5.2.2.2. *SituationComponents.* The SituationComponents divide the Base-Concepts in conceptually coherent clusters. The set of distinctions is therefore based on the diversity of the set of common Base-Concepts that has been defined. The following main components have been distinguished (where each component is followed by a formal definition and a short explanation):

Usage

Situations in which something (an instrument, substance, time, effort, force, money) is or can be used; e.g. *to use, to spend, to represent, to mean, to be about, to operate, to fly, drive, run, eat, drink, consume.*

Usage stands for Situations in which either a resource or an instrument is used or activated for some purpose. This covers both consumptive usage (the use time, effort, food, fuel) and instrumental operation (as in *to operate a vehicle, to run a program*). So far it has been restricted to Dynamic Situations only. It typically combines with Purpose, Agentive and Cause because we often deliberately use things to cause to some effect for some purpose.

Time

Situations in which duration or time plays a significant role; Static e.g. *yesterday, day, pass, long, period,* Dynamic e.g. *begin, end, last, continue.*

Time is only applied to BCs that strongly imply temporal aspects. This includes general BCs that only imply some temporal aspect and specific BCs that also denote some specific Situation. Typical 'aspectual' BCs, such as *begin, end,* only express the aspectual phase of situations but they abstract from the actual Situation.

Most of these also imply dynamicity. More specific BCs, such as *to attack*, *to depart*, *to arrive*, combine other SituationComponents but also imply some aspectual phase. Finally, all BCs that denote time points and periods, such as *time*, *day*, *hour*, *moment*, are all clustered below Time and Static.

Social

Situations related to society and social interaction of people: Static e.g. *employment, poor, rich*, Dynamic e.g. *work, management, recreation, religion, science*.

Social refers to our inter-human activities and situations in society. There are many Social activities (UnboundedEvent) which correlate with many different Social Interests or Purposes. These are not further differentiated in terms of TCs but using the Domain labels (Management, Science, Religion, Health Care, War, Recreation, Sports). In addition there are Static Social states such as *poverty, employment*.

Quantity

Situations involving quantity and measure; Static e.g. *weight, heaviness, lightness*; changes of the quantity of first order entities; Dynamic e.g. to *lessen, increase, decrease*.

Dynamic BCs clustered below Quantity typically denote increase or decrease of amounts of entities. Static Quantity BCs denote all kinds of measurements.

Purpose

Situations which are intended to have some effect.

Purpose is an abstract component reflecting the intentionality of acts and activities. This concept can only be applied to Dynamic Situations and it strongly correlates with Agentive and Cause, clustering mainly human acts and activities. Situation-Components such as Usage, Social and Communication often (but not always) combine with Purpose.

Possession

Situations involving possession; Static e.g. *have, possess, possession, contain, consist of, own*; Dynamic changes in possession, often to be combined which changes in location as well; e.g. *sell, buy, give, donate, steal, take, receive, send*.

Possession covers ownership and changes of ownership, but not physical location or meronymy or abstract possession of properties. The fact that transfer of Possession often implies physical motion or static location will be indicated by cross-classifying BCs for Possession, Location, and Static or Dynamic, respectively.

Physical

Situations involving perceptual and measurable properties of first order entities; either Static e.g. *health, a colour, a shape, a smell*; or Dynamic changes and perceptions of the physical properties of first order entities; e.g. *redden, thicken, widen, enlarge, crush, form, shape, fold, wrap, thicken, to see, hear, notice, smell.* Opposed to Mental.

Physical typically clusters Dynamic physical Changes, in which a Physical Property is altered, and Static Physical Properties. In all these cases a particular physical property is incorporated which, in many cases, can be made explicit by means of a causative relation (*to become red*) or a synonymy relation (*health and healthy*) with an adjective in the local wordnets. Another cluster is formed by Physical Experiences (see Experience).

Modal

Situations (only Static) involving the possibility or likelihood of other situations as actual situations; e.g. *abilities, power, force, strength.*

Modal Situations are always Static. Most Modal BCs denote some ability or necessary property needed to perform some act or activity.

Mental

Situations experienced in mind, including a concept, idea or the interpretation or message conveyed by a symbol or performance (*meaning, denotation, content, topic, story, message, interpretation*) and emotional and attitudinal situations; a mental state is changed; e.g. *invent, remember, learn, think, consider.* Opposed to Physical.

Mental Situations can be differentiated into Experiences (see Experience) and in Dynamic Mental events possibly involving an Agent. The latter cluster cognitive actions and activities such as *to think, to calculate, to remember, to decide.*

Manner

Situations in which way or manner plays a role. This may be Manner incorporated in a dynamic situation, e.g. ways of movement such *as walk, swim, fly,* or the static Property itself: e.g. *manner, sloppy, strongly, way.*

Manner as a SituationComponent applies to many specific BCs that denote a specific way or manner in which a Dynamic event takes place. Typical examples are ways of movement. General BCs that only refer to Manner as such and not to some specific Situation are Static nouns such as *manner, way, style.*

Location

Situations involving spatial relations; static e.g. *level, distance, separation, course, track, way, path*; something changes location, irrespective of the causation of the change; e.g. *move, put, fall, drop, drag, glide, fill, pour, empty, take out, enter.*

Location is typically incorporated in Dynamic BCs denoting *movements.* When combined with Static it clusters nouns that refer to Location Relations, such as *distance, level, path, space.* A Location Relation holds between several entities and cannot be seen as a property of single entity. This makes it different from Place, which applies to a 1stOrderEntity that functions as the location for an event or some other 1stOrderEntity.

Experience

> Situations that involve an experiencer: either mental or perceptual through the senses.

Situations with the TC Experience involve the mental or perceptual processing of some stimulus. In this respect there must be an experiencer implied, although it is not necessarily expressed as one of the arguments of a verb (it could be incorporated in the meaning). Typical Experience BCs are: *to experience, to sense, to feel, pain, to notice.* Experiences can be differentiated by combining it with Physical or Mental. Physical Experiences are external stimuli processed by the senses: *to see, to hear.* Mental Experiences are internal only existing in our minds: *desire, pleasance, humor, faith, motivation.* There are many examples of BCs that cannot be differentiated between these, e.g. *pain* that can be both Physical and Mental. Another interesting aspect of Experiences is that there is unclarity about the dynamicity. It is not clear whether a *feeling* or *emotion* is static or dynamic. In this respect Experience BCs are often classified as SituationType, which is undifferentiated for dynamicity.

Existence

> Situations involving the existence of objects and substances; Static states of existence e.g. *exist, be, be alive, life, live, death*; Dynamic changes in existence; e.g. *kill, produce, make, create, destroy, die, birth.*

Dynamic Existence Situations typically refer to the coming about, the dying or destruction of both natural and artifact entities. This includes artificial production or creation, such as *to make, to produce, to create, to invent*, and natural *birth.* Static Existence is a small cluster of nouns that refer to existence or non-existence.

Condition

> Situations involving an evaluative state of something: Static, e.g. *health, disease, success* or Dynamic e.g. *worsen, improve.*

Condition is an evaluative notion that can be either positive or negative. It can be combined with Dynamic changes (Social, Physical or Mental) or Static Situations which are considered as positive or negative (again Social, Physical or Mental).

Communication

> Situations involving communication, either Static, e.g. *be_about* or Dynamic (Bounded and Unbounded); e.g. *speak, tell, listen, command, order, ask, state, statement, conversation, call.*

Communication verbs and nouns are often speech-acts (bounded events) or denote more global communicative activities (unbounded events) but there are also a few Static Communication BCs. The Static Communication BCs (e.g. *to be about*) express meaning relations between PhysicalRepresentations (such as written language) and the propositional content (3rdOrderEntities). The Dynamic BCs below the TC Communication form a complex cluster of related concepts. They can represent various aspects of Communication which correlate with the different ways in which the communication is brought about, or different phases of the communication. Some Communication BCs refer to causation of communication effects, such as *to explain, to show, to demonstrate*, but not necessarily to the precise medium (graphical, verbal, body expression). These BCs combine with the TCs Cause and Mental. Other BCs refer to the creation of a meaningful Representation, *to write, to draw, to say*, but they do not necessarily imply a communicative effect or the perception and interpretation of the Representation. They typically combine with Existence, Agentive, and Purpose. Yet other BCs refer to the perceptual and mental processing of communicative events, *to read, to listen* and thus combine with Mental.

Cause

> Situations involving causation of Situations (both Static and Dynamic); *result, effect, cause, prevent.*

Causation is always combined with Dynamic and it can take various forms. It can either be related to a controlling agent which intentionally tries to achieve some change (Agentive), or it can be related to some natural force or circumstance (Phenomenal). Another differentiation is into the kind of effect as a perceptive or mental Experience, which makes the cause Stimulating. The different ways of causation have been subdivided in terms of an extra level of TCs:

Agentive

> Situations in which a controlling agent causes a dynamic change; e.g. *to kill, to do; to act*. Opposed to other causes such as Stimuli, Forces, Chance, Phenomena.

Stimulating

> Situations in which something elicits or arouses a perception or provides the motivation for some event, e.g. sounds (*song, bang, beep, rattle, snore*), views, smells, appetizing, motivation. Opposed to other causes such as Agents, Forces, Chance.

Phenomenal

> Situations that occur in nature controlled or uncontrolled or considered as a force; e.g. *weather, chance*. Opposed to other causes such as Stimuli, Agents.

As far as the set of Base Concepts is representative for the total wordnets, this set of SituationComponents is also representative for the whole. Note that adjectives and adverbs have not been classified in EuroWordNet yet. In this respect we may need a further elaboration of these components when these parts-of-speech are added. The last three SituationComponents are subdivided, which are discussed in the following subsections. As said above, a verb or 2ndOrder noun may thus be composed of any combination of these components. However, it is obvious that some combinations make more sense than others. Situations involving Purpose often also involve Cause, simply because it is in the nature of our behavior that people do things for some purpose. Furthermore, there may be some specific constraints that some components are restricted to some SituationTypes. Cause and Purpose can only occur with Dynamic Situations. When there is no constraint we will thus get various combinations, such as Dynamic and Physical for *to colour* or Static and Physical for *colour*, where word meanings can still be grouped on the basis of the shared component: Physical.

The more specific a word is the more components it incorporates. Just as with the 1stOrderEntities we therefore typically see that the more frequent classifying nouns and verbs only incorporate a few of these components. In the set of common Base-Concept, such classifying words are more frequent, and words with many SituationComponents are therefore rare. In total 314 combinations of TCs have been used to classify 500 2ndOrder BCs. Below are some examples of typical combinations of SituationComponents:

Experience + Stimulating + Dynamic + Condition (undifferentiated for Mental or Physical)

Verbs: *cause to feel unwell; cause pain*

Physical + Experience + SituationType (undifferentiated for Static/Dynamic)

Nouns: *sense; sensation; perception;*
Verbs: *look; feel; experience;*

Mental + (BoundedEvent) Dynamic + Agentive

Verbs: *identify; form an opinion of; form a resolution about; decide; choose; understand; call back; ascertain; bump into; affirm; admit defeat*
Nouns: *choice, selection*

Mental + Dynamic + Agentive

Verbs: *interpret; differentiate; devise; determine; cerebrate; analyze; arrange*
Nouns: *higher cognitive process; cerebration; categorization; argumentation*

Mental + Experience + SituationType (undifferentiated for Static/Dynamic)

Verbs: *consider; desire; believe; experience*
Nouns: *pleasance; motivation; humor; feeling; faith; emotion; disturbance*

Finally, it is important to realize that the Top Ontology does not necessarily correspond with the language-internal hierarchies. Each language-internal structure has a different mapping with the Top-Ontology via the ILI-records to which they are

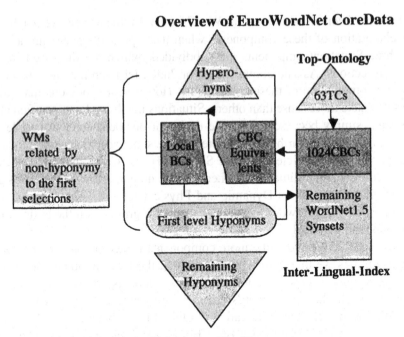

Figure 3. Vocabularies and modules in EuroWordNet.

linked as equivalences. For example there are no words in Dutch that correspond with a technical notion such as 1stOrderEntity, but also not with more down-to-earth concepts such as the Functional 1stOrder concept Container. These levels will thus not be present in the Dutch wordnet. From the Dutch hierarchy it will hence not be possible to simply extract all the *containers* because no Dutch word meaning is used to group or classify them. Nevertheless, the Dutch 'containers' may still be found either via the equivalence relations with English 'containers' which are stored below the sense of *container* or via the TopConcept clustering Container that is imposed on the Dutch hierarchy.[10]

6. Conclusions

In this paper we have described the general approach for building the EuroWordNet database. The discussion has focussed on the way we control the building of the separate wordnets at separate sites, where there has to be a maximum of flexibility, and still compatible results. On the one hand we want to allow for the development of unique language-specific wordnets, using different tools and methodologies, and on the other hand, we need to ensure that the same vocabulary is covered and the same decisions are made across the different sites. We have therefore developed a top-down approach where the building is divided into two phases: 1) covering a shared set of common Base Concepts, 2) extending from these Base Concepts using semi-automatic techniques.

The Base Concepts represent the shared cores of the different wordnets, where we try to achieve a maximum of consensus and overlap. Still, the local wordnets can differ in the exact way in which the vocabulary is lexicalized around these Base Concepts. We further specified the definition and selection of the Base Concepts. The main criterion has been the relevance of meanings for the local wordnets. This relevance has been measured mainly in terms of the number of relations and the position in the hierarchy. The local selections have been translated to WordNet1.5 synsets and merged into a shared set of concepts. This set has been critically assessed and evaluated which resulted in a final set of 1024 Common Base Concepts.

To get to grips with the Base Concepts they have been classified using a Top Ontology. The Top Ontology, which is organised using the relations subtype and opposition, provides a language-independent structuring of the Base Concepts in terms of 63 fundamental semantic distinctions, which are more like semantic features than like common conceptual classes – BCs are cross-classified in terms of multiple top concepts . This classification is used as a common framework to further guide the encoding of the language-internal relations at each site.

Figure 3 gives an overview of the different data types and subvocabularies discussed in this paper.

Notes

[1] (Procter, 1987).

[2] (Sinclair, 1987).

[3] Eq_Synonym and Eq_Near_Synonym.

[4] Cf. Peters et al. (this volume).

[5] These figures correspond to the number of WN 1.5 synsets which include one or more rejected word forms.

[6] Relations hold between lexicalized units (words and phrases) of a language, and not, as is often the case in language-neutral ontologies, between artificial node that are introduced just of the sake of creating a better ordering of hierarchies. The wordnets should therefore not contain levels or synsets for concepts which are not considered to be natural expressions in a language; this to the contrary of the common practice in WordNet1.5. as linguistic-structures the wordnets can provide valuable information on the expressiveness of languages, as conceptual-structures this is not guaranteed.

[7] In a later stage the EWN ontology will be compared with language-neutral ontologies such as CYC, Sensus (Knight and Luk, 1994), MikroKosmos. This will take place in the framework of the Eagles-project and in collaboration with the ANSI ADHOC Group on Ontology Standards.

[8] Cross-Part-of-Speech-Synonymy (cf. Alonge et al., this volume).

[9] This relation may be expressed in the language-internal wordnet by means of a specific role-relation with a verb or noun denoting the event.

[10] See Peters et al. (this volume) for a further discussion on accessing the different modules in the database.

References

Alvar M. (ed.) *Diccionario General Ilustrado de la Lengua Española VOX*. Barcelona: Biblograf S.A., 1987.

Agirre E. and G. Rigau. "Word Sense Disambiguation using Conceptual Density". In *Proceedings of the 16th International Conference on Computational Linguistics (COLING'96)*. Copenhagen, 1996.

Bateman, J., B. Magnini and J. Rinaldi. "The Generalised Upper Model". *Proceedings of ECAI*. 1994.

Boersma, P. *The Sift Lexical Database, Sift LRE 62030, Deliverable D10b*. University of Amsterdam, Amsterdam, 1996.

Dowty, D.R. *Word Meaning and Montague Grammar*. Dordrecht: Reidel, 1979.

Gangemi, A., G. Steve and F. Giacomelli. "Onions: An Ontological Methodology for Taxonomic Knowledge Integration". In *Proceedings of Workshop on Ontological Engineering, ECAI'96*. Budapest, 1996, pp. 29–40.

Guarino, N. "Semantic Matching: Formal Ontological Distinctions for Information Organization, Extraction, and Integration". In *Information Extraction: A Multidisciplinary Approach to an Emerging Information Technology*. Ed. M. T. Pazienza, Springer Verlag, 1997, pp. 139–170.

Gruber, T. R. *Ontolingua: a Mechanism to Support Portable Ontologies. Report KSL 91-66*. Stanford University, 1992.

Knight, K. and S. Luk. "Building a Large-Scale Knowledge Base for Machine Translation". *Proceedings of AAAI'94*. 1994.

Lakoff, G. *Women, Fire and Dangerous Things*. Chicago/London: University of Chicago Press, 1987.

Lenat, D. and R. Guha. *Building Large Knowledge-based Systems*. Representation and Inference in the CYC Project. Addison Wesley, 1990.

Levin, B. *English Verb Classes and Alternations*. Chicago: University of Chicago Press, 1993.

Lyons, J. *Semantics*. London: Cambridge University Press, 1977.

Martin W. and J. Tops. *Groot woordenboek Engels-Nederlands*. Utrecht: Van Dale Lexicografie, 1986.

Miller, G., R. Beckwith, C. Fellbaum, D. Gross and K. Miller. *Five Papers on WordNet. CSL Report 43*. Cognitive Science Laboratory, Princeton University, 1990.

Procter, P. (ed.) *Longman Dictionary of Contemporary English*. Harlow and London: Longman, 1987.

Pustejovsky, J. "The Syntax of Event Structure". *Cognition*, 41 (1991), 47–81.

Pustejovsky, J. *The Generative Lexicon*. Cambridge, MA: The MIT Press, 1995.

Rosch, E. "Human Categorisation". In *Studies in Cross-Cultural Psychology*, Vol. I. Ed. N. Warren, London: Academic Press, 1977, pp. 1–49.

Sinclair, J. (ed.) *Collins COBUILD English Dictionary*. London: Harper Collins Publishers, 1987.

Sowa, J. *Knowledge Representation: Logical, Philosophical, and Computational Foundations*. Boston: PWS Publishing Co., forthcoming.

Vendler, Z. *Linguistics and Philosophy*. Ithaca: Cornell University Press, 1967.

Verkuyl, H. *On the compositional Nature of the Aspects*. Dordrecht: Reidel, 1972.

Verkuyl, H. "Aspectual Classes and Aspectual Distinctions". *Linguistics and Philosiphy*, 12 (1989), 39–94.

Vossen P. and A. Bon. *Building a Semantic Hierarchy for the Sift Project, Sift LRE 62030, Deliverable D20b*. University of Amsterdam, Amsterdam, 1996.

Vossen, P. (ed.) *Encoding the Semantic Relations for basic Nouns and Verbs. Deliverable D010D011. LE-4002*. Amsterdam, 1997.

VOX-HARRAP'S *Diccionario Esencial Español-Inglés Inglés-Español*. Barcelona: Biblograf S.A., 1992.

Computers and the Humanities **32**: 153–184, 1998.
© 1998 *Kluwer Academic Publishers.*

Compatibility in Interpretation of Relations in EuroWordNet

PIEK VOSSEN[1,2], LAURA BLOKSMA[1,3], ANTONIETTA ALONGE[4,5],
ELISABETTA MARINAI[4,6], CAROL PETERS[7], IRENE CASTELLON[8,9],
ANTONIA MARTI[8,10] and GERMAN RIGAU[11]
[1]*Universiteit van Amsterdam, Faculteit Geesteswetenschappen, Spuistraat 134, 1012 VB
Amsterdam, The Netherlands; E-mail:* [2]*Piek.Vossen@hum.uva.nl,* [3]*lbloks@hum.uva.nl;* [4]*Istituto di
Linguistica Computazionale, CNR, Via della Faggiola 32, 56100 Pisa, Italy; E-mail:*
[5]*aalonge@pg.tecnonet.it,* [6]*elisabetta@ilc.pi.cnr.it;* [7]*Istituto di Elaborazione della Informazione,
CNR, Via S. Maria, 46, 56126 Pisa, Italy; E-mail: carol@iei.pi.cnr.it;* [8]*Universitat de Barcelona,
Departament de Filologia,Romanica Linguistica General, Gran Via 505, 08007 Barcelona, Spain;
E-mail:* [9]*castellon@lingua.fil.ub.es,* [10]*amarti@lingua.fil.ub.es;* [11]*Universitat Politècnica de
Catalunya. Jordi Girona Salgado, 1-3, 08034 Barcelona Spain; E-mail: g.rigau@lsi.upc.es*

Key words: overlapping relations and lexical gaps, sense differentiation

Abstract. This paper describes how the Euro WordNet project established a maximum level of consensus in the interpretation of relations, without loosing the possibility of encoding language-specific lexicalizations. Problematic cases arise due to the fact that each site re-used different resources and because the core vocabulary of the wordnets show complex properties. Many of these cases are discussed with respect to language internal and equivalence relations. Possible solutions are given in the form of additional criteria.

1. Introduction

The main objective of Euro WordNet is to build a multilingual database with wordnets for several languages. This multilingual database can be used directly in applications such as cross-language information retrieval or for comparison of the different wordnets. However, comparison and cross-linguistic retrieval only make sense when the separate wordnets are compatible in coverage and interpretation of relations. In (Rodriguez et al., this volume) it is described how we established compatibility in coverage of vocabulary. This paper deals with the compatibility in the interpretation of the relations.

We ensured a minimal level of consensus on the interpretation of lexical semantic relations by using explicit tests to verify the relations across words (as detailed in (Alonge et al., this volume)). This interpretation is in principle given by substitution tests (comparable to the diagnostic frames, (Cruse, 1986)) for each relation. Despite these tests it is nevertheless often difficult to decide on how the relations should be encoded. The tests do not always yield a clear intuition and in some cases there are still several possibilities open.

Especially the more fundamental and frequently used Base Concepts often turn out to be very complex. Typically, these Base Concepts have the following properties:

- They belong to high polysemous entries, having many and often vaguely-distinguished meanings (e.g. *make* which has 31 senses as a verb, *go* which has 28 senses as a verb, *head* which has 23 senses as a noun).
- They belong to large synsets; having more than average number of synonyms (e.g. *human body* 1 which has 14 synset members).
- They have poor definitions exhibiting circularity, co-ordination of genus words, void genus words.
- They have inconsistent patterns of hyponyms and hyperonyms across resources.
- They have a variety of syntactic properties.
- They are frequently used in daily language.

Still, these words make up the core of the wordnets, representing major semantic implications and clusters, which are carried over to the rest of the vocabulary. It is therefore extremely important that we still achieve a maximum of consensus on the encoding of these concepts across the sites, without loosing the possibilities to encode language-specific lexicalizations. For this we exchanged and compared specific problematic cases and had discussions on principles and strategies in order to deal with classes of problems.

This paper is a report on these discussions. We have given the solutions in the form of additional criteria, which can be used to make a decision, and by giving typical examples, which can be used for comparison. In Section 2 we discuss the problems with encoding the language-internal relations, especially with respect to our core vocabulary. In subsections we describe the typical problems that may arise, caused by differences in sense distinction, incompleteness and/or inconsistency in information and overlapping relations. In Section 3 we discuss the problems related to specifying the correct equivalence relations with the Word-Net1.5 synsets, caused by lexical gaps, differences in sense distinction across wordnets and mismatches of senses.

It is important to note that the procedure outlined and the problems discussed are not typical for the encoding process. In most cases, the relations are obvious and the encoding is straightforward. In this document we focus on the problematic cases and describe the (possible) solutions we found to ensure maximum compatibility. Finally, we assume that the reader is familiar with the other papers in this volume.

2. Strategies for Encoding Language-internal Relations

In EuroWordNet we re-use existing Machine Readable Dictionaries and Lexical Databases as far as possible, which is more cost-effective than starting from scratch. Therefore the information in the resources serves as a starting point for encoding the semantic relations. The general approach towards defining the relations for a word meaning can be described as a set of steps:

1. determine the appropriate division for the relevant senses of a word
2. determine the synsets
3. determine the hyperonyms for a synset
4. determine the hyponyms for a synset
5. determine the near synonyms
6. determine the other relations relevant to the synset
7. determine the equivalence relations with the WordNet1.5 synsets

Obviously, the order of these steps is not mandatory. Each site builds their wordnet according to the scheme that fits best their resources and tools. In some cases, sites may arrive at step 1 after having worked on step 2 up to 4, and in other cases, they may start with the translation from WordNet1.5 (step 7). The Spanish group, for example, first translates the WN1.5 synsets into Spanish (step 7), next they create the Spanish synsets (step 2) and take over the hyponymy relations from WN1.5 (steps 3 and 4). After that, steps 5 and 6 are performed and if necessary step 1. The order in this document is only given as a rule of thumb for clarification purposes, it is by no means prescriptive.

In the next subsections we will discuss the problems that arise when determining the appropriate sense distinction (step 1). Next, we will look at the problem of deriving comprehensive and consistent patterns of relations for word meanings. Finally, we will discuss various border cases where the choice between the semantic relations appears less clear (steps 2–6). Step 7 is discussed in Section 3.

2.1. DIFFERENCES IN SENSE DISTINCTION

As already mentioned, all sites use the information in their resources as a starting point for building the wordnets. This means that the sense distinction made by the resources is in principle accepted and then verified. In most cases there is no reason to alter the distinction. However, in other cases, the differences are very subtle, which can lead to many closely related senses, or condensed to only a single sense (as discussed by Jacobs, 1991; Atkins and Levin, 1988). Here, we would like to discuss those cases that are problematic when building our wordnets. We distinguish between two types of problems:

• over-differentiation of senses
• under-differentiation of senses

2.1.1. *Over-differentiation of senses*

In the case of over-differentiation the motivation for distinguishing different senses is not clear or intuitions vary. In the following examples the definitions of the different senses are more or less similar.

(1.) a *draaien*   1   functioneren
      (to run)   (to function)

                     2   aan de gang zijn
                          (working)

   b *scuola*   3a   attivit á rivolta a far apprendere una o piú discipline
     (school):   (activity aimed at causing to learn one of more disci-
                          plines);

                     3b   l'insegnamento
                          (teaching)

                     3c   indirizzo di studio o metodo didattico e pedagogico
                          adottato
                          (line of study or didactical and pedagogical method
                          adopted).

Although formulated in a different way the two senses of *draaien* (to run) in Dutch boil down to the same thing. Another example is represented by the Italian word *scuola* (school). In the main Italian source, there are 11 word-senses for this term, distributed variously over 5 principal word-meanings, of which a few distinctions are very subtle. In these cases it might be helpful to look at the rest of the information provided for the senses.

If a sense does not provide any really different information, we assume that there is an over-differentiation and one of the senses can be removed. This is the case of the Spanish entry *sopa* (soup):

(2.) *sopa*   1   Pedazo de pan empapado en cualquier líquido
                          (A piece of bread soaked in any liquid)

                     2   Plato compuesto de un líquido alimenticio y rebanadas
                          de pan
                          (Dish composed by a nutritive liquid and pieces of bread)

                     3   Plato compuesto de rebanadas de pan, fécula, arroz,
                          fideos, etc., y el caldo de la olla u otro análogo en que
                          se han cocido
                          (Dish composed of pieces of bread, starch, rice, noodle,
                          etc. and stock ...)

4   Pasta, fécula o verduras que se mezclan con el caldo en el plato de este mismo nombre

(Pasta, starch or vegatables mixed with the stock in the dish with the same name)

5   Comida que dan a los pobres en los conventos

(Meal served to the poor in a religious establishment in the convent)

6   Rebanadas de pan que se cortan para echarlas en el caldo

(Slices of bread cut and added into the stock)

Sense 6 is related to sense 1 by a hyponymy relation (where stock is a particular portion of "any liquid") both describing the main ingredients of the soup. This is also the case for sense 4 where, the ingredients added to the stock are different. On the other hand, sense 2 is included in sense 3 describing both the complete dish. Sense 5 is describing the same dish as sense 2 and 3 but is related to a particular situation. We can thus merge sense 1, 4 and 6 into a single meaning, and sense 2, 3 and 5 into another meaning. If the senses differ in any other kind of information, it is more difficult to make a decision. There are numerous reasons why a dictionary might split an entry into multiple senses, only some of which have to do with meaning (Gale et al., 1993). Often, senses are distinguished because of differences in morpho-syntactic properties:

- part-of-speech (nouns vs. adjectives, etc.).
- syntactic features (person, number, gender, etc.).
- valency structures (transitive vs. intransitive verbs, etc.).

The relevance of different grammatical and stylistic properties for distinguishing senses depends on the strictness of the definition of synonymy, where stylistic differences are usually not considered as differences of meaning. As a rule of thumb, we can state that morpho-syntactic properties that correlate with semantic differences, or with one of the semantic relations distinguished, should certainly be taken seriously. This is the case for many of the alternations of verbs (e.g. transitive/intransitive-causative/inchoative alternations, see (Levin, 1993) for an overview of English verbs):

(3.) a *cambiare*   1   intransitive

(to change)   to become different

2   transitive

to make different

cambiare   2   causes cambiare 1

b *bewegen*	1	intransitive
(to move)		(to change place or position)
	2	transitive
		(to cause to change place or position)
	6	reflexive
		((of people, animals) to change place or position)
bewegen	2	causes bewegen 1

Here we see that Italian *cambiare* 1 and 2 (change) exhibit a transitive/intransitive alternation which correlates with a difference in causation. Something similar holds for different senses of *bewegen* (move) in Dutch, which refer as intransitive verbs to a non-causative change-of-position and as transitives to the causation of such a change (this also holds for *mover* (move) in Spanish and *muovere* (move) in Italian).

Another typical example is given by countable/uncountable variation of nouns. For example, the uncountable Italian word *acqua* (water) signifies specific/specialized senses when it is used in the plural, such as: *acque territoriali* (coastal waters), *acque termali* (thermal waters), *acque minerali* (mineral waters). Another case is given by Dutch *zaad* (seed) which, as a countable noun, refers to *a single mature fertilized plant ovum* and as an uncountable noun to an amount of this. Clearly, the relation between these senses can be expressed by one of the semantic relations in EuroWordNet: *zaad* 2 HAS_MERONYM *zaad* 1.

In other cases, differences in morpho-syntactic features do not carry any semantic distinction as, for example, the change of gender in the Italian word *zucchino* or *zucchina* which means the same vegetable and is used indifferently in both morpho-syntactic forms. Another typical example is formed by Dutch plural variants, such as *aardappels* (potatoes) and *aardappelen* (potatoes). There may be a difference in style but these are typically seen as variants of the same meaning. If such stylistic or formal properties are the only reason for making a distinction in different senses we follow the strategy of collapsing the senses and storing the variations as stylistic or formal variation of a single sense:[1]

(4.) Variant

    key = aardappel

    pos = NOUN

    plural-form = aardappels; aardappelen

    countable = true

In all cases, where there is still some doubt about the similarity or equivalence of different senses, either due to subtle differences in the information or examples, the senses can be connected by a NEAR_SYNONYM relation. In this way, we at least ensure that very close meanings are grouped together in contrast to other co-hyponyms (words that have the same hyperonym or class) which are clearly considered as distinct.

At times we find that two senses have very different definitions but can still be considered as cases of over-differentiation. Two specific situations are often encountered:

- pragmatic specialisation
- different conceptualisation

Pragmatic specialisation is the phenomenon where a general word is used as a variant to refer to a more specific concept: a *car* can also be referred to using *vehicle* or even *thing*. In some cases this usage has lead a lexicographer to distinguish a separate sense for the specific use of such a general word, e.g. in WordNet1.5:

(5.) mixture 1   (a substance consisting of two or more substances mixed together (not in fixed proportions and not with chemical bonding))

    HAS_HYPERONYM

        substance, matter   (that which has mass and occupies space; "an atom is the smallest indivisible unit of matter")

mixture 2

    HAS_HYPERONYM

        foodstuff   (a substance that can be used or prepared for use as food)

In this case, a hyponymy-relation holds between the specific sense of *mixture* used for food and the general sense of the word *mixture*. Whenever the specific sense is fully predictable the sense is strictly speaking superfluous. Predictability follows from the fact that no idiosyncratic properties are implied (no specialisation) and the principle can productively be applied to any other specific referent: *mixture* can also be used to refer to other substances with some function *paint, explosives, gases*. Predictable specialisations can be omitted (Roventini, 1993). This was clearly the case for the Spanish entry of *sopa* soup shown above, where sense 5 describes a specific pragmatic difference with respect senses 2 and 3 because it refers to the people who receives the soup and the place where the soup is served.

Another possibility is that the different senses reflect different perspectives or conceptualisations of the same thing. In Italian, for example, some pieces of cutlery or chinaware can both be seen as containers and as the quantity of food or drink contained. So we find this double sense for terms such as *cucchiaio* (spoon), *tazza* (cup), *bicchiere* (glass), *piatto* (plate), etc. Traditional dictionaries often do not allow for the expression of multiple perspectives and the traditional way of defining words does not promote this. This either results in the omission of one perspective (e.g. certain items of *cutlery* are either classified as a *quantity* or as a *container*) or in the separation in different senses. However, in EuroWordNet (and also in WordNet1.5), it is possible to have multiple hyperonyms reflecting these perspectives of the same concept or meaning (possibly by using disjunction or conjunction), as is illustrated by the WordNet1.5 solution for *spoon*:

(6.) *spoon*   (a piece of cutlery with a shallow bowl-shaped container and a handle; used to stir or serve or take up food)

HAS_HYPERONYM

    cutlery   (implements for cutting and eating food)
    container   (something that holds things, especially for transport or storage)

The co-ordination-test (Zwicky and Sadock, 1975) shows that both conceptualisations can easily be combined, e.g. "It is a spoon therefore it is a piece of cutlery and a container". In this case it is valid to merge the information of the two senses in a single sense, as is done for *spoon* in WordNet1.5. Especially when it turns out that multiple sources classify the same concept differently it may be possible to merge multiple senses in a particular source in which these different classifications are split.

2.1.2. *Under-differentiation of senses*

The opposite situation in which different senses are collapsed in a single definition also occurs frequently in dictionaries. Mostly this is done using co-ordination, e.g.:

(7.) a *automatisering* 1   het automatisch *maken* of *worden*
        (automation)   (to *make* automatic or *become* automatic)
        beleefdheid 1   beleefde *handeling* of *uiting*
        (politeness)   (polite *act* or *utterance*)
        beroepsopleiding 1   *cursus* of *school*
        (occupational-training)   (*course* or *school*)
     b abombar 1   Dar o adquirir forma convexa [alguna cosa]
                                   (to give or to adopt [something] a convex shape)

        absorber 7   Retener o captar energía por medio de un material.
                                   (to *keep* or to attract energy by means of a material)

        achicharrar 1   *Freír, asar* o *tostar* [un manjar] hasta que tome sabor a quemado.
                                   (to *fry*, to *roast* or to *toast* [a food] until it takes a burned flavour)

For some of these examples it appears difficult to combine the hyperonyms of the definitions (underlined):

(8.) *de ene beroepsopleiding heeft een nieuw adres en de andere wordt twee keer gegeven.

(the one occupational-training has a new address and the other is given twice)

Since something cannot be an *institute* with an *address* and an *event* at the same time it seems to make more sense to distinguish two senses here. Furthermore, as separate senses it is possible to express the semantic relation between them; *beroepsleiding* 1 ROLE_LOCATION *opleiding* 2. In the case of verbs such as *maken* (make) and *worden* (become) we can state that they represent alternations of meanings which can be related using a CAUSES relation.[2]

Another pattern of co-ordination is illustrated by the following examples:

(9.) a *uitdaging* 2   *zaak, daad* of *uiting* die prikkelt tot een reactie
          (challenge)   (a *thing, act* or *utterance* which calls for a response)
          toevlucht 1   *persoon, zaak, plaats* waar men bescherming zoekt.
          (resort)   (*person, thing, place* where one hopes to find protection)
     b *antecedente* 2   *acción, dicho* o *circunstancia* anterior, que sirve para
                            juzgar hechos posteriores (previous *act, saying* or *circum-stance*, which can be used to judge posterior events)
          audición 2   Concierto, recital o lectura en público
                            (public *concert, recital* or *reading*)
          batido 4   *Claras, yemas* o *huevos* batidos
                            (white, yolk or shake eggs)
          bodrio 5   *Objeto, persona* o *actividad* desagradable o fea
                            (ugly *object, person* or *activity*)
     c *disperazione* 2   cosa o persona che causa infelicità
                            (thing or person causing unhappiness)
          problema 2   cosa o persona che causa problemi
                            (thing or person causing trouble)

Just as with the previous disjunctive hyperonyms we see that the test for distinguishing senses shows that the hyperonyms are incompatible:

(10.) *If it is a challenge then it is a thing and a person at the same time.

Strictly speaking, we should therefore split the sense into separate senses. However, how many senses do we have to distinguish here? The difference with the previous examples is that the range of entities is not restricted at all. There is an open range of referents for which some examples are listed: the list can easily be extended without changing the meaning. Conceptually, the test causes anomaly but in the case of the open denotation range the classifications do not motivate a separation of senses. Apparently, there is not one way to classify the referent, and the semantics of the word fully depends on the role or involvement it has with the event or situation expressed.

Since there may be an open range of entities it does not make much sense to split these in different senses. We therefore maintain a single sense for the definition where we can indicate the range of entities with disjunction of the hyperonym relation, but more important than the hyponymy-relation is the ROLE-relation with the predicate denoting the event:

(11.) *uitdaging* 2 (a challenge)

HAS_HYPERONYM disjunct:	*zaak* 1 (thing)
HAS_HYPERONYM disjunct:	*daad* 1 (deed)
HAS_HYPERONYM disjunct:	*uiting* 1 (utterance)
ROLE_AGENT:	*uitdagen* 1 (to challenge)

As long as the fundamental role relation is captured, the hyponymy relation may also be omitted.

The same problem also arises when no explicit genus term appears in definition. Consider for instance the following Spanish examples:

(12.) comida 1   lo que se come.

                      (*food, whatever that may be eaten*).

    denunciante 1   que hace una denuncia.

                      (*informer, who makes a report*).

The genus words *lo que* and *que* are pronouns that hardly differentiate. There are 2,362 noun definitions (2%) in the Spanish monolingual resource with such void heads. Similar patterns have also been found in the resources for the other languages (Vossen, 1995). In the case of a void head or genus word the denotational range is not even specified and the role/involved relation is the only relation that can be used.

Obviously, it will not always be possible to distinguish cases where co-ordinated hyperonyms should be split for different senses or combined in a single sense. To some extent, the decision to split or merge senses depends on common practice.

2.2. COMPLETENESS AND CONSISTENCY OF INFORMATION

After establishing a good view on the different senses of a word, the next step is to identify all the relevant words that should be related to such a meaning. One of the challenges for building a consistent lexical database is perhaps not so much the quality of the data but more its incompleteness: i.e. what information is not given. It is an inherent property of our minds that we cannot easily recall all possible information and relevant meanings actively, but that we can very easily confirm information presented to us. Especially, when dealing with large coverage resources such as generic lexical databases it is impossible to predict the total potential of relations.

The general way of overcoming the problem of completeness is to combine information from different resources. It is for example possible to treat the definitions in different monolingual dictionaries as a corpus and to collect those definitions that have relevant co-occurrences of words. Following (Wilks et al., 1993) two words are co-occurrent if they appear in the same definition (word order in definitions is not taken into account). This method has been applied to a monolingual Spanish dictionary, from which a lexicon of 300,062 co-occurrence pairs for 40,193 word forms was derived (stop words were not taken into account). Table I, for example, shows the first eleven words (ordered by Association Ratio[3] score) out of 360 that co-occur with *vino* (wine). In this sample, we can see many implicit relations. Among others, hyponyms (*vino tinto*), hyperonyms (*licor or bebida*), sisters (*mosto or jerez*), inter-category relations (*beber*), places were the wine are maked/stored (*cubas*), fruit from which the wine is derived (*uva*), properties (*sabor*), etc. Such a raw list can be used as a starting point for establishing the construction of comprehensive lists of relations or it can be used to verify the completeness of present relations.

In addition to such a global list, it is also possible to apply specific strategies for extracting more comprehensive lists of word meanings related in a specific way. The most important relation in this respect is synonymy. In some cases these synonyms are explicitly listed in dictionaries but these specifications are not always complete or comprehensive. Several techniques are available for finding more candidates for synonymy:

- expanding from WordNet1.5.
- word meanings with similar definitions; one-word-definitions; circular definitions.
- overlapping translations in bilingual dictionaries.

The first technique is rather obvious. By directly translating the synset members in WordNet1.5 it is possible to derive synsets in another language. The second technique looks at definitions that are the very similar, and, in particular, definitions consisting of a single word or circularly defining words in terms of each other. This is illustrated by the following Dutch examples:

Table I. Association rate for *vino* (wine) in Spanish Dictionary

Association rate	Frequency in dictionary	Paired word
11.1655	15	*tinto* (red)
10.0162	23	*beber* (to drink)
9.6627	14	*mosto* (must)
8.6633	9	*jerez* (sherry)
8.1051	9	*cubas* (cask, barrel)
8.0551	16	*licor* (liquor)
7.2127	17	*bebida* (drink)
6.9338	12	*uva* (grape)
6.8436	9	*trago* (drink, swig)
6.6221	12	*sabor* (taste)
6.4506	15	*pan* (bread)

(13.)	*apparaat*	min of meer samengesteld **werktuig**
	(apparatus)	(more or less assembled tool)
	instrument	min of meer samengesteld of fijn **gereedschap** of **toestel** ...
	(instrument)	(more or less assembled or delicate tool or apparatus)
	toestel	**apparaat**
	(apparatus)	(apparatus)
	werktuig	stuk **gereedschap**
	(tool)	(piece of tools)
	gereedschap	**werktuig**
	(tools, instruments)	(tool)

Here we see 5 different meanings that are circularly defined, suggesting a synonymy relation.

Another possibility is to look for words that have the same translations and/or occur as translations for the same words in bilingual dictionaries. The procedure is more or less as follows. Starting with a set of closely related Dutch words extracted on the basis of other techniques, such as the previous instrument examples *apparaat* (apparatus), *toestel* (apparatus), and *werktuig* (tool), and *gereedschap*(tools), we extract all the English translations for all their meanings from the bilingual Dutch-English dictionary. Next all these English translations are looked up in the reverse English-Dutch dictionary to see what Dutch words are given as translations for all the different meanings. The result is a very large list of translation-sets, covering very different meanings. However, we keep only those sets of Dutch translations that include at least two of the original words with which the search was started. These sets form a so-called translation-cycle via two bilingual resources. The co-occurrence of pairs of source words is thus used as a filter to select the correct meaning of the word. The automatically-generated result for the above words is the following list:

(14.) Potential Equivalents generated from bilingual dictionaries:

gebruiksvoorwerp 1	(implement, appliance, utensil)
comfort 1	(comfort)
mechanisme 2	(mechanism)
inrichting 5	(construction, installation)
tuig 1	(gear, equipment)
uitmonstering 3	(equipment, outfit, kit)
uitrusting 1	(equipment)
outillage 1	(equipment)
apparatuur 1	(apparatus, machinery)
materieel 1	(material, equipment)
machinerie 1	(machinery)
systeem 10	(system)
mechaniek 1	(mechanism)

Among them are a few synonyms but also words that can be related in other ways. (Atserias et al., 1997) describe a similar method for generating Spanish synsets.

Each of these techniques gives different results and requires further manual processing to achieve a coherent integration of the output. For example, the main source of data for the Italian wordnet is a combination of data from monolingual machine dictionary synonym fields and from a synonym dictionary, integrated with data from monolingual synonym-type definitions, and the semantic indicators in a bilingual Italian/English Lexical Data Base. All the data are extracted automatically but must be revised manually. Very briefly (and simplifying), the procedure for constructing the Italian synsets mainly operates in 3 steps:

1. Explicitly tagged synonyms contained in the machine-readable dictionary entries and synonym dictionary are grouped to form a first proposal of a synset. The output is revised manually.
2. Candidate synonyms extracted from synonym-type definitions (one-word definitions, similar definitions) are associated with all members of the synset under construction. The output is revised manually.
3. Each candidate for the synonym set is searched in the bilingual dictionary: semantic indicators and translation equivalents are associated and matched

against each other. The output is revised manually. A useful test for deciding whether a candidate belongs to a given synset is to examine the translation equivalent. If the translation equivalent for the doubtful item is very different from the translations of the other items in the synset, then it is likely that this item does not belong to the synset under construction.

The manual revision at the end of each stage is essential (see Roventini et al., 1998). After establishing a reasonable set of synonyms, the next problem is to find the relevant set of hyponyms. A selection of all words with the same genus word from a definition does not necessarily result in a coherent and comprehensive class. Due to alternative ways of defining or classifying meanings, words are spread over the hierarchies. The following main variations tend to occur (Vossen, 1995):

- Similar words are classified at different levels of abstraction.
- Different but more-or-less equivalent words have been used to classify the same meanings.
- Other perspectives have been chosen to classify similar meanings.

The first two variations are illustrated by the following examples from the Italian subset:

(15.) *forchetta* (fork)   HAS_HYPERONYM   *arnese* (tool)
      coltello (knife)   HAS_HYPERONYM   *strumento* (tool)
      cucchiaino (teaspoon)   HAS_HYPERONYM   *posata* (piece of cutlery)

Here *cucchiaino* (spoon) is classified at an intermediate level as *posata* (piece of cutlery) which is then linked to the nearly equivalent classes *arnese* (tool) and *strumento* (tool), where you would expect to find all types of cutlery at the same level. The next example shows a variation in perspective:

(16.) *avvelenare*   HAS_HYPERONYM   *uccidere*
      (to kill by poisoning)   (to kill)
      lapidare (to stone)   HAS_HYPERONYM   *colpire*
      (to kill by stoning)   (to hit)

Here we see that *avvelenare* (to poison) and *lapidare* (to stone) are classified within different hierarchies. This is the result of the way in which they have been defined in the monolingual dictionaries. Whereas *avvelenare* (to poison) is defined as "uccidere con il veleno" (to kill by means of poison), *lapidare* (to stone) is defined as "colpire con sassate per uccidere" (to hit with stones in order to kill). In both cases the result and the manner of achieving this are relevant but the Italian resources describe the events from different perspectives.

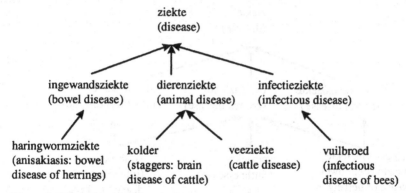

Figure 1. Hierarchical relations in the Van Dale database.

In the next hierarchy (Figure 1) containing Dutch words for diseases we see a typical combination of the phenomena, where multiple perspectives and levels have been missed. We see here that *haringwormziekte* (anisakiasis) is only linked to *ingewandziekte* (bowel disease) and *vuilbroed* (infectious disease of bees) is only linked to *infectieziekte* (infectious disease), while both are diseases of animals: *herrings* and *bees* respectively. In both cases, the classification as *dierenziekte* (animal disease) has been omitted. Within the same part of the hierarchy we see the opposite situation for *kolder* (staggers) which is directly linked to *dierenziekte* (animal disease) while it is also a disease of *cattle* and should be linked to *veeziekte* (cattle disease).

The hierarchy of diseases contains some typical examples of restructuring that are required because sub-levels of hyperonyms have been skipped and multiple classifications have been missed. Such variation in levels and multiple classifications can be detected by applying the Principle-of-Economy to the hyponyms (Dik, 1978). This principle states that it is not allowed to relate a word W1 to a word W3 when there is a word W2 linked to W3 to which W1 can be linked in the same way. In practice this means that all hyponyms of *ziekte* (disease) have to be cross-checked to see whether they represent hyperonyms of each other.[4] This then also reveals multiple category membership. When applied to the above cases we obtain the restructuring in Figure 2. Extracting information from different resources or merging different classification schemes gives a more comprehensive picture of a lexical semantic field but it also causes another problem. In some cases, the information given for these meanings is not coherent or exchangeable. This may either follow from the definitions of words which are supposed to be synonymous or be caused by the fact that the hyperonyms and/or hyponyms (or other semantic relations if present) do not apply to all the members of a synset. To some extent these problems are being tackled by individual measures such as the more-systematic encoding of multiple hyperonyms and the use of the so-called NEAR_SYNONYM relation.

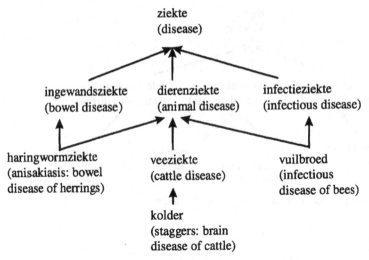

Figure 2. Restructured hierarchical relations.

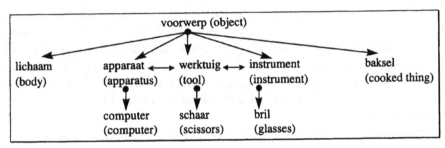

Figure 3. Near-synonymy relations between co-hyponyms.

In the case of the above example, where the Dutch words *apparaat* (apparatus), *toestel* (apparatus), *werktuig* (tool), and *gereedschap* (tools) have very similar and circular definitions, we may consider grouping them into a single synset. However, intuitively, they are not completely interchangeable, as is shown by the different clusters of hyponyms linked to them. Electrical devices are mostly classified as *apparaat* (apparatus), *instrument* (instrument), possibly as *toestel* (apparatus) but not as *werktuig* (tool) or *gereedschap* (tool). Instead of joining such closely-related meanings in a synset they can be related as NEAR_SYNONYMs so that they are distinguished from other co-hyponyms at the same level which are clearly not equivalent, while at the same time their hyponyms can be kept apart when they form different clusters. In Figure 3, we see that *apparaat* (apparatus), *werktuig* (tool) and instrument (*instrument*) still represent different clusters of hyponyms. The NEAR_SYNONYM relation expresses closeness, as opposed to other very different co-hyponyms like *baksel* (cooked thing) and *lichaam* (body).

2.3. OVERLAPPING RELATIONS

We have found that the tests do not always discriminate between all relations. This first of all shows itself in the subtypes of relations. As explained in (Alonge et al., this volume) the meronymy and role relations are differentiated into more general relations and more specific subtypes, such as HAS_MERO_MEMBER, has MERO_PORTION or HAS_ROLE_AGENT, HAS_ROLE_INSTRUMENT, etc. The more general relations are used when the more specific subtypes cannot clearly be assigned. Unclear cases of meronymy are the following examples:

(17.) a vlam 1   Portion?   *vuur* 2
         (flame)   (fire)

      b *bloedfactor* 1   Made of?   *bloed* 1
         (blood factor)   (blood)

      c *wijkgebouw* 1   Location?   *wijkcentrum* 1
         (building of community centre)   (community centre)

Portions normally are quantities of substances, e.g. a beer, two coffees, a snack. In the case of *vlam 1* (flame) and *vuur 2* (fire) it is however not clear whether we are dealing with a substance or with an event and hence it is unclear whether the meronymy relation portion can apply. In the case of (17)b it is not clear whether *bloedfactor 1* (blood factor) is a genuine component or a property, and a *wijkgebouw* 1 is both located at a *wijkcentrum* 1 and it is a part of it as well (they could even be synonymous). In such non-prototypical cases, where there is doubt about the specific relation, the most general relation HAS_MERONYM and HAS_HOLONYM is used.

As described in (Alonge et al., this volume), EuroWordNet distinguishes different roles or involvements of first-order-entities (concrete things) indicating arguments 'incorporated', or word meanings strongly implied, within the meaning of high-order entities (events). Most of these relations are (semi-)automatically extracted from regular definition patterns, such as "used for", "which causes", "a person who", "a place where", "made for", etc. However, we find examples where the extracted semantic roles are not prototypical, e.g.:

(18.) a *aardappelmoeheid*   Force/Cause   *aaltje*
         (potato disease)   (eelworms)

         antracose   Force/Cause   *steenkool*
         (anthracosis, miner's lungs)   (coal)

         betrekken   Force/Cause   *bewolking*
         (to cloud over)   (clouds)

	storen (to disturb)	Force/Cause	*hinder* (disturbance)
b	*baarmoederhalskanker* (cancer of the cervix)	Location/Patient	*baarmoederhals* (cervix)
	borstkanker (breast cancer)	Location/Patient	*borst* (breast)
	bellenblazen (blow bubbles)	Patient/Result	*zeepbel* (soap bubble)
	bespannen1 (to string)	Patient/Result	*bespanning* (stringing)
c	*verliezen2* (to loose)	Agent/Patient	*verliezer* (a looser)
	winnen1 (to win)	Agent/Patient	*winnaar* (a winner)

In (18)a we see some examples where a concrete entity causes a situation but it cannot be seen as an Agent having any control or intention of doing this. However, since the causes relation is restricted to higher-order-entities (events, states) it cannot be applied here. The relation between e.g. *aaltjes* (eelworms) and the disease is in fact more indirect. The *eelworms* only create the circumstances, which result in the disease. The same holds for *clouds*, *coal* and *disturbance*, they are Factors, Forces or Causes but not Agents. Here we can either broaden the interpretation of Agent or add new roles. In (18)b we see cases where the Patient-role interferes with other roles. In the first two examples we see an entity with a double role as the affected entity (by a disease) but also as the location where the disease is active. They could be considered as Location or as Patient. Another group of dubious Patients are entities which are created by some event. As concrete entities, they cannot be related by means of a CAUSES relation but they can still be seen as the result of an event. Again we can choose to broaden the interpretation of Patient or add a new relation. Finally, in (18)c we see two typical examples where an entity is actively involved in a (competition) event, but has no control over the outcome and is conceptualised as the affected entity (positive or negative) as well. In this case, we can decide to allow both the Patient and Agent relation, although it is still not a prototypical Agent having control over the action. In all the above cases, we have now decided to use the under-specified relation ROLE. The advantage of the under-specified relation is clear. The lexicographer does not have to solve a complex problem to continue with an isolated case, whereas all the undifferentiated relations can be collected at a later stage and regular patterns can be differentiated after reaching agreement with the other sites in the project.

More serious than under-differentiation of relations are cases where incompatible relations still show some overlap in interpretation. This is the case for two classes of relations: hyponymy/synonymy versus meronymy/subevent, and agent/instrument roles versus CAUSES. In the following examples we see meanings where one entity or event consists of components or subevents but is also hardly distinguishable from it:

(19.) a sports   HAS_SUBEVENT?   sport-game
    b bevolkingsgroep   HAS_PART_MEMBER   bevolking
      (group of people)   (people)
      gebladerte   HAS_PART_MEMBER   blad
      (leafage)   (leaf)
      gesteente   HAS_PART   steen
      (stones)   (stone)

In (19)a we see a complex event or activity which consists of the subevent *sport-game*, but the difference is subtle. Especially when pluralized, a subevent can easily be used to replace the larger event that includes it. Differences in number are not reflected by one of the semantic relations in EuroWordNet. The same holds for the meronymy relation in (19)b. The group-noun *bevolkingsgroep* and the collective *bevolking*, as well as *gebladerte* and the plural form *bladeren* (leaves) are denotationally equivalent (can refer to the same type of entities), but differ in grammatical reference. In the case of the collective *gesteente* (stones, especially as a kind of stone) and the mass noun *steen* (stone), we see that the difference is only the genericity of reference. In all these cases, it is difficult to decide on synonymy/hyponymy on the one hand and meronymy/subevent on the other (Vossen and Copestake, 1993; Vossen, 1995). Because of the homogeneity of the composition we often see that both the complex concepts and the component are linked to the same hyperonym as well. For example, both *mood* and *feeling* are subtypes of mental state, and both *gesteente* (stones) and *steen* (stone) are linked to *stof* (substance).

When discussing the role/involved-relations we more or less suggested that there is a close relation between agents and instruments on the one hand and CAUSES-relations on the other hand. So far we have stated that the former relate first-order-entities to dynamic events, whereas the latter can only be used to relate high-order-entities. However, the distinction between first-order-entities and high-order-entities is not always clear-cut, and this results in cases where the difference between agent-roles and CAUSES starts to fade as well. There are three ways in which there can be lack of clarity about the status of an entity:

1. words may refer to properties and to concrete entities having that property.
2. non-concrete words such as thoughts, ideas, opinions still have entity-like properties.
3. words may vary over both types of entities.

We have discussed examples where some process or change results in a concrete entity and a similar change or process may also result in a state as in (20)a. However, in some cases the word naming the result refers to both the state or an entity in such a state, as in (20)b:

(20.) a	verwoestijnen	INVOLVED	woestijn
	(to become a desert)		(desert)
	evaporar		vapor
	(to evaporate)		(vapour)
	natworden	CAUSES	nat
	(to become wet)		(wet)
	afear		feo
	(to make ugly)		(ugly)
b	mineralize	CAUSES/INVOLVED	mineral
	liquidify	CAUSES/INVOLVED	liquid
	solidificar	CAUSES/INVOLVED	sólido
	(to become solid)		(solid)

Here we see that *mineral* and *liquid* can be both a noun and an adjective denoting a substance or a state of a substance and the intuitive interpretation does not differ much from both examples in (20)a. For such resultative events we have taken an arbitrary position that the classification of the result as first or high-order-entity is the only criterion: i.e. if *mineral* is disambiguated as a noun the relation will be INVOLVED, just as for *desert*, if it is an adjective the relation will be CAUSES, just as for *wet*.

A second problematic case is represented by words denoting sounds, mental states or objects which are not concrete first-order-entities but share a lot of properties with them:

(21.) a	musiceren1	CAUSES/INVOLVED	muziek
	(make music)		(music)
	zingen1		lied
	(sing)		(song)
	cantar		canción
	(sing)		(song)
b	bekeren 5	CAUSES/INVOLVED	mening
	(convert, reform)		(opinion)
	bedenken 1		gedachte
	(think up)		(thought)

	juzgar		*juicio*
	(to judge)		(judgement)
c	*nominaliseren*	CAUSES/INVOLVED	*naamwoord*
	(nominalize)		(noun)
	nominalizar		*nombre*

In (21)a we see that the relation for production of sound depends on how sounds are treated. In EuroWordNet they are classified as higher-order-entities so strictly speaking the relation should be CAUSES. However, if considered as a physical signal the same criterion would predict that there should be an INVOLVED relation. In (21)b we see that a mental or communicative event results in a mental state or thought and again the status of these as entities determines the type of relation. Metaphorically, thoughts and opinions are very much like concrete entities. You can work on them, create them, keep them, multiply them, etc. Therefore we have applied the relation INVOLVED here. Finally, (21)c represents a difficult case because the result is a word which can be a symbolic representation, a sound, or a concept in the mind, where the former is a first-order-entity and the latter two are high-order-entities.

Another example where ROLE and CAUSE relations converge is represented by words referring to the initiator of an event without implying further information on the status of the entity. For example, the Dutch noun *middel 1* (means) can stand for any event, method, or instrument leading to some change:

(22.) *middel*1   INSTRUMENT/CAUSES   *veranderen*

(any means or method to achieve something)   (to change, alter)

Clearly, the level-of-entity criterion does not work here. Related to this are so-called Modal-states which are properties or situations which are necessary conditions or qualities to make a change or event possible. Typical examples of these states are mental and physical abilities:

(23.) *gehoor*   CAUSES   *horen*

(hearing: the capability to hear)   (to hear)

mogelijkheid   CAUSES   *gebeuren* 2

(possibility)   (to take place)

visión   CAUSES   *ver*

(vision)   (to see)

sentido   *sentir*

(sense)   (to feel)

The relation between the capacity and the associated event is now expressed by means of a CAUSES relation in EuroWordNet.

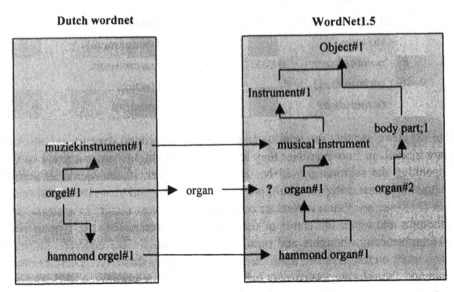

Figure 4. Selecting translations to WordNet1.5 by conceptual distance measuring to the translated context in the Dutch wordnet.

Concluding, we can say that the notion of causality applies to a wide range of relations, from genuine cause relations between events and results, to agents and instruments, to modal states or abilities. In between the clearer cases, there are many meaning relations which are not easy to classify.

3. Establishing Equivalence Relations

The second type of problems regard the specification of equivalence relations. As stated in the introduction of this volume, each synset in the monolingual wordnets will have at least one equivalence relation to a concept in the Inter-Lingual-Index (ILI). Especially, at the start of the project this ILI mainly consisted of synsets taken from WordNet1.5 synsets. The linking to WordNet1.5 is partly done using automatic techniques and partly manually. For example, the translations for most Spanish nouns are generated automatically on the basis of the following criteria:

- monosemous translations of synsets with a single sense are directly taken over as translations.
- polysemous translations are disambiguated by measuring the conceptual-distance in the WordNet1.5 between the senses of multiple translations (Agirre and Rigau, 1996; Rigau et al., 1997).

The latter technique calculates the distance between two senses by counting the steps to their closest shared node in the network, taking into account the level of the hierarchy and the density of nodes relative to the average density. When two translations are given for a Spanish word and these translations have multiple

Table II. Reliability of the automatically-generated equivalence relations in the Dutch wordnet

Matching Rank	Nouns		Verbs	
	No. of synsets	Percentage	No. of Synsets	Percentage
1st score	70	70.71%	20	40.82%
2nd score	14	14.14%	13	26.53%
3rd score	5	5.05%	9	18.37%
>	1	1.01%	3	6.12%
lexical gaps	7	7.07%	1	2.04%
no correct	20	20.20%	12	24.29%
Total of synsets	99[5]		58	

senses in WordNet1.5, those senses are selected which have the shortest distance in the hierarchy. A similar approach has been applied to the Dutch and Italian wordnet but in this case we took advantage of the translated context in the hierarchy as well (Vossen et al., forthcoming; Peters et al., forthcoming), as is illustrated in Figure 4 for Dutch. Here we see that *orgel* in Dutch is translated as *organ*, which can either be a musical instrument or a body part. Since the hyperonym and a hyponym of *orgel* in the Dutch wordnet have already been translated it is possible to measure the distance of the two senses of organ to the translations of the hyperonym and hyponym.

The distance measuring of the translations to the context in the Dutch wordnet, leads to a ranking of all the senses of a translation. Table II gives the reliability of this methodology for a random sample of 99 nominal and 49 verbal synsets. The score for each ranking indicates the number of synsets that are the correct translations. In most cases of the nouns (71), the highest translation is the correct one. In 20% of all nouns, the correct translation was not among the proposed translations at all. In 7% of all nouns, there was no good translation possible (lexical gaps), because the meaning does not exist in English or in WordNet1.5. For the verbs the results are considerably worse. Only 41% of the highest ranking was correct. This difference is the result of the fact that the verb-hierarchies are more shallow and diverse. If many verbs are linked to the same hyperonym or too many different but unrelated tops in WordNet1.5 this results in a poor matching for all candidates. Note, however, that by taking the top-3 ranking, the results for nouns and verbs are about the same (90% versus 85.6%). In the case of verbs, it appears to be difficult to choose and several senses of the translations could apply. It thus makes sense to select the best 3 translations for verbs instead of trying to select a single best sense.

As these figures show, a manual revision of suspect cases is necessary. Furthermore, crucial meanings are encoded manually in the first place. There are three main problems that play a role when establishing these equivalence relations which we will discuss in more detail below:

Table III. Matching of Spanish-English bilingual dictionary with WordNet1.5

	English nouns	Spanish nouns	synsets	connections[6]
WordNet1.5	87,642	—	60,557	107,424
Spanish/English	11,467	12,370	—	19,443
English/Spanish	10,739	10,549	—	16,324
Merged Bilingual	15,848	14,880	—	28,131
Maximum Reachable Coverage[7]	12,665	13,208	19,383	66,258
Of WordNet	14%	—	32%	—
Of bilingual	80%	90%	—	—

- lexical gaps;
- differences in sense-differentiation;
- fuzzy-matching;

These problems not only show up in the automatic matching of synsets to WordNet1.5 but also when we try to assign the equivalence relations manually.

3.1. LEXICAL GAPS

Gaps may either be due to inadequacy of the resources or to differences in lexicalization across the languages. Four specific problems may occur (Copestake et al., 1995):

- there may be no entry
- there may be a phrasal translation in a bilingual dictionary (phrases, compounds, derivations, inflected forms).
- the translation is not an entry in WN1.5,
- the intended sense of a translation is not present in WN1.5 (although the word itself is).

We will illustrate these problems for the Spanish lexical resources (see Atserias et al., 1997, for further details). By merging both directions of the nominal part of the Spanish/English bilingual dictionaries we obtained an homogeneous bilingual dictionary (that is, both directions of a bilingual dictionary are normally not symmetric). As is shown in the Table III, the maximum coverage we can expect using this small bilingual dictionary, ranges from 14% of all WN1.5 nouns to 32% of WN1.5 synsets (including errors). On the other hand, this mapping does not yield a connection to WN1.5 for 20% of the English nouns appearing in the homogeneous dictionary and 10% of the Spanish words.

The simplest mapping presented in (Atserias et al., 1997) is the situation where a Spanish word has a unique English translation in both directions and this English

Table IV. Overlap in lexical units across monolingual and bilingual sources

A	Noun Definitions	93,394	
B	Noun Definitions with Genus Word	92,693	
C	Genus Words	14,131	
D	Genus with Bilingual translation	7,610	54% of c)
E	Genus with WordNet translation	7,319	52% of c)
F	Headwords	53,455	
G	Headwords with Bilingual translations	11,407	21% of f)
H	Headwords with WordNet translations	10,667	20% of f)
I	Definitions with Bilingual translations	30,446	33% of b)
J	Definitions with WordNet translations	28,995	31% of b)

word has only one sense in WN1.5. Only 92% of the connections produced by this method were considered correct. Another 2% of the connections were considered hyponyms of the correct ones, 2% nearly correct and 2% fully incorrect. Examples of correct and incorrect connections are the following. For instance *horn* could be translated in Spanish as *asta, bocina, claxon, cuerno,* etc. *Horn* in Spanish has (at least) two meanings: part of an animal and part of a car. As the homogeneous bilingual dictionary only connects words (not meanings) the following connections could be produced.

00740047 05 *horn asta* OK of an animal
00740047 05 *horn bocina* ERROR of an animal (OK of a car)
00740047 05 *horn claxon* ERROR of an animal (OK of a car)
00740047 05 *horn cuerno* OK of an animal

Another problem relates to differences in size of monolingual and bilingual resources that are merged. Table IV shows the overlapping across lexical units and resources. The monolingual dictionary contains 93,394 noun definitions (a), relating 53,455 headwords (f) and 14,131 genus words (c). Whereas there is a bilingual translation for 54% of the genus words, the bilingual dictionary only covers 21% of the headwords. The mapping only produces fully connected definitions (both headword and genus word) for 33% of the whole monolingual source. Furthermore, approximately 2% of the Spanish lexical units cannot be mapped to WN1.5 because the English translation was not found.

If there is no translation or only a phrasal translation for a sense in the dictionary it may be the case that we are dealing with a lexical gap. There may be different types of lexical gaps:

- Cultural gaps, e.g. the Dutch verb: *klunen* (to walk on skates) refers to an event not known in the English culture.
- 'Pragmatic gaps', e.g. the Dutch compound verb form *doodschoppen* (to kick to death), the Spanish *alevín* (young fish), or the Italian verb *rincasare* (to go

back home), which all refer to concepts known in the English culture but not expressed by a single lexicalized form. In these cases the lexicalization patterns in the languages are different from English.

- Morphologic mismatches: e.g. in Dutch the adjective *aardig* is equivalent to the verb *to like* in English.

In all these cases the Source Synset is linked to the closest Target-equivalent using a so-called complex-equivalence relation. Complex-equivalence relations parallel the language-internal relations (HAS_EQ_HYPERONYM, HAS_EQ_MERONYM, etc.). In most cases a lexical gap will be related to a more general concept with a HAS_EQ_HYPERONYM relation. In the case of the morphological gap EuroWordNet provides the possibility to encode a cross-part-of-speech equivalence relation. Likewise there can still be an EQ_SYNONYM relation between *aardig* Adjective and *like* Verb:

(24.) Equivalence relations for Gaps

Dutch WordNet	Equivalence Relation	WordNet1.5
klunen (to walk on skates)	HAS_EQ_HYPERONYM	*Walk*
aardig	EQ_SYNONYM	*Like*

3.2. SENSE-DIFFERENTIATION ACROSS WORDNETS

The second problem is that matching entries across resources shows differences in the differentiation of senses. Obviously, this problem is related to the sense-differentiation problems discussed above. Again we can make a distinction between under-differentiation and over-differentiation, which can occur either at the source wordnet or the target wordnet (in the case of EuroWordNet synsets taken from WordNet1.5):

Over-differentiation

- multiple targets: Dutch *schoonmaken* has only 1 sense whereas English *clean* has 19 senses. Here WN1.5 gives senses for different pragmatic uses that should not be distinguished as separate senses. The target is clearly over-differentiated.
- multiple sources: Dutch *versiersel* and *versiering* are both linked to the same WN1.5 synset *decoration* but are still distinguished as different synsets in the Dutch resource. There is however no difference in their definition or any other information. Here the source is over-differentiated.

Under-differentiation

- multiple targets: The Dutch sense *keuze* is defined as the *act* or *result* of choosing, likewise it can be linked both to *choice* 1 the act of choosing and *choice* 2 what is chosen. Two incompatible Dutch senses are conflated: the source is under-differentiated.

- multiple sources: *hout 1* (wood as substance), *houtsoort 1* (kind of wood) / wood 4. WN1.5 gives only one sense for wood, which has to capture both meanings *kinds* of wood and a *portion*. The target is under-differentiated (although it is less clear whether this is a mistake).

To solve these matching problems we are taking some specific measures. First of all the EQ_SYNONYM relation is only used when there is a clear and simple equivalence relation with a single synset in another resource (either at the source-side or the target-side). When there is no partial overlap or matching with a target synset, the source-synset is treated as a lexical gap in WordNet1.5 until we find evidence to the contrary. In the case of too many and too fine-grained sense-distinctions in the target or source-wordnet we agreed to apply the EQ_NEAR_SYNONYM relation. This would apply to the above case where a single sense in Dutch matches multiple senses of *clean*:

(25.) Near-Equivalence relations to multiple targets

Dutch WordNet	Equivalence Relation	WordNet1.5
schoonmaken 1	EQ_NEAR_SYNONYM	Clean 1 (making clean by removing filth, or unwanted substances)
shoonmaken 1	EQ_NEAR_SYNONYM	Clean 2 (remove unwanted substances from, such as feathers or pits, as of chickens or fruit)
schoonmaken 1	EQ_NEAR_SYNONYM	Clean 7 (remove in making clean)
schoonmaken 1	EQ_NEAR_SYNONYM	clean 8 (remove unwanted substances from – (as in chemistry))
hout 1 (wood as substance)	EQ_NEAR_SYNONYM	wood 4.
houtsoort 1 (kind of wood)	EQ_NEAR_SYNONYM	wood 4.

Obviously, judging the differences in sense-differentiation as over-differentiation or under-differentiation will eventually lead to a restructuring of the sense-differentiation of the source-wordnets and WordNet1.5. The cases of under-differentiation have in fact already been discussed in the previous section. Whenever conflated hyperonyms are incompatible (e.g. according to a co-ordination test) the sense will have to be split into two separate senses. In the case of over-differentiation we will see to what extent it is possible to globalise the sense-differentiation. In the case of WordNet1.5 this is particularly important because over-differentiation may cause equivalent meanings across wordnets to be linked to different WordNet1.5 senses.

Another sense-differentiation problem has again to do with the inconsistent treatment of regular polysemy across resources. In the next examples we see that the Dutch resource lists two senses for both *ambassade* (embassy) and *academie* (academy), one as the building and one as the institute, while WordNet1.5 specifies only one sense for each, but a different one:

(26.) **NL-WordNet**   **WordNet1.5**

    ambassade   *1 <organization>*   0

                   2 <building>   *embassy*

    academie   *1 <organization>*   academy

                   2 <building>   0

These regular patterns of polysemy can also be generated to partially overcome the inconsistent listing of senses across resources. This solution has been applied by (Hamp and Feldweg, 1997) in the building of the German wordnet, by encoding a polysemy-relation between classes of concepts that exhibit regular meaning-shifts (animal-food, institute-building, animal-human, etc.). The advantage is not only that omissions may be corrected but also that mismatchings across resources may be resolved. If for example the Dutch resource represents *universiteit* (university) as the institute and the Spanish resource represent *universidad* as the building, the regular polysemy pointer will generate the missing senses for both resources:

(27.) Metonymic Equivalence relations

Dutch WordNet	**WordNet1.5 Equivalents**	**Spanish WordNet**
universiteit	University the institute	<extended meaning>
<extended meaning>	University the building	*universidad*

In EuroWordNet we will extend the ILI with global synsets that represent groups of senses related either as specializations of a more general meaning or by means of regular polysemy as above. In (Peters et al., this volume) we discuss in detail how specific synsets in the wordnets can be related to these more global synsets.

3.3. MISMATCHES OF SENSES

A final case of mismatching to be discussed is the situation in which there is a close match with a specific target synset but the information across the wordnets does not match. The mismatching information could be:

- the way the meanings are classified (their hyperonyms are not equivalent or different hyponyms are listed), e.g.:

(28.)   a   **NL-WordNet**

hond	HYPERONYM	*huisdier*
(dog)		(pet)

WordNet1.5

dog	HYPERONYM	*canine*

   b   **SP-WordNet**

queso	HYPERONYM	*masa*
(cheese)		(substance)

WordNet1.5

cheese	HYPERONYM	dairy_product

Here the mismatching depends on the compatibility of the hyperonyms (see discussion above). Only when the hyperonyms cannot be combined as conjuncted predicates may it be necessary to reconsider the equivalence relation. In these examples both classifications are acceptable (*a dog is a pet and a canine; cheese is a mass and a dairy product*).

Obviously, differences in classification also lead to situations in which two equivalent hyperonyms have different sets of hyponyms below them. In the above cases we can expect that Dutch *huisdier* and English *pet*, or Spanish *masa* and English *substance* will differ in the hyponyms but may still have equivalent definitions and hyperonyms themselves. The differences in these examples do not falsify the equivalence relations but only show that the classifications differ (either as an inconsistency or as a language-specific property).

- their definitions may deviate in some way;

(29.)   **IT-WordNet**   **WordNet1.5**

seguace, descepolo	*follower*
(=who strongly believes)	(=who accepts)

Here we see that the gloss for the Italian synset is more specific than the English gloss, despite the equivalence relation in bilingual dictionaries. This difference may still fall within the limits of acceptable variation and the equivalence relation is legitimate.

- they may differ in the synset-members;

This is very likely to happen when large synsets are mapped. Comparison of both wordnets shows that in many cases there are large synsets in both languages for the same concepts, but these often are not parallel. Differences are mostly due to unbalanced differentiation in both wordnets. For example *onzin 1* (nonsense) in the Dutch wordnet has 36 synset members, possible candidates as equivalents in WN1.5 are *humbug 1* (10 synset members) and *bullshit 1* (13 synset members). These are however represented in different synsets in WordNet1.5:

(30.)   <subject matter1, message2, content3, substance4>

what a communication that is about something is about

HAS_HYPONYM:

—

<nonsense2, meaningless2, nonsensicality1>

HAS_HYPONYM

<humbug1, baloney1, bilgewater1, boloney1, bosh1, drool2,

tarradiddle1, tommyrot1, tosh1, twaddle1>

<drivel2>

a worthless message

HAS_HYPONYM

<Irish bull1, bull3, *bullshit1*, buncombe1, bunk2, bunkum1,

crap1, dogshit1, guff1, hogwash1, horseshit1, rot1, shit3>

To distinguish *bullshit 1* as a worthless message from *baloney 1* as *nonsense 2* looks like over-differentiation of WordNet1.5. In the Dutch wordnet however the synset of *onzin 1* is extremely large. It contains words like *gekakel 2* (cackle/chatter), *gezwam* (empty talk), which are not synonyms of *onzin* (nonsense) but more specific hyponyms. So here there is under-differentiation as well at the Dutch side.

Obviously, in all the above cases there must be something in common to seriously consider an equivalence relation. In general we follow the policy that we take the concept or gloss as the starting point. Differences in hyperonyms or hyponyms can also be caused by other reasons. To indicate a less precise matching these synsets should always be linked with an EQ_NEAR_SYNONYM relation.

4. Conclusions

In this paper we have described a general procedure for building wordnets in Euro-WordNet, discussing the major problems that may be encountered, especially when dealing with the more complicated Base Concepts. The decisions taken for these words have an effect on the structure of the database as a whole. By following a common strategy and shared solutions we ensure that these fundamental building blocks are encoded in a similar way across the different wordnets.

Usually, a summary of problematic examples is a disappointing enterprise. However, it is important to realise that not all meanings and relations are as complicated as suggested here. In many cases the relations are obvious and most words only have one or two meanings. Large fragments of the wordnets are therefore generated (semi-)automatically looking for patterns in definitions, mapping synsets via bilingual dictionaries or comparing taxonomies. These procedures are not discussed here, but will be described in a separate deliverable of the project on the tools and methods for building the wordnets.

Notes

[1] Note that it is not allowed to list two senses of the same entry in the same synset. Two senses can therefore only be merged in a variant of the same synset by deleting one sense and adding the related information to the remaining sense.

[2] We often see that disjunctive hyperonyms (hyperonyms that cannot apply simultaneously) form a regular metonymic pattern or alternation pattern. In principle their senses should be separated although it is possible to keep the collapsed meaning as well. In Peters et al. (this volume) we will discuss how these regular polysemy patterns can be captured via collapsed synsets in the Inter-Lingual-Index, regardless of the way they are treated in the individual wordnets.

[3] Association Ratio can be defined as the product of Mutual Information by the frequency. Given two words w1 and w2 which co-occurs in some definitions:

$$AR(w1,w2) = Pr(w1,w2)*log(Pr(w1,w2)/Pr(w1)*Pr(w2))$$ where $Pr(w1,w2)$ is the estimation of the probability of w1 and w2 co-occur in some definitions and $Pr(w)$ is the estimation of the probability of w occur in some definition.

[4] Some practical strategies for finding similar meanings which are classified differently, is by making use of the morphology of the entries (e.g. compounds ending with *disease*), or by looking for other, alternative definition patterns (e.g. containing phrases such as *infectious*).

[5] The total of scores exceeds the total of synsets because in some cases multiple senses or translations appear to be correct.

[6] Connections can be word/word or word/synset. When there are synsets involved the connections are Spanish-word/synset, (except for WordNet itself), otherwise Spanish-word/English-word.

[7] Maximum Reachable Coverage. Given the translations placed in the bilingual we can only attach Spanish words to 32% of WN1.5 synsets, 14% of WN1.5 nouns, etc. This is the maximum we can reach (most of these connections could be wrong).

References

Antelmi D. and A. Roventini. "Semantic Relationships within a Set of Verbal Entries in the Italian Lexical Database". In *Proceedings of EURALEX '90*, IV International Congress, Benalmadena (Malaga), 28–8/1–9, 1990.

Agirre E. and G. Rigau. "Word Sense Disambiguation using Conceptual Density". In *Proceedings of the 16th International Conference on Computational Linguistics* (COLING'96). Copenhagen, Denmark, 1996.

Atkins B. and B. Levin. "Admiting Impediments". In *Proceedings of the 4th Annual Conference of the UW Centre for the New OED*, Waterloo, Canada, 1988.

Atserias J., S. Climent, X. Farreres, G. Rigau and H. Rodríguez. "Combining Multiple Methods for the Automatic Construction of Multilingual WordNets". In *Proceedings of International Conference "Recent Advances in Natural Language Processing"*, Tzigov Chark, Bulgaria, 1997.

Cruse, D. A. *Lexical Semantics*. Cambridge: CUP, 1986.

Dik, S. *Stepwise Lexical Decomposition*. Lisse: Peter de Ridder Press, 1978.

Gale W., K. Church and D. Yarowsky. "A Method for Disambiguating Word Senses in a Large Corpus". *Computers and the Humanities*, 26 (1993), 415–439.

Hamp, B. and H. Feldweg, "GermaNet: a Lexical-Semantic Net for German". In *Proceedings of the ACL/EACL-97 workshop on Automatic Information Extraction and Building of Lexical Semantic Resources for NLP Applications*. Eds. P. Vossen, N. Calzolari, Adriaens, Sanfilippo and Y. Wilks, Madrid, 1997.

Jacobs, P. "Making Sense of Lexical Acquisition". *Lexical Acquisition: Exploiting On-line Resources to Build a Lexicon*, Ed. Zernik U., Hillsdale, New Jersey: Lawrence Erlbaum Associates, publishers, 1991.

Levin, B. *English Verb Classes and Alternations*. Chicago: University of Chicago Press, 1993.

Peters, C., A. Roventini, E. Marinai and N. Calzolari. "Making the Right Connections: Mapping between Italian and English Lexical Data in EuroWordNet". In *Proceedings of the Joint International Conference ALLC/ACH '98 "Virtual Communities"*, 5–10 July 1998, Lajos Kossuth University, Debrecen, Hungary (forthcoming).

Rigau G., J. Atserias and E. Agirre. "Combining Unsupervised Lexical Knowledge Methods for Word Sense Disambiguation". *Proceedings of the 34th Annual Meeting of the Association for Computational Linguistics* (ACL'97). Spain: Madrid, 1997, pp. 48–55.

Roventini, A. "Acquiring and Representing Semantic Information from Place Taxonomies". *Acta Linguistica Hungarica*, 41(1–4) (1992), 265–275.

Roventini, A., F. Bertagna, N. Calzolari and C. Peters. "Building the Italian component of EuroWord-Net: A Language-specific Perspective". *Proceedings of Euralex '98*, August, Brussels, Belgium (forthcoming).

Vossen P. and A. Copestake. "Untangling Definition Structure into Knowledge Representation". *Default Inheritance in Unification Based Approaches to the Lexicon*. Eds. E.J. Briscoe, A. Copestake and V. de Paiva. Cambridge: Cambridge University Press, 1993.

Vossen P. *Grammatical and Conceptual Individuation in the Lexicon*, PhD. Thesis University of Amsterdam, Studies in Language and Language Use, No. 15. IFOTT, Amsterdam, 1995.

Vossen, P., L. Bloksma and P. Boersma. "Generating Equivalence Relations to WordNet1.5 by Aligning the Hierarchical Context". In *Proceedings of the Workshop on Cross-language Semantic Links*, organized by the Institut fuer Deutsche Sprache, Pescia, 19th–21st June 1998 (forthcoming).

Wilks Y., D. Fass, C. Guo, J. McDonal, T. Plate and B. Slator. "Providing Machine Tractable Dictionary Tools". *Semantics and the Lexicon*. Ed. J. Pustejowsky, Dordrecht: Kluwer Academic Publishers, 1993, pp. 341–401.

Zwicky A. and J. Sadock. "Ambiguity Tests and How to Fail Them". *Syntax and Semantics 4*. Ed. J. Kimball, New York: Academic Press, 1975.

Computers and the Humanities **32**: 185–207, 1998.
© 1998 *Kluwer Academic Publishers.*

Applying EuroWordNet to Cross-Language Text Retrieval

JULIO GONZALO[1], FELISA VERDEJO[1], CAROL PETERS[2] and NICOLETTA CALZOLARI[3]

[1]*UNED, Ciudad Universitaria, s.n., 28040 Madrid, Spain, E-mail: julio,felisa@ieec.uned.es;*
[2]*Istituto di Elaborazione della Informazione, Consiglio Nazionale delle Ricerche, Via S. Maria, 46, 56126 Pisa, Italy, E-mail: carol@iei.pi.cnr.it;* [3]*Istituto di Linguistica Computazionale, Consiglio Nazionale delle Ricerche, Via della Faggiola, 32, 56100 Pisa, Italy, E-mail: glottolo@ilc.pi.cnr.it*

Key words: cross-language text retrieval, multilingual lexical resources, large-scale ontologies

Abstract. We discuss ways in which EuroWordNet (EWN) can be used in multilingual information retrieval activities, focusing on two approaches to Cross-Language Text Retrieval that use the EWN database as a large-scale multilingual semantic resource. The first approach indexes documents and queries in terms of the EuroWordNet Inter-Lingual-Index, thus turning term weighting and query/document matching into language-independent tasks. The second describes how the information in the EWN database could be integrated with a corpus-based technique, thus allowing retrieval of domain-specific terms that may not be present in our multilingual database. Our objective is to show the potential of EuroWordNet as a promising alternative to existing approaches to Cross-Language Text Retrieval.

Abbreviations: CLTR – Cross-Language Text Retrieval; EWN – EuroWordNet; ILI – Inter-Lingual-Index; IR – Information Retrieval; NLP – Natural Language Processing; POS – Part of Speech; WSD – Word Sense Disambiguation

1. Introduction

The current challenge for Natural Language Processing (NLP) technology is to demonstrate its cost-effectiveness for real-world tasks. Although it is widely recognized that reusable linguistic resources and tools are needed to address the complexity of building large-scale NLP applications, our task now is to reduce the distance between the research lab and the marketplace. Experience tells us that already available resources can be exploited by software developers to improve their products by including, for instance, some language component. A good example of this is the growing number of applications using WordNet (Miller et al., 1990) mentioned in the literature, since it first became freely available.

Multilinguality has been a central concern from the very beginning of NLP research. In particular, substantial efforts have been dedicated to machine translation, perceived as a major priority in the building and exploiting of applications.

However, the recent global diffusion of computers in both the work place and at home, together with the dramatic increase in computer network users, is opening opportunities for many other kinds of applications involving multilingual resources. We can mention, for example, the improvement of access to international multimedia information services, the enhancement of language learning aids, the assisted production of multilingual manuals, technical or legal documents, or the automatic generation of reports in highly structured domains, such as traffic bulletins or weather information. For all these activities, and many more, a generic multilingual database with wordnets for different languages will be a key resource.

In our opinion, one of the most interesting applications for the EuroWordNet (EWN) database is probably in the area of Cross-Language Text Retrieval (CLTR). The explosive growth of universally accessible information over the international networks – information that is unstructured, heterogeneous and multilingual by nature – has made CLTR one of the currently most compelling challenges for information technology. For this reason, we have decided to focus the last article in this collection on a description of how it will be possible to apply the EuroWordNet multilingual database in CLTR activities.

The main approaches to CLTR being experimented today use either knowledge-based or corpus-based techniques:

Knowledge-based approaches apply bilingual or multilingual dictionaries, thesauri or general-purpose ontologies to cross-language text retrieval.

USING THESAURI: So far, the best known and tested approaches to CLTR are thesaurus-based, although these are generally used in controlled-text retrieval, where each document is indexed (mainly by hand) with keywords from the thesaurus. A thesaurus is an ontology specialized in organizing terminology; a multilingual thesaurus organizes terminology for more than one language. ISO 5964 gives specifications for the incorporation of domain knowledge in multilingual thesauri and identifies alternative techniques. There are now a number of multilingual thesaurus-based systems available commercially. However, controlled text retrieval demands resource-consuming thesaurus construction and maintenance, and user-training for optimum usage. In addition, domain-specific thesauri are not very useful outside of the particular domain for which they have been designed. In the remainder of the paper, we will refer mainly to free-text retrieval, where queries are compared against full documents, rather than pre-built keyword descriptions of the documents.

USING DICTIONARIES: Some of the first methods attempting to match the query to the document for free-text (as opposed to controlled-text) retrieval have used bilingual dictionaries. It has been shown that dictionary-based query translation, where each term or phrase in the query is replaced by a list of all its possible translations, represents an acceptable first pass at cross-language information retrieval although such – relatively simple – methods clearly show performance below that of monolingual retrieval. Automatic machine readable dictionary (MRD) query translation, on its own, has been found to lead to a drop in effectiveness of 40–60% of monolingual retrieval (Hull and Grefenstette, 1996; Ballesteros and Croft, 1996). There are three main reasons for this: general purpose dictionaries do not normally contain specialized vocabulary; failure to translate multiword terms; and the presence of spurious translations (a problem derived from polysemy which is further discussed in Section 2).

Corpus-based approaches : The above considerations have encouraged an interest in corpus-based techniques in which information about the relationship between terms over languages is obtained from observed statistics of term usage. Corpus-based approaches analyze large collections of texts in multiple languages and automatically extract the information needed to construct application-specific translation techniques. The collections analyzed may consist of parallel (translation equivalent) or comparable (domain-specific) sets of documents. The main approaches that have been experimented using corpora are vector space and probabilistic techniques. A recent, comparative evaluation of some representative approaches to corpus-based cross-language free-text retrieval (Carbonell et al., 1997) showed that such approaches – and in particular some applications of example-based machine translation – significantly outperformed the simple dictionary-based term translation used in the evaluation.

The first tests with parallel corpora were on statistical methods for the extraction of multilingual term equivalence data which could be used as input for the lexical component of MT systems. Some of the most interesting recent experiments, however, are those using a matrix reduction technique known as Latent Semantic Indexing (LSI) to extract language independent terms and document representations from parallel corpora (Dumais et al., 1996). LSI applies a singular value decomposition to a large, sparse term document co-occurrence matrix (including terms from all parallel versions of the documents) and extracts a subset of the singular vectors to form a new vector space. Thus queries in one language can retrieve documents in the other (as well as in the original language).

The problem with using parallel texts as training corpora is that test corpora are costly to acquire – it is difficult to find already existing translations of the right kind of documents and translated versions are expensive to create. For this reason, there has been a lot of interest recently in the potential of comparable corpora. A comparable document collection is one in which documents are aligned on the basis of the similarity between the topics they address rather than because they are translation equivalent. Methods have been studied to extract information from such corpora on cross-language equivalences in order to translate and expand a query formulated in one language with useful terms in another (Sheridan and Ballerini, 1996; Picchi and Peters, 1996).

Again, as with the parallel corpus method reported above, it appears that such strategies are very application dependent. A new reference corpus would have to be built to perform retrieval on a new topic.

From this discussion, we can conclude that any single method currently being tried presents limitations. Existing resources – such as electronic bilingual dictionaries – are normally inadequate or insufficient for the purpose; the building of resources like domain-specific thesauri and training corpora is expensive and such resources are generally not fully reusable; a new multilingual application will require the construction of new resources or considerable work for the adaptation of previously built ones.

It should also be noted that most of the systems and methods in use so far concentrate on pairs rather than multiples of languages. This is hardly surprising. The situation is far more complex when an attempt is made to achieve effective retrieval over a number of languages than over a single pair; it is necessary to study some kind of interlingual mechanism – at a more or less conceptual level – in order to permit multiple cross-language transfer. This is why we feel that a large-scale, multilingual semantic database such as EWN offers an interesting alternative: it can be used to perform conceptual, language-neutral retrieval without training and without parallel corpora. This paper thus proposes ways in which EWN can be applied in order to achieve this goal, and discusses why a resource of this type should be particularly effective in CLTR and what can be learned from it.

We begin, in the following section, by considering previous WordNet-based monolingual text retrieval experiments. We also mention ways that WordNet has been used in tasks such as word-sense disambiguation or acquisition of semantic information, which can be seen as component tasks of information systems in a multiple language (and not only English) context. Although such experiments have not always been completely successful, we show that a cross-language scenario can retain the advantages of a WordNet approach without its major drawback (an unnecessary exacerbation of problems of polysemy). Section 3 reviews the major features of the EWN database from the point of view of Text Retrieval, highlighting its advantages over WordNet 1.5.

In Sections 4 and 5, we discuss two proposals that examine the application of EWN in CLTR for different retrieval contexts. The first approach, studied at UNED, Madrid, is to index documents in terms of the Inter-Lingual-Index of the database, turning term weighting and query/document comparison into language-independent tasks and taking full advantage of EWN features for text retrieval. This approach seems especially well-suited for searches over unrestricted, heterogeneous collections, such as World-Wide-Web searches, as it does not require training or parallel corpora. The second approach suggests how knowledge from the EWN database could be integrated with a corpus-based strategy, being developed at ILC-CNR, Pisa. This integration with corpus-based techniques seems best-suited for searches over homogeneous corpora with domain-specific vocabulary that is not likely to be found in the EWN database.

2. Lessons from WordNet-Based Monolingual Text Retrieval

WordNet 1.5 is a large-scale lexical database configured as a semantic net of 91,587 *synsets* (sets of synonymous word-senses) containing 119,217 words and with the encoding of basic semantic relations (such as synonymy, hyponymy, meronymy). A large-scale semantic database such as WordNet would appear to have a great potential for text retrieval. There are, at least, two obvious reasons:

- It contains information (encapsulated in the *synsets*) that should make it possible to discriminate word senses in documents and queries. This could prevent matching *spring* in its "metal device" sense against documents mentioning *spring* in the sense of *springtime*. Thus retrieval accuracy could be improved.
- Similarly, it makes it possible to identify semantically related words. For instance, *spring, fountain, outflow, outpouring*, in the appropriate senses, can be identified as occurrences of the same concept, '*natural flow of ground water*'. Going beyond synonymy, WordNet can be used to measure semantic distance between terms in order to obtain more sophisticated ways of comparing documents and queries.

However, the general feeling within the information retrieval community is that dealing explicitly with semantic information does not significantly improve the performance of text retrieval systems. This impression is based on the results of certain experiments measuring the role of Word Sense Disambiguation (WSD) for text retrieval, on one hand, and attempts to exploit the features of WordNet and other lexical databases, on the other hand.

In Sanderson (1994), word sense ambiguity is shown to produce only minor effects on retrieval accuracy, apparently confirming the idea that query/document matching strategies already perform an implicit disambiguation. Sanderson also estimates that if explicit WSD is performed with less than 90% accuracy, the results are worse than with no disambiguation at all. In his experimental set-up, ambiguity is introduced artificially in the documents, substituting randomly chosen pairs of words (for instance, *banana* and *kalashnikov*) with artificially ambiguous terms (*banana/kalashnikov*). While his results are interesting, it remains unclear, in our opinion, whether they would be corroborated with real occurrences of ambiguous words. There is also another minor weakness in Sanderson's experiments. When he "disambiguates" a term such as *spring/bank* to obtain, for instance, *bank*, he has only achieved a partial disambiguation, as *bank* can be used in more than one sense in a text collection.

In addition to disambiguation, many attempts have been made to exploit WordNet for monolingual text retrieval purposes. Two aspects have mainly been addressed: the enrichment of queries with semantically-related terms, on one hand, and the comparison of queries and documents via conceptual distance measures, on the other.

Query expansion with WordNet has been shown to be potentially helpful to recall enhancement, as it makes it possible to retrieve relevant documents that do not contain any of the query terms (Smeaton et al., 1995). However, it has produced few successful experiments. For instance, Voorhees (1994) manually expanded 50 queries over a TREC-1 collection (Harman, 1993) using synonymy and other semantic relations from WordNet 1.3. Voorhees found that the expansion was useful with short, incomplete queries, and rather useless for complete topic statements – where other expansion techniques worked better. For short queries, the problem remained of selecting the expansions automatically; doing it badly could degrade retrieval performance rather than enhancing it. In Richardson and Smeaton (1995), a combination of rather sophisticated techniques based on Word-Net, including automatic disambiguation and measures of semantic relatedness between query/document concepts resulted in a drop of effectiveness. Unfortunately, the effects of WSD errors could not be discerned from the accuracy of the retrieval strategy. However, in Smeaton and Quigley (1996), retrieval on a small collection of image captions – that is, on very short documents – is reasonably improved using measures of conceptual distance between words acquired from WordNet 1.4. Captions and queries were previously manually disambiguated against WordNet. The reason for this success is that with very short documents (e.g. *boys playing in the sand*) the chance of finding the original terms of the query (e.g. of *children running on a beach*) are much lower than for average-size documents (that typically include many phrasings for the same concepts). These results are in agreement with Voorhees (1994), but the question remains as to whether the conceptual distance matching would scale up to longer documents and queries. In addition, the experiments in Smeaton and Quigley (1996) only consider nouns, while WordNet offers the chance to use all open-class words (nouns, verbs, adjectives and adverbs).

However, if it is true that WordNet has potential capabilities with respect to Text Retrieval tasks, it also clearly suffers from certain weaknesses. The most apparent (as of version 1.5) are:

- It lacks cross-part-of-speech relations. This means, for instance, that *paint* and *painting* or *adornment* and *adorn* are not related in WordNet, whereas the connection between them is of great relevance in text retrieval.
- It lacks topic or domain information. For instance, *tennis shoes* and *tennis racquet* have no semantic connection in WordNet; they belong to different parts of the hierarchy. This is another dimension of relatedness that is crucial for text retrieval, as the topic determines the context of a word within a document to a large extent.
- The WordNet hierarchy is unbalanced; the coverage of the sub-domains is not homogeneous. This causes a distortion of most measures of semantic distance used in the literature.
- Sense distinctions in WordNet are excessively fine-grained. For instance, *people* has four different senses in WordNet:
    1. people – any group of persons (men or women or children) collectively.
    2. citizenry, people – (the body of citizens of a state or country)

3. people – (members of a family line)

(a) multitude, masses, mass, hoi polloi, people – (the common people generally)

This degree of fine-grainedness does not favor retrieval, as queries do not usually imply such distinctions from a human-judgment point of view (which is the only gold standard!).

But above and beyond these reasons, a major problem when using WordNet for Information Retrieval (IR) purposes is that WordNet-based approaches augment exponentially the problem of polysemy. Let us suppose that the query contains the word *spring* in the sense of *spring, springtime – season of growth*. The standard problem caused by polysemy when retrieving by exact term matching is that, besides pertinent documents, we will also retrieve others talking about metal devices, fountains, etc., that correspond to other meanings of *spring*. Now, what happens if we expand the query with WordNet? We will obtain a set of words *spring, springtime, fountain, leap, outflow, bound, give, springiness, outpouring* of which only the first two correspond to the intended meaning; unfortunately, the other words are probably polysemous as well, and none of their senses will be related to the original idea of the query. So the problem of ambiguity is expanded, by adding terms for the wrong meanings of the query term. Recall may be slightly improved by the addition of *springtime*, but precision will be very much affected by the large set of irrelevant words that have also been added.

The interesting point is that this is exactly what happens – either explicitly or implicitly – within any approach to cross-language text retrieval. When translating a query from the source to the target language, the task of finding equivalent terms in the target language is identical to finding synonyms; in fact we are looking for synonyms, but in another language. For instance, when we translate *spring* to Spanish, we obtain a set of words *primavera(season), salto(leap), brinco(leap), elasticidad(springiness), manantial(source of water), fuente(source), resorte(metal device)* where only one meaning of one of the words is related to the intended meaning of the query. This expansion of ambiguity makes cross-language text retrieval much harder than its monolingual counterpart.

Thus a WordNet-based (or better, a EuroWordNet based) approach to cross-language text retrieval expands ambiguities just as any other cross-language approach, *but no more*. From the term *spring* we may obtain its synonyms in any of the project languages – e.g. for Spanish, we have the above set of words. While WordNet introduces an often excessive level of expansion in monolingual retrieval, EuroWordNet expands ambiguity in the same way as any other cross-language approach. Thus, the disadvantages of using a WordNet-like structure should be less significant in a multilingual setting. This makes WordNet-based retrieval probably more interesting in a multilingual setting than in a monolingual one. We will further discuss this question in Section 3.

However, before concluding this section, we feel that it is important to observe that a semantic net such as WordNet can be used in a number of techniques and tasks related to the disambiguation and acquisition of semantic information, i.e. in tasks that are clearly subsidiary to, or components of, the broad application goal of Text Retrieval discussed in this paper. We briefly list here applications where WordNet has been tested in such tasks for English, as we can safely infer from this the usability and usefulness of similar semantic nets for other languages in both a monolingual and a multilingual setting.

As is known, WordNet, or other thesauri, are being used extensively in word similarity measurement techniques (Kurohashi and Nagao, 1994; Li and Abe, 1995), which are at the basis of a number of NLP applications and tasks. The intuitive underlying assumption is that words closer to each other in a hierarchical structure can be considered to have a higher degree of semantic similarity. After evaluation of the results of statistics-based and human-crafted thesaurus-based approaches, Fujii et al. (1997) claims that better results can be obtained by an integration of the two approaches. This combined technique is evaluated also in its application to a word sense disambiguation task, where it is also shown to be effective. The use of WordNet helps to solve problems of data sparseness suffered by semantic disambiguation tasks based on probabilistic models.

The advantages of using WordNet in the task of automatic acquisition of lexical information (e.g. selectional preferences) are reported in McCarthy (1997), as part of the LE-SPARKLE project, but go back to Grishman et al. (1992), Ribas (1995), Li and Abe (1995). In these approaches, WordNet is used, in different ways, to obtain classes at an appropriate level of generalization, thus reducing again the sparseness problem. However, in lexical acquisition tasks there is also the problem of having to acquire information from an ambiguous input, and therefore the problem of semantic disambiguation. McCarthy tries to tackle the lack of semantic disambiguation in the input, which causes, due to the presence of various erroneous senses, a sort of over-generalization or dispersion in non-appropriate semantic areas. Sense disambiguation is handled, although in a crude manner, using WordNet as a classification tool to disambiguate heads in parsed texts.

It is clear that these two tasks of word-sense disambiguation and acquisition of semantic preferences are strictly, and somehow circularly, interconnected, but a bootstrapping and iterative approach can be adopted, where even crude disambiguation can help acquisition.

Semantic similarity, assessed with reference to WordNet (Resnik, 1995), is also used by Sanfilippo (1997), again within LE-SPARKLE, to disambiguate syntactic collocates; the preliminary results are encouraging, considering the reduction of input data requirements with respect to statistical techniques. Here too the task at stake is the automatic acquisition of semantic co-occurrence restrictions from text corpora.

Semantic tagging using WordNet associated with the Hidden Markov disambiguation method (as used in POS-tagging), is described in Segond et al. (1997) as improving the baseline from 81% to 89%.

WordNet has also been used to enhance information extraction systems. For example, Chai and Bierman (1997) uses WordNet hierarchies to automatically generalize patterns in the training of one information extraction system in new domains.

Once EuroWordNet is publicly available, all these techniques can be experimented or applied in a multilingual setting.

3. EWN Features for Text Retrieval

As has already been stated in other articles in this collection, EuroWordNet (which is scheduled for the first public release in Spring 1999), consists of a set of monolingual wordnets for several European languages, linked through the ILI. This means that it will be possible to experiment all those applications which can profitably use WordNet for English in a multiple language setting. In addition, such applications will be able to profit from the additional features of the EWN databases with respect to WordNet.

A number of these features are particularly important from the point of view of text retrieval. The database is described in detail in this volume (Alonge et al., this volume; Rodríguez et al., this volume; Peters et al., this volume), but here below we will review those issues that are relevant for CLTR.

- EWN will contain about 50,000 word meanings correlating the 20,000 most frequent words (only nouns and verbs in the first stage) in each language. This size should be sufficient to experiment with generic, domain-independent text retrieval in a multilingual setting without the need for training with bilingual parallel corpora. The individual monolingual databases will be considerably smaller than WordNet 1.5, but the difference in coverage is only for specific sub-domains; the coverage of most frequent words and more generic terms will be similar in both databases. The EWN database will be expanded to a higher level of detail for one specific domain, in order to test its adequacy to incorporate domain-specific thesauri.
- Synsets have domain labels that relate concepts on the basis of topics or scripts rather than classification. This means that *tennis shoes* and *tennis racquet* will be related through a common domain label *tennis*. As we have mentioned above, topic relations are very important for word-sense disambiguation and retrieval tasks.
- Nouns and verbs do not form separate networks. EWN includes cross-part-of-speech relations:
  - noun-to-verb-hyperonym: *angling* → *catch* (from angling: sport of catching fish with a hook and line)
  - verb-to-noun-hyponym: *catch* → *angling*
  - noun-to-verb-synonym: *adornment* → *adorn* (from *adornment: the act of adorning*)
  - verb-to-noun-synonym: *adorn* → *adornment*

Again, these relations establish links that are significant from the point of view of text retrieval. In particular, *adorn* and *adornment* are nearly equivalent for retrieval purposes, regardless of their different Parts-of-Speech.

The multilingual architecture of EWN is described in detail in Vossen (this volume) and Peters et al. (this volume); we summarize here its components:

Monolingual Wordnets. Each language has its individual wordnet with internal relations that reflects specific properties of that language. However, each monolingual wordnet is being built from a common set of 1024 *base concepts* (concepts which are relatively high in the semantic hierarchies and which have many relations with other concepts). These have been verified manually to fit all monolingual wordnets. This is one of the measures that guarantees overlap and compatibility between wordnets, reducing spurious mismatches in the hierarchy.

Inter-Lingual-Index(ILI). A superset of all concepts occurring in the monolingual wordnets. The ILI began as a collection of records that matched WordNet 1.5 synsets, and is growing as new concepts are added. It will also be modified with respect to WordNet 1.5, as too fine-grained sense distinctions will be collapsed. (see section 2). Peters et al. (this volume) describes this process in detail. All interlingual relations and language-independent information is linked to the ILI, as explained below.

Cross-language relations. Each wordnet is linked to the ILI via cross-language equivalence relations, namely:

- cross-language synonymy: *It:anitra EQ-NEAR-SYNONYM duck*
- cross-language hyperonym: *Dutch:hoofd (human head) EQ-HAS-HYPERONYM head*
- cross-language hyponym: *Sp:dedo (finger or toe) EQ-HAS-HYPONYM finger, Sp:dedo EQ-HAS-HYPONYM toe*

Cross-language complex relations (hyperonyms and hyponyms) indicate potential new ILI records. After each building stage, all complex relations are collected and compared across languages and new ILI records will be added if appropriate. These relations facilitate cross-language retrieval.

Top-concept Ontology. A hierarchy of 63 language-independent concepts reflecting explicit opposition relations (e.g. *object* vs. *substance*). This ontology is linked to the base concepts through the ILI, see Rodríguez et al. (this volume).

Hierarchy of domain labels. Also linked to the ILI and thus inherited by every monolingual wordnet.

4. Language-Independent Text Retrieval with EWN

Our first proposal as to how EuroWordNet can be effectively applied to CLTR is to index documents in terms of the Inter-Lingual-Index records (which, in practice, serves as a language-independent ontology) rather than expanding queries with terms for all languages. This approach has been studied at UNED, Madrid, see Gilarranz et al. (1997) for a first description. We use the vector space model, but instead of a vector of weighted terms, each document is represented as a vector of weighted Inter-Lingual-Index records. This means that we can consider language-independent criteria for term weighting and query/document comparison.

This approach combines two benefits for retrieval, regardless of multilinguality: (i) terms are fully disambiguated as ILI records represent word senses (this should improve precision); (ii) equivalent terms can be identified, as terms with the same sense map to the same ILI record (this should improve recall). Note that query expansion does not satisfy the first condition, as the terms used to expand a query are, themselves, words and, therefore, can be in their turn ambiguous. On the other hand, plain word sense disambiguation does not satisfy the second condition, as equivalent senses of two different words are not recognized. Thus, indexing by synsets enables a maximum of word sense matching while reducing spurious matching and seems to be a good starting point to study text retrieval using either WordNet or EuroWordNet.

Two major processes have to be considered: document indexing and query/document matching.

4.1. DOCUMENT INDEXING

Document indexing is performed in two stages: a language-dependent one that maps terms to ILI records, and a language-independent one that assigns weights to the representation.

Language-dependent stage

1. **Part of Speech Tagging.** This is a first step towards disambiguation and should not cause problems. POS tagging can be performed with more than 96% precision for many languages, see, for example, Brill (1992) and Màrquez and Padró (1997).

2. **Term Identification.** This step includes stemming and reconstruction, and the identification of multiwords. The detection of multiwords is known to be beneficial to text retrieval tasks; WordNet is rich in multiword information, thus offering a potential for retrieval refinement that should be exploited. However, an appropriate treatment of multiwords from a multilingual perspective is not at all simple.

   As has been stated, the detection of lexicalized multiwords in a monolingual setting can enhance precision. For instance, *hot spring* can be identified in a document as a lexicalized multiword simply by inspecting WordNet 1.5 entries. We can thus assign a single meaning to *hot spring*, avoiding a separate inclusion of meanings for *hot* and *spring*, which would not reflect the content of the document. Even when WordNet 1.5 includes non-lexicalized phrases such as *a great distance* or *fasten with a screw*, it would seem helpful to use these in order to refine term identification and matching for monolingual text retrieval. In fact, such non-lexicalized phrases are very common in WordNet 1.5, which oscillates between lexical and conceptual criteria when constructing the synsets. However, with many of such phrases the best solution is probably to search for the lexically significant words in close co-occurrence, e.g. for *fasten* near to *screw*.

The handling of non-lexicalized phrases is not a simple task in the cross-language setting, partly because the situation is not symmetric over languages and this asymmetry frequently reflects important differences in conceptualization between languages which must not be lost. Consider, for instance, lexical items in one language that do not have equivalents in another. In order to provide an exact translation equivalent, recourse is normally made to a phrase. An example is *toe*, which does not have a direct equivalent in Spanish. The closest lexical item is *dedo*, which means *finger or toe*. Thus going from one language to the other we appear to lose information on specificity; a solution could be to introduce a Spanish synset containing a phrase, even if it is not lexicalized, to describe the concept in Spanish. The appropriate phrase in Spanish would be *dedo del pie* (*del pie = of the foot*). However, we have to consider whether this is the most correct way to deal with this kind of situation. When a Spanish document is talking about toes, it will probably just use the term *dedo*. A retrieval system looking for *dedo del pie* as a single bound item could miss relevant information. The best solution is probably that already suggested above for monolingual retrieval: to search for both *dedo* and *pie* in close proximity and also just *dedo*; *pie* can be used as a weight for document ranking.

The question of the treatment of multiwords and lexicalized/non lexicalized translation equivalents is one that affects other possible applications of the EuroWordNet database. The decision taken by the project has been to include only lexicalized concepts in each monolingual wordnet. For CLTR, this means that we should look for cross-language hyponyms or hyperonyms when a lexical item does not have a lexicalized equivalent in some target language.

3. **Word-Sense Disambiguation.** It is usually assumed that information retrieval systems perform an implicit disambiguation when comparing queries and documents, because the adequate senses for a term are reinforced by the terms in the context (Krovetz and Croft, 1992; Sanderson, 1994). So how should we index in terms of ILI records? Is it better to disambiguate with a certain error ratio, or can we assign all possible ILI records for each word form. Would

conceptual indexing improve retrieval in a monolingual setting, or would it have only a subtle effect, as previous experiments suggest?

In Gonzalo et al. (1998), we report on some experiments that address this and other questions related to our approach in a monolingual setting. On one hand, it was observed that using WordNet synsets as indexing terms improved performance when compared to standard word indexing. We also observed that with less than 10% disambiguation errors retrieval performance was not affected, and with between 30% and 60% errors the performance was neither clearly better nor worse than standard word indexing. These results were obtained for a manually disambiguated test collection (of queries and documents) derived from the SEMCOR (Miller et al., 1993) semantic concordance. Errors were introduced randomly over the hand-tagged documents in order to evaluate the role of disambiguation errors.

Automatic WSD is still very much an open research problem in NLP; there currently is much on-going work aimed at experimenting new methodologies and, specially, at improving evaluation methods. An example of the current state-of-the art on a comparable setting (namely, disambiguating against WordNet, evaluating on a subset of the Brown Corpus, and treating the 191 most frequently occurring and ambiguous words of English) can be the one reported in Ng (1997). They achieve 58.7% accuracy on a Brown Corpus subset and 75.2% on a subset of the Wall Street Journal Corpus. In order to know if this is sufficient for our purposes we need more careful evaluation of the role of WSD.

4. **Mapping into Inter-Lingual-Index.** Once the terms in the documents have been disambiguated in terms of the relevant monolingual wordnet, they can be mapped to the Inter-Lingual-Index via cross-language equivalence relations.

Language-independent stage

5. **Weighting.** Using a classical vector-space model, synset weighting can be done employing language-independent criteria. Standard weighting schemes combine within-document term frequency, (TF) – a term is more relevant in a document if it appears repeatedly – and inverted documents frequency (IDF) – a term is more relevant if its frequency in the document is significantly higher than its frequency in the collection. Such weighting schemes (nnn, atc, etc.) can be rendered language-independent when WordNet synsets are used as indexing terms for the documents in each language.

Besides standard weighting, depth in the conceptual hierarchy can also be used to weight synsets, as synsets deeper in the hierarchy are more specific and therefore more informative. It follows that the uppermost synsets are the least informative and can probably be removed, thus providing a list of *stop synsets*. This is an interesting possibility provided by the WordNet hierarchy, but its effectiveness has to be carefully evaluated, as this may well depend on the homogeneity of the database. It is known that the WordNet hierarchy is not well balanced and thus a simple measure of hierarchical depth might not be reliable for weighting. The building strategy used for the EuroWordNet database is expected to provide a more evenly balanced hierarchy (Rodríguez et al., this volume), but only an evaluation of the final database will be able to guarantee this.

The same process will be applied to queries, although performing disambiguation is much more difficult because queries are very short compared with documents and thus offer little contextual information.

4.2. QUERY/DOCUMENT MATCHING

We will experiment with three approaches to query/document comparison. Each approach adds some information to the previous one:

a) **Cosine comparison.** As formally we have a classical vector model, we use classical cosine comparison as a baseline. Thus we can evaluate separately the impact of the indexing process and the methods for comparison. The experiments in Gonzalo et al. (1998) cited above gave better results for this approach in a monolingual setting (up to 29% better) than standard word indexing with the SMART (Salton, 1971) system. This result is obtained for a manually disambiguated test collection, but it strongly suggests that performance can be very good if we can overcome problems of ambiguity resolution.

b) **Weighted expansion.** The vector can be expanded – still in a language-independent manner – by including related ILI records. The first candidates are cross-POS synonyms, which usually have strongly related meanings (see previous sections). Meronyms also seem to be good candidates, as they are likely to appear in context. However, we are aware that expansions beyond synonymy are not guaranteed to improve performance, and so careful evaluation of all kinds of expansion is required.

c) **Measure of semantic relatedness.** Instead of simply matching identical concepts, it is possible to measure the semantic relatedness of query and document indexing concepts. A similar approach gave good results for monolingual retrieval in Smeaton and Quigley (1996). In addition, the domain labels could be used to score occurrences of words related to the same topics.

4.3. EVALUATION STEPS

It is unlikely that a multilingual corpus, manually disambiguated against the EuroWordNet database, will be available very soon. Therefore, our plan is to investigate issues related to disambiguation in a monolingual setting, with a manually disambiguated test collection. In this way we can distinguish the effects of our retrieval approach, on one side, and of disambiguation accuracy, on the other. Once the best scenario for concept retrieval is reached in a monolingual setting, we will evaluate the system in bilingual and multilingual collections which will probably not be disambiguated.

1. *Monolingual experiments with WordNet.* As mentioned above, our first experiments, reported in Gonzalo et al. (1998), use a manually disambiguated test collection adapted from SEMCOR. We found that our methodology can give excellent results for disambiguated collections. The role of disambiguation is not entirely clear yet, but it seems that with less than 30% errors, synset indexing outperforms word indexing, whereas between 30% and 60% it is not clearly either better or worse than word indexing. Our goal is now to find the best way to disambiguate automatically with sufficient precision, and without high computational costs, which would be unfeasible for real-scale retrieval collections. We will then have to evaluate the performance of the system with the different query/comparison methods and query expansion techniques mentioned above.

2. Bilingual experiments (English-Spanish). Once WSD is tuned, one of the best corpora for cross-language retrieval evaluation would be the one described in Carbonell et al. (1997), where several different approaches (specially corpus-based ones) have been tested in identical conditions for English-Spanish retrieval.

3. Multilingual experiments. At the moment, we are unaware of the existence of an adequate test collection for multilingual experiments. Ideally, such a collection would reflect the variety of topics and styles, heterogeneous and multilingual, of the World Wide Web (WWW). Experimenting with such a corpus would be a difficult task for retrieval, but it should provide the most suitable test-bed to evaluate the effectiveness of EuroWordNet in CLTR.

4.4. SUMMING UP

This proposal for cross-language text retrieval has attractive advantages over other techniques:

- It performs language independent indexing, providing
  - A semantic structure to perform explicit WSD for indexing.
  - Language-independent weighting criteria.
- It permits language-independent retrieval, by
  - Concept comparison rather than term comparison.
  - Topic comparison.

– It does not require training or the availability of parallel corpora (a great advantage when thinking of more than two languages or when performing retrieval on unrestricted texts, such as WWW searches).
– the EuroWordNet architecture seems better suited for text retrieval than WordNet 1.5:
   • Words can be conceptually related even if they have different POS.
   • Besides classification relations, synsets have also topic information (domain labels), which is especially useful for text retrieval.

5. Using EWN in a Corpus-Based Cross-Language Query System

The previous section described a way in which EWN could be used for cross-language text retrieval which is well-suited for retrieval over sparse, heterogeneous document collections where training is impractical, the best example being a WWW search. This approach is not feasible for technical corpora, because the relevant domain-specific vocabulary is not likely to be found in the EWN database. In this section we will discuss how the EWN database could be integrated with a corpus-based approach to overcome this limitation, making it possible to find target language query terms even when the source language search item is not included as an entry in the database.

In the Introduction, we mentioned the main approaches to CLTR: knowledge-based and corpus-based. A recent trend is to experiment the integration of different approaches. At ILC-CNR, Pisa, the combination of a lexicon with a corpus-based strategy has already been experimented (Picchi and Peters, 1996). However, we feel that the integration of a multilingual ontology such as EWN with corpus-based techniques could prove particularly effective for two reasons. Up until now, tests have generally been on pairs of languages; EWN offers the possibility of testing retrieval in a multiple language setting (querying in one language, and retrieving documents from collections in several languages). So far tests have generally been made using bilingual dictionaries; the features included in EWN mean that it is far more than a dictionary – it is a semantic database with a high level conceptual top ontology and domain information. It should be possible to exploit the wide-range of cross-language equivalence relations encoded, retrieving not just cross-language synonyms but also other kinds of related words including cross-POS equivalents.

In this section, we describe the methodology for cross-language retrieval that has been developed in Pisa and discuss why we feel that an approach of this type could be strengthened by employing EWN instead of the bilingual database on which our tests have been made so far. Unfortunately, at the time of writing, a sufficiently complete version of EWN was not ready for experimentation, and thus it has not been possible to test this hypothesis. We can only describe how the special features of EWN could be exploited when integrated in the corpus-based strategy.

5.1. A CORPUS-BASED SYSTEM FOR DOMAIN-SPECIFIC DOCUMENT BASES

As stated above, the design of a cross-language query system for a text collection containing documents in more than one language has been studied at Pisa. This system integrates a lexicon-based search with a corpus-based strategy. The aim is to be able to match a query formulated in one language against documents stored in other languages, even when the query terms themselves are not included in the multilingual lexicon. Systems of this type are important for retrieval in domain-specific collections which tend to contain special language and terminology, but for which a specifically designed multilingual thesaurus does not exist.

This corpus-based strategy is based on the concept of comparable corpora. Comparable corpora are sets of texts in pairs (or multiples) of languages with the same communicative function, i.e. generally on the same topic or domain. Such corpora are sources of natural language lexical equivalences across languages. Collections of documents on the same topic in more than one language constitute the equivalent of a comparable corpus. In our information dominated society, such collections are becoming increasingly available and the need for effective methods for searching them in a user-friendly way is growing, i.e. it should be possible to formulate queries in one language and retrieve all relevant documents matching the query in whatever language they are stored.

The comparable corpus query system is based on the assumptions that (i) words acquire sense from their context, and (ii) words used in a similar way throughout a sub-language or special domain set of documents will be semantically similar. It follows that, if it is possible to establish equivalences between several items contained in two different contexts, there is a high probability that the two contexts themselves are to some extent similar. Lexical knowledge is thus extracted from a domain-specific document collection in one language and projected onto comparable collections in other languages; i.e. given a particular term or set of terms in the document collection in one language, the aim is to be able to identify contexts which contain equivalent or related expressions in the collections in other languages. To do this, the vocabulary related to that term in the documents in the first language (which we call the source language) is isolated – hypothesising that lexically equivalent terms will be associated with a similar vocabulary in the target languages. However, so far, this system has only been tested for a pair of languages: Italian and English, using a bilingual Italian/English dictionary and an Italian/English corpus (Picchi and Peters, 1996). The multilinguality of EWN will give us the opportunity to extend this methodology and apply it to document collections in more than two languages; we will also be able to test the effectiveness of the additional features offered by EWN with respect to the bilingual lexicon that has been used so far.

5.2. METHODOLOGY

If we have a collection of documents on a given topic in two or more of the EWN languages, for any term of interest, T, searched in one language, the objective is to be able to retrieve a ranked list of documents containing equivalent terms in the other languages. Thus when T is entered, the system will automatically construct a context window containing T and up to n lexically significant words (nouns and verbs only) to the right and left of T for the set of documents in the collection. The value for n can be varied. For each of these co-occurrences of T, morphological procedures identify the base lemma(s), i.e. each word-form is stemmed in order to match it against equivalent forms and to identify the relevant entry that will be looked up in the EWN database. The significance of the correlation between its collocates and T is then calculated using a statistical procedure. Church and Hanks' Mutual Information Index (Church and Hanks, 1990) is currently used in these procedures, although a different measure based on the likelihood ratio as formulated by Dunning (1993) is also being tested.

The set of most significant collocates derived makes up the vocabulary, V, that is considered to characterize the term, T, in the particular document collection being analyzed. The next step is to establish equivalent target-language vocabularies for T in each different set of documents being searched. These vocabularies represent the potential significant collocates for T in the target languages. This will be done by looking up each item of vocabulary V in the EWN database and extracting the entire set of potential cross-language equivalents, including all equivalent synonyms and cross POS equivalents. The target language vocabularies for T are thus significantly larger than the source language vocabulary. Words or expressions that can be considered as lexically equivalent to the selected term in the source language texts will then be searched in the document sets in other languages, i.e. this is done by searching for those contexts in the target language collections in which there is a significant presence of the target language vocabulary for T. The significance is determined on the basis of a statistical procedure that assesses the probability for different sets of target language cooccurrences to represent lexically equivalent contexts for T. The target language contexts retrieved are written in a file and listed in descending order of relevance to the original query term. Information extracted from EWN can be used to weight the term in the target language vocabulary for T, e.g. cross-language equivalent synonyms will be given a higher value than cross-language equivalents with a different part-of-speech.

In the experiments performed so far, the creation of target language vocabularies for any term of interest, T, has been performed on-line. In a real-world retrieval context, the creation of such vocabularies would be done off-line, periodically, as a multilingual document collection increases, in order to optimize the on-line search times.

In this way, we can develop a multilingual search tool which combines the features of a knowledge-based tool with that of a corpus-based procedure and thus searches for both terms for which multilingual equivalences can be identified in

EWN but also for cross-language lexical equivalences which are not included in our multilingual database.

5.3. SEARCH TERM DISAMBIGUATION

Although the problem of polysemy is greatly reduced in a domain specific corpus, it is still present – to a varying degree depending on the type of texts being treated. The construction of the source language vocabulary which characterizes the term T permits us to obtain a clustering of the most relevant terms connected to T. If the corpus contains a predominant sense for the term then the vocabulary should represent this sense – secondary senses that appear rarely will not interfere with this. If, in the corpus, there is more than one relevant sense for T then we would expect two or more distinct clusterings of significant collocates. For example, the Italian noun *accordo* has two distinct senses in the Italian component of EuroWordNet: the general sense which is mapped to the ILI synset *agreement; understanding*, and the very specific musical sense mapped to *chord*. Testing the system on a corpus of parliamentary debates, no examples of the second sense were found. However, if there had been a significant occurrence of the second sense too, two distinct clusterings of significant collocates with little or no overlap should be found. A technique is now being studied which should make it possible to separate distinct senses of the same word in a text collection on the basis of their collocates; the sets of most strongly related words will be built for each collocate and then compared to identify overlapping. In this way, it should be possible to distinguish between common technical terms which are used with different meanings in different scientific areas. Think, for example, of the different usage of *protocol* in the medical and software engineering domains. Very different sets of collocates would be constructed for the different acceptions of this term and thus searching for the appropriate sense would be facilitated.

5.4. TARGET TERM DISAMBIGUATION

When constructing the target language vocabularies of significant collocates for the source language term being searched, the procedure will take as input all the cross-language equivalent synonyms provided by EWN, regardless of sense distinctions. Spurious or inappropriate translations are eliminated by the fact that they are not normally found together with a significant number of other items from the target language vocabularies for the term being searched. This makes it possible to perform a sense disambiguation on the target terms proposed. For example, examining all the occurrences of the Italian noun *sicurezza* in the test corpus, we find that the sense is that of *safety*, or *security*. This is confirmed by the set of significant collocates for this term; the top ten are the Italian equivalents of toy, hygiene, reactor, health, nuclear, maritime, council, road, provisions, Euratom.

The EWN entries for *safety*, and *security* include the following possible synonyms in the different senses: for the six senses of *safety*, we have *refuge, guard, base hit, condom, rubber, prophylactic*; for the seven senses of *security*, we find *protection, certificate, surety, guarantee, warranty*. Of these potential synonyms, only *protection* is actually relevant, as a cross-language equivalence of the Italian term *sicurezza* that we are searching. Most of the irrelevant word senses are not found in the test corpus; but even if they should appear, the contexts containing them are ranked very low as they will not contain significant collocates from the target language vocabulary of related cooccurrences constructed for the source language search term: *sicurezza*. Thus, this approach helps us to identify the correct sense of the target terms offered by EWN and to provide a ranking of the best target language matches for the term searched.

5.5. SUMMING UP

In this proposal for integrating EWN in a corpus-based approach, queries are translated using the multilingual database and extended by including cross-language synonyms and cross-POS equivalents, but they are also expanded by applying the comparable-corpus based strategy in order to associate with each query term, not only its direct translations but also a vocabulary which defines its probable immediate context, in the query language and in the target language(s).

In this way, we search for both pre-identified translation equivalents and also cross-language lexical equivalences. When EWN offers no translation equivalent, the search for cross-language equivalent contexts is still possible. Documents retrieved are ranked with respect to (i) translation equivalents of query terms, (ii) statistical values assigned to associated significant collocates, on the basis of their status in the EWN database with respect to the query term.

A limitation of this type of statistically-based querying over domain-specific archives is that it is only feasible when the text collection is sufficiently large and sufficiently homogeneous to be able to derive a statistically meaningful set of collocates for the terms queried.

6. Conclusions

The existence of large-scale semantic databases, such as EuroWordNet, opens new and challenging possibilities for cross-language text retrieval, among other applications.

We began this paper by discussing why we feel that the additional features of the EWN database mean that it will probably be more effective for cross-language text retrieval than WordNet has proved so far in monolingual retrieval experiments.

In order to illustrate this thesis, we presented two approaches that describe how EWN can be applied to CLTR. The first approach indexes documents and queries in terms of the EuroWordNet Inter-Lingual-Index, thus turning term weighting and query/document matching into language-independent tasks. The second one integrates the information in the EWN database with corpus-based techniques, thus allowing retrieval for domain-specific terms that may not be present in our multilingual database.

Each methodology addresses a different aspect of text retrieval: Our first approach is well-suited for querying over heterogeneous document collections such as WWW searches, as it is language-independent and does not require training with multilingual corpora. The second approach, on the other hand, is best suited for retrieval over domain-specific collections, where the document sets are homogeneous and technical vocabularies play an essential role.

Considering the two approaches that we have discussed here, we are convinced that the building of the EuroWordNet database offers an excellent opportunity to experiment with truly multilingual (rather than just bilingual or cross-language) text retrieval and information extraction. And vice versa: CLTR is an excellent testbed to measure the quality of the EWN database.

Acknowledgements

This research is being supported by the European Community, project LE #4003 and also partially by the Spanish government, project TIC-96-1243-CO3-O1.

References

Alonge, A., N. Calzolari, P. Vossen, L. Bloksma, I. Castellon, T. Marti and W. Peters. "The Linguistic Design of the EuroWordNet Database". *Computers and the Humanities, Special Issue on EuroWordNet* (this volume) (1998).

Ballesteros, L. and W. Croft. "Dictionary-based Methods for Cross-lingual Information Retrieval". In *Proceedings of the 7th International DEXA Conference on Database and Expert Systems Applications*, 1996, pp. 791–801.

Brill, E. "A Simple Rule-based Part of Speech Tagger". In *Proceedings of the Third Conference on Applied Natural Language Processing*, 1992.

Carbonell, J., Y. Yang, R. Frederking, R. Brown, Y. Geng and D. Lee. "Translingual Information Retrieval". In *Proceedings of IJCAI'97*, 1997.

Chai, J. and A. Bierman. "The Use of Lexical Semantics in Information Extraction". *Proceedings of the ACL/EACL'97 Workshop on Automatic Information Extraction and Building of Lexical Semantic Resources.* Eds. P. Vossen, G. Adriaens, N. Calzolari, A. Sanfilippo and Y. Wilks, 1997.

Church, K. and P. Hanks. "Word Association Norms, Mutual Information and Lexicography". *Computational Linguistics*, 16(1) (1990), 22–29.

Dumais, S., T. Landauer and M. Littman. "Automatic Cross-linguistic Information Retrieval Using Latent Semantic Indexing". In *Working Notes of the Workshop on Cross-Linguistic Information Retrieval, ACM SIGIR'96*, 1996, pp. 16–23.

Dunning, T. "Accurate Methods for the Statistics of Surprise and Coincidence". *Computational Linguistics*, 19(1) (1993).

Fujii, A., T. Hasegawa, T. Tokunaga and H. Tanaka. "Integration of Hand-crafted and Statistical Resources in Measuring Word Similarity". *Proceedings of the ACL/EACL'97 Workshop on*

Automatic Information Extraction and Building of Lexical Semantic Resources. Eds. P. Vossen, G. Adriaens, N. Calzolari, A. Sanfilippo and Y. Wilks, 1997.

Gilarranz, J., J. Gonzalo and M. Verdejo. "An Approach to Cross-language Text Retrieval with the EuroWordNet Semantic Database". In *AAAI Spring Symposium on Cross-Language Text and Speech Retrieval.* AAAI Press SS-97-05, 1997, pp. 49–55.

Gonzalo, J., M. F. Verdejo, I. Chugur and J. Cigarrán. "Indexing with WordNet Synsets can Improve Text Retrieval". In *Proceedings of the ACL/COLING Workshop on Usage of WordNet for Natural Language Processing,* 1998.

Grishman, R., C. Macleod and J. Sterling. "New York University Description of the Proteus System as Used for MUC-4". In *Proceedings of the Fourth Message Understanding Conference,* 1992, pp. 223–241.

Harman, D. K. "The First Text Retrieval Conference (trec-1)". *Information Processing and Management,* 29(4) (1993), 411–414.

Hull, D. and G. Grefenstette. "Querying across Languages. A Dictionary-based Approach to Multilingual Information Retrieval". In *Proceedings of the 19th ACM SIGIR Conference,* 1996, pp. 49–57.

Krovetz, R. and W. Croft. "Lexical Ambiguity and Information Retrieval". *ACM Transactions on Information Systems,* 10(2), 1992, 115–141.

Kurohashi, S. and M. Nagao. "A Method of Case Structure Analysis for Japanese Sentences Based on Examples in Case Frame Dictionary". *IEEE Transactions on Information and Systems,* E77-D(2) (1994), 227–239.

Li, H. and N. Abe. "Generalizing Case Frames Using a Thesaurus and the Mdl Principle". In *Proceedings of Recent Advances in Natural Language Processing,* 1995, pp. 239–248.

McCarthy, D. "Word Sense Disambiguation for Acquisition of Selectional Preferences". In *Proceedings of the ACL/EACL'97 Workshop on Automatic Information Extraction and Building of Lexical Semantic Resources.* Eds. P. Vossen, G. Adriaens, N. Calzolari, A. Sanfilippo and Y. Wilks, 1997.

Miller, G., C. Beckwith, D. Fellbaum, D. Gross and K. Miller. Five Papers on WordNet, CSL Report 43. Technical report, Cognitive Science Laboratory, Princeton University, 1990.

Miller, G. A., C. Leacock, R. Tengi and R. T. Bunker. "A Semantic Concordance". In *Proceedings of the ARPA Workshop on Human Language Technology.* Morgan Kauffman, 1993.

Màrquez, L. and L. Padró. "A Flexible POS Tagger Using an Automatically Acquired Language Model". In *Proceedings of ACL/EACL'97,* 1997.

Ng, H. T. "Exemplar-based Word Sense Disambiguation: Some Recent Improvements". In *Proceedings of the Second Conference on Empirical Methods in NLP,* 1997.

Peters, W., P. Vossen, P. Díez-Orzas and G. Adriaens. "The Multilingual Design of the EuroWordNet Database". *Computers and the Humanities, Special Issue on EuroWordNet* (this volume), 1998.

Picchi, E. and C. Peters. "Cross Language Information Retrieval: A System for Comparable Corpus Querying". In *Working Notes of the Workshop on Cross-Linguistic Information Retrieval, ACM SIGIR'96.* Ed. G. Grefenstette, 1996, pp. 24–33.

Resnik, P. "Using Information Content to Evaluate Semantic Similarity in a Taxonomy". In *Proceedings of IJCAI,* 1995.

Ribas, F. "On Learning more Appropriate Selectional Restrictions". In *Proceedings of the Seventh Conference of the European Chapter of the Association for Computational Linguistics,* 1995, pp. 112–118.

Richardson, R. and A. Smeaton. "Using WordNet in a Knowledge-based Approach to Information Retrieval". In *Proceedings of the BCS-IRSG Colloquium, Crewe,* 1995.

Rodríguez, H., S. Climent, P. Vossen, L. Bloksma, A. Roventini, F. Bertagna, A. Alonge and W. Peters. "The Top-down Strategy for Building EuroWordNet: Vocabulary Coverage, Base Concepts and Top Ontology". *Computers and the Humanities, Special Issue on EuroWordNet* (this volume), 1998.

Salton, G. (ed.). *The SMART Retrieval System: Experiments in Automatic Document Processing.* Prentice-Hall, 1971.

Sanderson, M. "Word Sense Disambiguation and Information Retrieval". In *Proceedings of 17th International Conference on Research and Development in Information Retrieval*, 1994.

Sanfilippo, A. "Using Semantic Similarity to Acquire Co-occurrence Restrictions from Corpora". In *Proceedings of the ACL/EACL'97 Workshop on Automatic Information Extraction and Building of Lexical Semantic Resources*. Eds. P. Vossen, G. Adriaens, N. Calzolari, A. Sanfilippo and Y. Wilks, 1997.

Segond, F., A. Schiller, G. Grefenstette and J. Chanod. "An Experiment in Semantic Tagging Using Hidden Markov Model Tagging". *Proceedings of the ACL/EACL'97 Workshop on Automatic Information Extraction and Building of Lexical Semantic Resources*. Eds. P. Vossen, G. Adriaens, N. Calzolari, A. Sanfilippo and Y. Wilks, 1997.

Sheridan, P. and J. Ballerini. "Experiments in Multilingual Information Retrieval Using the Spider System". In *Proceedings of the 19th ACM SIGIR Conference*, 1996, pp. 58–65.

Smeaton, A., F. Kelledy and R. O'Donnell. "TREC-4 Experiments at Dublin City University: Thresolding Posting Lists, Query Expansion with WordNet and POS Tagging of Spanish". In *Proceedings of TREC-4*, 1995.

Smeaton, A. and A. Quigley. "Experiments on Using Semantic Distances between Words in Image Caption Retrieval". In *Proceedings of the 19th International Conference on Research and Development in IR*, 1996.

Voorhees, E. M. "Query Expansion Using Lexical-semantic Relations". In *Proceedings of the 17th Annual International ACM-SIGIR Conference on Research and Development in Information Retrieval*, 1994.

Vossen, P. "Introduction to EuroWordNet". *Computers and the Humanities, Special Issue on EuroWordNet* (this volume), 1998.

Computers and the Humanities **32:** 209–220, 1998.
© 1998 *Kluwer Academic Publishers.*

A Semantic Network of English: The Mother of All WordNets

CHRISTIANE FELLBAUM

Cognitive Science Laboratory, Princeton University, and Rider University, Princeton, NJ, USA

Key words: lexicon, semantic network, Natural Language Processing

Abstract. We give a brief outline of the design and contents of the English lexical database WordNet, which serves as a model for similarly conceived wordnets in several European languages. WordNet is a semantic network, in which the meanings of nouns, verbs, adjectives, and adverbs are represented in terms of their links to other (groups of) words via conceptual-semantic and lexical relations. Each part of speech is treated differently reflecting different semantic properties. We briefly discuss polysemy in WordNet, and focus on the case of meaning extensions in the verb lexicon. Finally, we outline the potential uses of WordNet not only for applications in natural language processing, but also for research in stylistic analyses in conjunction with a semantic concordance.[1]

1. Introduction

WordNet began more than a decade ago as an experiment, the brainchild of George A. Miller (Miller, 1986). Miller and his co-workers in the Cognitive Science Laboratory at Princeton University wanted to find out whether a semantic network could be constructed not just for a handful of words but for the better part of the vocabulary of a natural language. Over the years WordNet has grown into a large lexical database that has become the tool of choice for researchers in many areas of computational linguistics in dozen of countries. But people are not just using WordNet; some are reproducing it for languages other than English. As WordNet became synonymous with a particular kind of lexicon design, the proper name shed its capital letters and became a common designator for semantic networks of natural languages.

While the second-generation wordnets retain the underlying design of the English WordNet, they differ in a number of aspects, reflecting choices that were made with an eye towards specific goals and applications (see Alonge et al., this volume). As can be seen from G. A. Miller's (1998a) account of the history of WordNet, the aspirations of the project more than a decade ago were quite different and far more modest than what is needed for ambitious applications in natural language processing today. WordNet represented an original experiment that could not benefit from the experience of predecessors. Miller (1998a) chronicles the modifications and enlargements that WordNet underwent over the years to accommodate both our growing understanding of the lexicon's properties when viewed through a relational lens, and the applications that the research community was eager to explore with the help of WordNet.

This paper outlines some of the ideas behind WordNet, as well as some of the unresolved problems.[2] In addition, we discuss some applications of WordNet that have not yet been fully explored but that have a potential for new research.

2. Design and Contents of WordNet

WordNet's coverage extends over the four major parts of speech, nouns, verbs, adjectives, and adverbs. The current version (1.6) contains approximately 94,000 distinct noun forms, 10,000 verb forms, 20,000 adjective forms, and 4,500 adverb forms.

Like a standard dictionary, WordNet includes not just single words, but also compound nouns (like *water wheel*) and collocations (like *kick the bucket*). Unlike a standard dictionary, WordNet does not take the word, or lexeme, as its elementary building block. Instead, WordNet resembles a thesaurus in that its units are concepts, lexicalized by one or more strings of letters, or word form. A group of words that can all refer to the same concept is dubbed a synonym set, or synset.[3]

In WordNet's web structure, words and synsets are linked to other words and synsets by means of conceptual-semantic and lexical relations. The user of WordNet finds a word's meaning given not only in terms of the other members of the same synset, but, in addition, via its relations to other words, that is, in terms of its location within the net. For example, one meaning of *dog* is given, in part, by all the terms that refer to kinds of *dog*, including *corgi*, *poodle*, and *dalmatian*. The meanings of *corgi*, *poodle*, and *dalmatian*, in turn, are given partly in terms of their superordinate concept, *dog*.

2.1. NOUNS IN WORDNET

The conceptual-semantic relations are not the same for the different parts of speech. Noun synsets are connected to one another principally by the superordinate relationship, or hyponymy (Miller, 1990, 1998b), illustrated above by the *corgi – dog* example. Hyponymy, or the IS-A relation, builds hierarchical structures that can have as many as twelve levels, ranging from a very generic concept to highly specific, often technical ones. Arranging concepts in terms of this class inclusion relation also seems to capture an important priciple of knowledge representation in human lexical memory (Miller, 1998b).

The other major relation between noun synsets is the part-whole relation, or meronymy. For example, *book* and *binding* are linked by means of meronymy, as are *keratin* and *hair*. While Chaffin, Hermann, and Winston (1988) noted the polysemy of the meronymy relation and identified seven semantically distinct types of parts and wholes, WordNet limits itself to three kinds. WordNet distinguishes separable parts such as *blade* and *head*, which are parts of *knife* and *body*, respectively; members of groups (like *professor – faculty*), and substances such as *oxygen*, which is a component of *air* and *water* (Miller, 1990, 1998b).

Hyponymy is a transitive relation, in that a *miniature poodle* is a kind of *dog* by virtue of the fact that its direct superordinate, *poodle*, is a kind of *dog*. By contrast, the transitivity of the meronomy relations coded in WordNet is limited; while a *fingernail* is a part of *finger*, which in turn is part of a *hand*, which is part of an *arm*, it sounds odd to say that a *fingernail* is part of an *arm* (see Miller, 1998b, for a detailed discussion).

Linguists, psychologists, and philosophers generally have paid more attention to nouns and the concepts associated with them than to words from other lexical categories. Nouns could be represented in a fairly straightforward way in WordNet, and their clear organization has made them the favorite target for NLP applications (see Fellbaum, 1998a, for a representative selection).

The noun lexicon is also a good place to look for lexical gaps, in particular when comparing the noun component of WordNet with those of the languages that make up EuroWordNet (see Vossen, this volume; Peters et al., this volume). In many cases, one language has a label for a certain concept that is referred to in another language by a compound noun or a phrase. For example, the meaning of the French noun *rentrée* can be expressed in English only by an entire phrase, "the start of the school or university year", although the concept is probably equally salient in both cultures. On the other hand, French does not have a simple word corresponding to *schedule* (as in the sentence "I have a busy schedule") and must do with the complex expression *emploi du temps*, literally "use of time."

These two examples pertain to fairly specific concepts. An interesting question is whether lexical gaps can be found on the more generic levels in noun hierarchies of one or more languages or whether missing words tend to be confined to more specialized concepts that are located towards the bottom of hierarchies (see the other papers in this volume). In any case, the construction of multilingual word-nets might yield some generalizations pertaining to the lexicalization patterns in different languages and allow for a new perspective that WordNet alone could not afford.

2.2. ADJECTIVES IN WORDNET

Adjectives are part of the original WordNet, but they are not included in EuroWord-Net. As modifiers, the information conveyed by adjectives is perhaps less vital for understanding sentences in an NLP system than that carried by nouns and verbs. At the same time, adjectives are highly polysemous, and their meaning is determined, to a large degree, by the head noun that they modify. For example, in the phrase *big bank*, the adjective does not contribute anything towards resolving the ambiguity inherent in the noun, although the meaning of the adjective differs depending on whether one is talking about an embankment or a financial institution. Their polysemy makes the semantics of adjectives difficult to capture in an enumerative lexicon like WordNet, which attempts to capture and distinguish all the senses of a polysemous word form.

On the other hand, many of the less frequent (and less polysemous) adjectives are choosy with regard to the nouns that they co-occur with, and examining the adjective in a phrase containing a polysemous noun may help to disambiguate that noun. Thus, a *steep bank* can only denote a certain kind of slope or incline, whereas an *international bank* is unambiguously a financial institution. This suggests a division between a small group of highly polysemous (and highly frequent) core adjectives like *big, little, good, bad, old, new*, etc., and a larger group of less chameleon-like, more discriminating adjectives, including *steep* and *international*.

In WordNet, a distinction between highly frequent, highly polysemous adjectives and less frequent, less polysemous ones was not deliberately drawn with an eye towards noun sense disambiguation, but it is reflected in the differentiation between "direct" and "indirect" antonyms. This distinction arose from the recognition that, unlike nouns and verbs, adjectives do not lend themselves to a hierarchical organization. Instead, they fall into clusters centered around two antonymic ajectives. For example, *long* and *short* are considered "direct antonyms" in WordNet (Gross, Fischer and Miller, 1989; Miller, K., 1998).

Direct antonyms have a number of interesting properties. In addition to their promiscuity with respect to the choice of head nouns and the resulting polysemy, direct antonym pairs are psychologically salient. They occur with great frequency in the language and are acquired early by children; their members elicit each other in word association experiments, and they co-occur in the same sentence with frequencies much higher than chance (Justeson and Katz, 1991).

Direct antonym pairs constitute a conspicuous but small part of the adjective lexicon. Many more adjectives are classified in WordNet as "semantically similar" to the members of the direct antonym pairs. Thus, *brief, clipped*, and *abbreviated* are adjectives that are similar to (the temporal sense of) *short*, while *durable, eternal*, and *protracted* are similar to its direct antonym, *long*. Adjectives like *abbreviated* and *eternal* are considered "indirect antonyms" of *long* and *short*, respectively. The organization of adjectives in WordNet can thus be visualized in terms of barbell-like structures, with a direct antonym in the center of each disk surrounded by its semantically similar adjectives (which constitue the indirect antonyms of the adjectives in the opposed disk). Indirect antonyms are compatible with fewer head nouns; thus, they are less polysemous and probably contribute to the disambiguation of their head nouns when these are polysemous.

Direct antonymy links specific pairs of adjectives rather than synsets; while *long* and *brief* are semantic opposites, the salient relation exists only between *long* and *short*. The same is true for semantic opposition found elsewhere in the lexicon; the verbs *rise* and *fall* form a salient pair based on the semantic opposition between them; this is not the case for *rise* and *descend*. Antonymy, or, more generally, semantic opposition, is therefore a lexical relation, which holds between individual lexemes rather than between all the members of the synsets.

Finally, so-called relational adjectives like *atomic* and *industrial* are not organized like qualitative adjectives, because their semantics cannot be captured within the barbell model. In WordNet, these adjectives point to the nouns to which they pertain (*atom* and *industry*, respectively). Relational adjectives, too, are less polysemous than core adjectives like *big* and *old*. They can sometimes be replaced by the noun from which they are derived (*atomic/atom bomb, musical/music education*). Thus, a noun modified by a relational adjectives somewhat resembles a compound noun; the inclusion of this class of adjectives in a database that is largely intended for word sense disambiguation and information retrieval might be profitable.

2.3. ADVERBS

WordNet 1.6 contains 4,500 different adverbs. Most of these are derived via *-ly* affixation from the adjectives to which they are semantically related. Whenever possible, adverbs are linked to antonymic adverbs, following the organization of the adjectives from which they are derived. For lexical adverbs like *hard* and *even* no particular organization has been implemented.

2.4. VERBS

Verbs in WordNet are arranged primarily by a manner-of relation dubbed "troponymy" (Fellbaum, 1990, 1998). Troponymy relates two verbs such that one verb specifies a certain manner of carrying out the action referred to by the other verb. For example, *swipe, sock, smack,* and *tap* are troponyms of *hit*, because they refer to particular ways of hitting that are distinguished according to the degree of force with which someone hits someone or something. For verbs denoting events, troponymy similary relates a more general to a semantically more elaborate concept. Thus, *plummet* is a troponym of *drop*.

Troponymy builds hierarchical structures similar to the hyponymy relation among noun synsets. However, the verb trees are flatter than the noun trees and rather more like bushes, rarely exceeding four levels. Like meronymy, troponymy is a polysemous relation that subsumes many different kinds of manners, depending on the semantic field. Verbs of motion are semantically elaborated along such dimensions as speed (*walk – run*), direction (*rise – fall*), and means of displacement (*walk – drive*). Communication verbs like *talk* have troponyms that specify the volume (*whisper, murmur, shout, yell*) or the speed and fluency (*stammer, yack, spout*) of the talker. No distinction is made in WordNet between different kinds of troponymy.

Other relations among verbs include semantic opposition, which, like troponymy, is polysemous; motion verbs often form opposing pairs based on the direction of the motion (*rise – fall; come – go*), while the opposition found among

verbs in the semantic field of "possession" often is of a converse nature (*give –
take; buy – sell*).

Finally, verbs are related by various kinds of lexical entailment. For example,
eating entails *swallowing*: When people eat, they necessarily swallow. A different
kind of entailment is backward presupposition, exemplified by *untie* and *tie*: in
order to untie (something), someone must have tied (something) in the first place.
Finally, *snore* entails *sleep*, because when one snores, one necessarily sleeps. These
kinds of entailment differ from each other with respect to the temporal relations
between the two activities denoted by the verbs (Fellbaum, 1990).

Troponymy is a kind of entailment, too, because it is true that when one whis-
pers or shouts, one necessarily talks. But whereas the relation between whispering
or shouting can, in addition, be expressed in terms of manner, this is not the case
for the other kinds of entailment: snoring is not a kind of sleeping, swallowing is
not a manner of eating, etc.

In all cases, the entailment holds only in one direction. Swallowing does not
entail eating; going does not entail stopping, sleeping does not entail snoring, and
speaking does not entail whispering or shouting. This unilateral relation is similar
to some kinds of meronymy. Some nouns refer to groups, collections, or substances
that exist only by virtue of their parts, members, or ingredients. At the same time,
the entities that constitute the parts, members, or ingredients can exist outside of
these groups, collections, or substances. For example, a library is not a library
unless it contains books as its most important part. But a book is not necessarily
defined as a part of a library. Similarly, a forest must contain trees, but a tree is
not necessarily a part of a forest. And while a martini necessarily contains gin, gin
exists outside a martini.

3. Polysemy in WordNet

The semantic distinctions drawn in WordNet are rather fine-grained, and it turned
out that the different senses of many polysemous words were not clearly distinguishable when given only in terms of their relations to other words (also see Peters
et al., this volume). To make WordNet more informative and to better support on-
going efforts in automated sense disambiguation, definitional glosses and example
sentences were added. The content words in these glosses and definitions, in turn,
can all be found in WordNet's synsets, though we do not know at this point whether
all their senses are covered.

WordNet does not distinguish between polysemes and homonyms. On the other
hand, many cases of regular and predictable polysemy are grouped together to indicate the close semantic relation of the different senses. Weinreich (1972), Apresjan
(1973), Nunberg (1978), Ostler and Atkins (1991), and others have noted that a
word like *magazine* can refer to the printed product (as in (1)), the institution that
publishes the magazine (as in (2)), or the printed content (as in (3)) below.

(1) He held the magazine in his hands.

(2) The magazine was bought by the publishing tycoon.

(3) The magazine made some spectacular accusations against the politician.

Depending on the context, these readings can be distinguished or they can be conflated, as in a sentence like (4):

(4) I like this magazine.

The regularity of this kind of polysemy is reflected in the fact that many nouns referring to publications, including *book*, *newspaper*, and *journal*, display it. In many cases, the related senses are grouped together in WordNet to distinguish them from unrelated senses (such as the sense of *magazine* referring to a powder store).

In WordNet, polysemes like *magazine* and *newspaper* that exhibit the same kind or regular and predictable polysemy due to shared superordinates (*publication, publishing house* and *product* in this case), are called "cousins."

Related senses of polysemous verbs, too, are often grouped together. In many cases, these relations are regular and predictable as well. For example, many verbs denoting a change of state or motion have both a causative (transitive) and a intransitive use. For example, *walk* can be an intransitive verb ("The men walked up the hill") or a transitive, causative one ("They walked the prisoners down the hill/They walked their dogs"). These two senses are grouped together in WordNet and distinguished from less similar senses of *walk*, such as the one in the expression *walk in sadness*. Similarly, the verbs in the two sentences "He broke the vase" and "The vase broke" refer to the same event; the first verb has the added component of causativity. Such causative and intransitive (inchoative) verb pairs are often grouped together in WordNet and distinguished from other, unrelated senses (such as the sense of "break" in "The news broke"). English has hundreds of causative-inchoative verb pairs, showing that the relation here is not confined to a few cases, but that it is an important part of the verb lexicon (see Levin, 1993, for a list of such verb pairs and references).

Similarly, many transitive verbs have a so-called middle alternation, as illustrated in

(5) My students read Russian novels this semester.

(6) Russian novels read easily.

While (5) refers to an action or event, (6) is stative and has generic character. The middle refers to a property of the referent of the subject NP that allows any potential agent to carry out the action referred to by the transitive in the manner referred to by the adverb (Keyser and Roeper, 1984; Fellbaum, 1985a,b; and others). But the semantic relation between (5) and (6) is clearly there, and it is indicated in Word-Net by means of assigning these two senses to one semantic sub-group of senses. The hierarchical structure of WordNet does not allow for indicating the semantic relatedness in any other way. The verb in (5) is a verb of change, while the verb in (6) is a stative verb; thus, the two verbs are assigned to different superordinate concepts in different "trees" in the net (Fellbaum, 1998a).

3.1. NON-LITERAL LANGUAGE IN WORDNET

A special kind of polysemy is represented by lexemes that have both literal and non-literal reference. For example, consider two meanings of *heart*, exemplified in

(7) His heart stopped.

(8) He immediately won the hearts of the people.

While it is difficult to draw a categorical distinction between literal and non-literal language or to define the latter clearly, most speakers would probably classify the second meaning ("affection") as a metaphor, i.e., as a non-literal extension. WordNet is blind to this distinction; in each case, *heart* is a referring expression and can be represented in the semantic net like any other meaning-bearing noun. The user, when querying WordNet on the string *heart*, will get both senses (in addition to others). Similarly, idiomatic verb phrases like *kick the bucket* and *trip the light fantastic* are included in the appropriate synsets together with their literal synonyms (*die* and *dance*, respectively.)

Fellbaum (1998b) notes that sense extensions of verbs frequently share not only the meanings but also the syntax of their literal synonyms. Verbs that are classified as unaccusatives (ergatives), are believed, like passives, to have a derived, rather than an underlying, subject; moreover they show certain characteristics, such as the selection of the auxiliary *be* in most Romance and Germanic languages and the inability to take a direct object (Perlmutter, 1970, and others).

Semantically, they tend to denote changes of state or motions that are not controlled by their surface subjects. Unaccusative verbs in English include *fall, break, (dis)appear, die,* and *bloom.*

For example, an extended meaning of *die*, as in (9)

(9) My computer died last night.

can be found in the same synset with *break* and *go*, two unaccusative verbs. *Burst* in a sentence like (10)

(10) He burst into view.

means "emerge"; both are unaccusatives. It seems, therefore, that the meaning extension of verbs proceeds in a systematic and non-haphazard way: the extended sense(s) that a given verb takes on are syntactically similar to the literal senses of that verb. Thus, we would not expect a verb like *smoke*, a verb with transitive and unergative surface realizations, to be able to express the meaning of *break*, as *die* does in (9). Similarly, some unaccusative verbs that take on extended meanings do not have simple synonyms but can be paraphrased as passive phrases; both unaccusatives and passives are characterized by the absence of an underlying, agentive subject. For example, *appear* in the sentence

(11) Her book will appear this Fall.

means "will be published." Similarly, *fall* in

(12) This falls into a special category.

can be paraphrased as "is classified or included."

It is most unlikely that accusative verbs like *hit* or *buy* would ever take on meanings like "be published" or "be included."

Because WordNet structures the lexicon into synsets, it permits one to examine the particular kind of polysemy represented by nonliteral language. In the case of verbs, one can look for relations between literally and metaphorically referring members of a synset, as well as analyze the relation between literal and extended meanings of verb forms.

4. The Semantic Concordance

A considerable amount of work has been done in the area of semantic disambiguation in connection with the WordNet database. Automatic sense disambiguation is an important and difficult problem for NLP, yet determining the sense of a polysemous word that is intended in a particular context is vital for practical applications such as Information Retrieval and Machine Translation. One step towards teaching a computer to recognize the appropriate meaning of a polysemous word is to feed it information about the contexts in which a given sense appears. In order to obtain such information, one must of course examine a fairly large body of text and collect the contexts that are needed to sufficiently characterize the use of a particular word sense and that distinguish it from the use of other senses of the same word form. For example, the noun *line* most likely has the sense "queue" when it appears in close proximity to the verb *wait* (Leacock, Chodorow and Miller, 1998).[4]

To this end, the WordNet group has created a semantic concordance (Miller et al., 1995; Landes et al., 1998), a body of text where each content word (noun, verb, adjective, adverb) is linked to (one of) its particular sense(s) in the Word-Net database. The result is a semantically "tagged", disambiguated text, which is potentially useful for various kinds of NLP applications.

So far, the Princeton group has completely tagged one literary work, Stephen Crane's novella *The Red Badge of Courage*. In addition, large parts of the Brown Corpus were semantically annotated.

Semantic tagging continues at the Princeton Cognitive Science Laboratory with the aid of specially designed software and an interface ("ConText") that facilitate the tagging task. However, in contrast to the *Red Badge of Courage* and the Brown Corpus, which were tagged sequentially, specific nouns and verbs are now being selected and tagged, with the aim of creating a corpus of polysemous, high-frequency words and attested contexts for each of their different senses. These sets of contexts are expected to facilitate automatic disambiguation (Leacock et al., 1998).[5]

In addition to determining the linguistic environments of certain word senses for the purposes of automatic sense disambiguation, semantic concordances can be useful in areas outside computational linguistics and NLP.

4.1. STYLISTIC TEXT ANALYSES

Researchers can quickly search a text for occurrences of a particular sense of a polysemous word. Senses that are not relevant to the search will not be returned, making a search faster and more efficient. This feature is potentially useful for subtle text analyses.

People studying particular authors' styles or trying to determine authorship of a literary work on the basis of style and word usage often search the author's (or authors') text corpus for the use of word *forms* only, independent of the particular meaning of polysemous word forms. In the case where the author whose work is being studied does not use a polysemous word such as, for example, *flower* significantly more often or in different contexts than other authors, no conclusion can be drawn from his use of this word.

Semantic concordances allow for more fine-grained stylistic typing and let the researcher determine not only which word form a given author tends to use more frequently or in a particular way, but, more precisely, whether or not an author uses a given word form with a particular sense in a characteristic manner.

If an author's work has been semantically tagged, one can distinguish whether or not the author uses a particular sense of polysemous words like *flower* in a characteristic manner. For example, one may find that one author tends to use *flower* when referring to a plant, whereas another author characteristically uses this noun to refer to a period of life, which is referred to by the first author by the word *prime*. Thus, the two authors' styles may be distinguished by virtue of the way in which they use the polysemous noun *flower* to denote different entities. A semantic concordance therefore allows a more subtle analysis of authors' style and usage of words than an analysis that relies only in the use of word forms regardless of their meanings.

So far, the Princeton group has completely tagged only one literary work, *The Red Badge of Courage*. Once automatic sense tagging has become feasible and reliable, others should follow, and make possible a stylistic comparison between the different authors. The tagging of the newspaper corpus, including words from the *Wall Street Journal* and the *San Jose Monitor*, will permit comparisons concerning the use of polysemous words. A statistical analysis of the usage of polysemous word senses might firm up one's intuitions concerning genre (e.g., novella vs. newspaper) or topic matter (e.g., political vs. economic reporting). Thus, not surprisingly, the Wall Street Journal uses the string *line* overwhelmingly to refer to a product line (Leacock et al., 1998).

5. Conclusion

WordNet is a large lexical resource combining features of dictionaries and thesauruses in a unique way that allows for a fresh perspective on the semantics of nouns, verbs, and adjectives and offers new possibilities for exploring the internal structure of the lexicon. The English WordNet experiment demonstrated the feasibility of a large-scale relational lexicon and inspired the creation of wordnets for other languages. Their construction is likely to reveal interesting aspects of the different lexicons as well as crosslinguistic patterns of lexicalization. Its breadth, design, and availability have made the "Ur"-WordNet a valuable tool for a variety of applications in computational linguistics and NLP; we hope that its potential for interesting applications in literary and stylistic studies will soon be tested as well. The development and growth of Euro-wordnets should serve as the basis for further, crosslinguistic applications (see Gonzalo et al., this volume).

Notes

[1] Preparation of this paper was supported in part by contract N66001-94-C-6045 with the Advanced Research Project Agency, contract N6601-95-C-8605 with the Advanced Research Project Agency, Computer Aided Education and Training Initiative and grant IRI-9528983 from the National Science Foundation.

[2] Fellbaum (1998a) contains up-to-date descriptions and discussions of all aspects the WordNet database, as well as a representative overview of WordNet-based applications.

[3] The members of a synset are usually not absolute synonyms; most are interchangeable in some, but not all contexts.

[4] Before semantic disambiguation can be attempted, the syntactic category of the word that is to be disambiguated must be established; here, we will not be concerned with this important preliminary step.

[5] The tagged novella and the Brown Corpus, as well as ConText, are freely available to researchers.

References

Apresjan, Y. "Regular Polysemy". *Linguistics*, 142 (1973), 5–32.

Chaffin, R., D. J. Hermann and M. Winston. "An Empirical Taxonomy of Part-whole Relations: Effects of Part-whole Relation Type on Relation Identification". *Language and Cognitive Processes*, 3 (1988), 17–48.

Fellbaum, C. "Adverbs in Agentless Actives and Passives". In *Proceedings of the 21st Meeting of the Chicago Linguistic Society, Parasession on Agentivity and Causatives*. Eds. W. Eilfort et al., Chicago, IL: University of Chicago, 1985a.

Fellbaum, C. *On the Middle Construction in English*. Bloomington, IN: Indiana University Linguistics Club, 1985b.

Fellbaum, C. (ed.). *WordNet: An Electronic Lexical Database*. Cambridge, MA: MIT Press, 1998a.

Fellbaum. C. "A Semantic Network of English Verbs". In WordNet: An Electronic Lexical Database. Ed. C. Fellbaum, 1998a.

Fellbaum, C. "The English Verb Lexicon as a Semantic Net". *International Journal of Lexicography*, 3 (1990), 278–301.

Fellbaum, C. "Semantics via Conceptual and Lexical Relations". In *Breadth and Depth of the Lexicon*. Ed. E. Viegas, Dordrecht: Kluwer, in press.

Gross, D., U. Fischer and K. J. Miller. "The Organization of Adjectival Meanings". *Journal of Memory and Language*, 28 (1989), 92–106.

Justeson, J. and S. Katz. "Co-occurrences of Antonymous Adjectives and Their Contexts". *Computational Linguistics*, 17 (1991), 1–19.

Keyser, S. J. and T. Roeper. "On the Middle and Ergative Constructions in English". *Linguistic Inquiry*, 15 (1984), 381–416.

Landes, S., C. Leacock and R. Tengi. "Building Semantic Concordances". In WordNet: An Electronic Lexical Database. Ed. C. Fellbaum, 1998.

Leacock, C., M. Chodorow and G. A. Miller. "Using Corpus Statistics and WordNet Relations for Sense Identification". *Computational Linguistics*, 24 (1998), 1.

Levin, B. *English Verb Classes and Alternations*. Chicago, IL: University of Chicago Press, 1993.

Miller, G. A. "Dictionaries in the Mind". *Language and Cognitive Processes*, 1 (1986), 171–185.

Miller, G. A. "Nouns in WordNet". *International Journal of Lexicography*, 3 (1990), 235–264.

Miller, G. A., M. Chodorow, S. Landes, C. Leacock and R. G. Thomas. "Using a Semantic Concordance for Sense Identification". In *Proceedings of the ARPA Workshop on Human Language Technology*. San Francisco: Morgan Kaufman, 1994.

Miller, G. A. "Preface". WordNet: An Electronic Lexical Database. Ed. C. Fellbaum, 1998a.

Miller, G. A. "Nouns in WordNet". WordNet: An Electronic Lexical Database. Ed. C. Fellbaum, 1998b.

Miller, G. A., C. Leacock, R. Tengi and R. T. Bunker. "A Semantic Concordance". In *Proceedings of the ARPA Workshop on Human Language Technology*. San Francisco: Morgan Kaufman, 1993.

Miller, K. "Modifiers in WordNet". WordNet: An Electronic Lexical Database. Ed. C. Fellbaum, 1998.

Nunberg, G. *The Pragmatics of Reference*. Bloomington, IN: Indiana University Linguistics Club, 1978.

Ostler, N. and B. T. S. Atkins. "Predictable Meaning Shifts: Some Linguistic Properties of Lexical Implication Rules". In *Lexical Semantics and Knowledge Representation*. Eds. J. Pustejovsky and S. Association for Computational Linguistics, 1992, pp. 76–87.

Perlmutter, D. M. "Impersonal Passives and the Unaccusative Hypothesis". *Berkeley Linguistics Society*, 4 (1970), 157–189.

Weinreich, U. *Explorations in Semantic Theory*. Den Hague: Mouton, 1972.

Computers and the Humanities **32**: 221–251, 1998.
© 1998 *Kluwer Academic Publishers.*

Cross-linguistic Alignment of Wordnets with an Inter-Lingual-Index

WIM PETERS[1], PIEK VOSSEN[2], PEDRO DÍEZ-ORZAS[3] and GEERT ADRIAENS[4]

[1]*University of Sheffield, Computer Science Department, Portobello Street 211, Sheffield, S1 4DT, UK; E-mail: w.peters@dcs.sheffield.ac.uk;* [2]*Universiteit van Amsterdam, Faculteit Geesteswetenschappen, Spuistraat 134, 1012 VB Amsterdam, The Netherlands; E-mail: Piek.Vossen@let.uva.nl;* [3]*University of Madrid Alfonso X El Sabio, Madrid; E-mail: pdiez@uax.es;* [4]*Lernout & Hauspie, Potsleihof 1, Antwerp, Belgium; E-mail: Geert.Adriaens@lhs.be*

Key words: aligning wordnets, equivalence relations, multilingual database

Abstract. This paper discusses the design of the EuroWordNet database, in which semantic databases like WordNet1.5 for several languages are combined via a so-called inter-lingual-index. In this database, language-independent data is shared whilst language-specific properties are maintained. A special interface has been developed to compare the semantic configurations across languages and to track down differences.

1. Introduction

EuroWordNet is an EC-funded project (LE2-4003) that aims to build a multilingual database consisting of wordnets in several European languages. Each language specific wordnet is structured along the same lines as WordNet (Miller et al., 1990): i.e. synonyms are grouped in synsets, which in their turn are related by means of basic semantic relations. As explained in Vossen (this volume), the wordnets in EuroWordNet are treated as autonomous language-specific systems. This makes it possible to build the wordnets relatively independently, which is necessary because the construction takes place at different sites with very different starting points in terms of available resources and tools. Another advantage is that we are able to maintain language-specific properties of the individual wordnets. In principle, the wordnets contain relations only between lexicalized units (words and expressions) of each language. This gives the correct predictions on the expressibility of concepts in languages and it avoids endless discussion on the unification of the different structures in the languages. Each wordnet is thus a unique, language-specific structure. To create a multilingual database, we store the language-specific wordnets in a central lexical database while the equivalent word meanings across the languages are linked to each other. Via the equivalence relation it will thus be possible to compare the wordnets, so that we can learn from the differences. We can for instance assess what are inconsistent configurations across wordnets, or what are language-specific properties.

In this paper we will discuss in detail the multilingual design of the database and the ways in which it should give access to the resources to make this type of comparison possible. The structure of this paper is as follows. In the next section we will compare different multilingual design options for our database, and motivate our choice for a so-called Inter-Lingual-Index. This Inter-Lingual-Index is an unstructured list of concepts that only functions as a fund for interlinking word meanings across languages. We will then further explain the design and the way in which the equivalence relations are expressed. In section 3 we will discuss the different types of mismatches that can occur across the wordnets, and the way in which they can be compared in the database to extract the most important cases of mismatch.

Finally, in section 4 we describe how we improve the Inter-Lingual-Index (which is mainly based on WordNet1.5 synsets) to get a more consistent matching across the wordnets. Due to differences in the sense-differentiation across resources, many equivalent synsets may not be linked at all. By extending the Inter-Lingual-Index with coarser synsets that relate several, more specific meanings, we can improve the matching in an elegant and modular way.

2. The Multilingual Design

In the EuroWordNet database, large-scale lexical semantic resources for many languages are interconnected. Currently, resources are included for English (two resources), Dutch, Italian, Spanish, German, French, Czech and Estonian. Furthermore, we collaborate with other research groups developing wordnets for their national languages. In the future, the database will thus be further extended. The multilingual nature of such a database raises several methodological issues for its design and development. We have considered four possible designs for the database in which language specific wordnets are conceptually linked in different ways, most of which correspond with approaches in machine translation (Copeland et al., 1991; Nirenburg, 1989):

(a) by pairs of languages
(b) through a structured artificial language
(c) through one of the languages
(d) through a non-structured index

The first option (a) is to pair-wise link the languages involved (comparable to traditional transfer-based machine translation systems). This makes it possible to precisely establish the specific equivalence relation across pairs of languages, but it also multiplies the work by the number of languages to be linked. Furthermore, the addition of a new language will require the addition of new equivalence relations for all the other languages, with all the possible consequences. The second option

(b) is to link the languages through a structured language-neutral inter-lingua. A language-independent conceptual system or structure may be represented in an efficient and accurate way but the challenge and difficulty is to achieve such a meta-lexicon, capable of supplying a satisfactory conceptual backbone to all the languages. A drawback from a methodological point of view is that new words that are added in one of the languages or completely new wordnets that are added, might call for a revision of a part of the language-independent network.

As a third possibility the linking can be established via one language. This resolves the inconveniences and difficulties of the former two options, but forces an excessive dependency on the lexical and conceptual structure of one of the languages involved. The last possibility (d) is to link through a non-structured list of concepts (the Inter-Lingual-Index), which forms the superset of all concepts encountered in the different languages involved. This list does not satisfy any cognitive theory, because it is an unstructured index with unique identifiers for concepts that do not have any internal or language-independent structure. This has the advantage that it is not necessary to maintain a complex semantic structure that incorporates the complexity of all languages involved. Furthermore, the addition of a new language will minimally affect any of the existing wordnets or their equivalence relations to this index.

For pragmatic reasons we have chosen design (d), which is a variant of option (b) and (c). An unstructured index as a linking device is most beneficial with respect to the effort needed for the development, maintenance, future expansion and reusability of the multilingual database. The different language wordnets are given a maximal flexibility in connecting up to this list of concepts. This list starts off as the total set of WordNet concepts, which makes it a variant of option (c), but the lack of interlingual conceptual structure, as opposed to option (b), makes extension simple without having to take the conceptual structure of WordNet into account, and allows, if necessary, flexible adjustments of the level of granularity of WordNet sense distinctions (see section 4).

Of course, the adopted architecture is not without difficulties. These are especially crucial in the process of handling the index and creating tools for the developers to obtain a satisfactory result. Tasks such as identifying the right inter-lingual correspondence when a new synset is added in one language, or how to control the balance between the languages are good examples of issues that need to be resolved when this approach is taken.

2.1. THE INTER-LINGUAL-INDEX AND THE LANGUAGE-MODULES

As mentioned in the introduction, each wordnet represents a language-internal system of synsets with semantic relations such as hyponymy, meronymy, cause, roles (e.g. *agent*, *patient*, *instrument*, *location*) comparable to the structure of Word-Net1.5 (Miller et al., 1990). Equivalence relations between the synsets in different languages and WordNet1.5 are made explicit in the so-called Inter-Lingual-Index

(ILI). The ILI starts off as an unstructured list of WordNet1.5 synsets with their glosses, and will grow when new concepts are added, which are not present in WordNet1.5. In addition to the gloss, an ILI-record may have one or more domain-labels (e.g. *sports*, *water sports*, *winter sports*, *military*, *hospital*) or top-concepts (e.g. *Object* or *Dynamic*) linked to it. The latter are described in Rodriquez et al. (this volume), whereas Vossen (this volume) gives an overview of the different modules.

Each synset in the monolingual wordnets will have at least one equivalence relation with a record in this ILI. Language-specific synsets linked to the same ILI-record should thus be equivalent across the languages. This is illustrated in Figure 1, which is taken from the graphical interface to the EuroWordNet database, called Periscope (Cuypers and Adriaens, 1997). The top-half of the screen-dump shows a window with a fragment of the Dutch wordnet at the left and a similar fragment of WordNet1.5 at the right. The bottom window shows a similar parallel view for the Italian and Spanish wordnets. Each synset in these windows is represented by a rectangular box followed by the synset members. On the next line, the closest Inter-Lingual-Index concept is given, following the = sign (which indicates direct equivalence). In this view, the ILI-records are represented by an English gloss. Below a synset-ILI pair, the language-internal relations can be expanded, as is done here for the hypernyms. The target of each relation is again represented as a synset with the nearest ILI-equivalent (if present). The first line of each wordnet gives the equivalent of *cello* in the 4 wordnets. In this case, they are all linked to the same ILI-record, which indirectly suggests that they should be equivalent across the wordnets as well. We also see that the hypernyms of *cello* are also equivalent in the two windows, as is indicated by the lines connecting the ILI-records. Apparently, the structures are parallel across the Dutch wordnet and WordNet1.5 on the one hand and the Spanish and Italian wordnets on the other. However, we see that the intermediate levels for *bowed stringed instrument* and *stringed instrument* in the Dutch wordnet and WordNet1.5 are missing both in Italian and Spanish. Had we compared other wordnet pairs, the intermediate synsets would be unmatched across the wordnets. Because the ILI is unstructured, different parallelisms and structural mismatches can easily be expressed, without complicating the comparison. Note also that the actual internal organization of the synsets by means of semantic relations can still be recovered from the WordNet database, which is linked to the index as any of the other wordnets.

2.2. COMPLEX EQUIVALENCE RELATIONS

Next to the language-internal relations (discussed in Alonge et al., this volume]) there are six different types of inter-lingual relations. The most straightforward relation is EQ_SYNONYM, which applies to meanings which are directly equivalent to some ILI-record, as has been shown in Figure 1. In addition there are relations for complex-equivalent relations, among which the most important are:

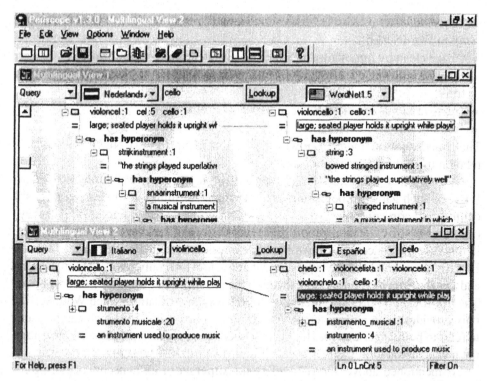

Figure 1. Parallel wordnet structures in EuroWordNet linked to the same ILI-records.[1]

- EQ_NEAR_SYNONYM when a meaning matches multiple ILI-records simultaneously,

- EQ_HAS_HYPERONYM when a meaning is more specific than any available ILI-record,

- EQ_HAS_HYPONYM when a meaning can only be linked to more specific ILI-records.

The complex-equivalence relations are comparable to the different kind of mismatches across word meanings as have been described in the Acquilex project in the form of complex *TLINKS* (Ageno et al., 1993; Copestake et al., 1995; Copestake and Sanfilippo, 1993). It is possible to manually encode these relations directly in the database, but they can also be extracted semi-automatically using the technology developed in Acquilex. In EuroWordNet, the complex relations are needed to help the relation assignment during the development process when there is a lexical gap in one language or when meanings do not exactly fit (see also Vossen et al., this volume).

The first situation, in which a single synset matches several ILI-records simultaneously, occurs quite often. The main reason for this is that the sense-differentiation in WordNet1.5 is much larger then in the traditional resources from which the other wordnets are being built. For example, in the Dutch resource there is only one sense for *schoonmaken* (to clean) which simultaneously matches with at least 4 senses of *clean* in WordNet1.5:

- {make clean by removing dirt, filth, or unwanted substances from}
- {remove unwanted substances from, such as feathers or pits, as of chickens or fruit}
- {remove in making clean; "Clean the spots off the rug"}
- {remove unwanted substances from – (as in chemistry)}

The Dutch synset *schoonmaken* will thus be linked with an EQ_NEAR_SYNONYM relation to all these senses of *clean*.

The EQ_HAS_HYPERONYM is typically used for gaps in WordNet1.5 or in English. Such gaps can be genuine, cultural gaps for things not known in English culture, e.g. *citroenjenever*, which is a kind of gin made out of lemon skin, or they can be caused by lexicalization differences between languages, in the sense that in this case the concept is known but not expressed by a single lexicalized form in English. An example of the latter are Dutch *hoofd* which only refers to human head and Dutch *kop* which only refers to animal head, while English uses *head* for both. The EQ_HAS_HYPONYM is then used for the reversed situation, when WordNet1.5 only provides more narrow terms. An example is Spanish *dedo* which can be used to refer to both *finger* and *toe*. In this case there can only be a pragmatic difference, not a genuine cultural gap.

As mentioned above, the ILI will be the **superset** of all concepts occurring in the separate wordnets. The main reasons for this are:

- it should be possible to link equivalent non-English meanings (e.g. Italian-Spanish) to the same ILI-record even when there is no English or WordNet equivalent;
- it should be possible to store domain-labels for non-English meanings, e.g.: all Spanish *bull-fighting* terms should be linked to ILI-records with the domain-label bull-fighting.

Initially, the ILI will only contain WordNet1.5 synsets but eventually it will therefore be updated with language-specific concepts, such as the gaps described above. The updating takes place according to the following procedure:

1. a site that cannot find a proper equivalent among the available ILI-concepts will link the meaning to another ILI-record using a so-called complex-equivalence relation [2] and will generate a potential new ILI-record (see Table I);
2. after a building phase all potential new ILI-records are collected and verified for overlap by one site;
3. a proposal for updating the ILI is distributed to all sites and has to be verified;
4. the ILI is updated and all sites have to reconsider the equivalence relations for all meanings that can potentially be linked to the new ILI-records.

After extending the ILI with the new concepts, each of the local synsets can directly be linked to the new concepts. These synsets will thus have two different equivalence relations, a complex equivalence relation to the closest WordNet1.5 synset and a simple equivalence relation to the new ILI-record.

Table I. Potentially new ILI records for gaps in WordNet1.5

Source Language	New ILI-synset	New ILI-gloss concept	Equivalence relation	Target-
Dutch	citroenjenever	kind of gin made from lemon skin	EQ_HAS_HYPERONYM	gin
Dutch	hoofd	human head	EQ_HAS_HYPERONYM	head
Dutch	kop	animal head	EQ_HAS_HYPERONYM	head
Spanish	dedo	finger or toe	EQ_HAS_HYPONYM	finger
Spanish	dedo	finger or toe	EQ_HAS_HYPONYM	toe

From what has been said so far it follows that there can be many-to-many mappings from local synsets to ILI-records. In all the above cases, a single synset is linked to multiple target synsets in the ILI. This may either be with an EQ_NEAR_SYNONYM relation or with an EQ_HAS_HYPONYM / EQ_HAS_HYPERONYM and with an EQ_SYNONYM to a new ILI-record. In the case of genuine, cultural gaps, the latter matching will probably also result in a situation, where multiple synsets in a local wordnet are linked to the same ILI-record. If a specific meaning, such as the Dutch *citroenjenever* is linked to a more general ILI-record with an EQ_HAS_HYPERONYM relation (e.g. *gin*), the hyperonym of this local synset (in this case the Dutch *jenever*) will probably also be linked to this more general meaning as well with a simple equivalent relation. In general, we can state here that a combination of a simple and a complex equivalence relation to an ILI-record should match the language-internal relation between local synsets.

Finally, a many-to-many mapping often arises when closely-related synsets in a local wordnet are related to multiple closely-related concepts in the ILI. As explained in Alonge et al. (this volume) and Vossen et al. (this volume), it is possible to encode a NEAR_SYNONYM relation between synsets, which are close in meaning but cannot be substituted as easily as synonyms: e.g. *machine, apparatus, tool*, which are members of different WordNet1.5 synsets. In this case it may very well happen that these near-synonyms are linked to the same target ILI-record, either with an EQ_SYNONYM or an EQ_NEAR_SYNONYM relation. Typically, we find such sets as *machine, apparatus, tool* in all the involved languages. We will then get a rather fuzzy matching from the wordnets to a global set of ILI-records as is illustrated in Figure 2 for Dutch and Italian. In this example, 3 near synonyms in the Dutch wordnet are linked to multiple ILI-records, from-top-to-bottom: *device, apparatus, instrument, implement, tool*. The ILI-records are again represented by their glosses, where the synset of the highlighted ILI-record (device:1) is shown in the small box at the bottom-right corner. In the Italian wordnet we see that 4 of these ILI-records are given as EQ_NEAR_SYNONYMS of a single synset *utensile:1* but *device* is linked to *ferrovecchio:2* by an EQ_HAS_HYPERONYM relation (as

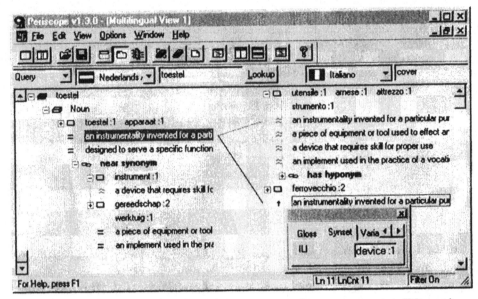

Figure 2. Many-to-many mappings of near synonyms of *apparatus* synsets to ILI-records.

indicated by the symbols). In section 4, we will discuss how we can exercise control over these cases.

3. Comparing the Wordnets via the Multilingual Index

The wordnets are built in different phases. In the first phase each site creates the language-internal structure, and the equivalence relations with Inter-Lingual-Index records (the order may vary from site to site). Once a substantial subset has been covered the next phase will be to load the wordnets in the multilingual database and to carry out systematic comparisons. It is important to realize that the relation with the other wordnets is only established indirectly. Each site only links their meanings to (mostly) English synsets in the ILI (using bilingual dictionaries, Dutch-English, Italian-English and Spanish-English) and comparison is possible when the other wordnets link meanings to the same ILI-records.

Comparison can give information on the consistency of the wordnets and it will reveal areas where there is a mismatch. In principle, the comparison is done separately by the sites, where each site uses the other wordnets (including WordNet1.5) as a reference (Reference wordnets) to learn about their local wordnet (the Source wordnet). When comparing a local Source wordnet with a Reference wordnet, the following general situations can occur (Vossen, 1996):

1. a set of word-meanings across languages has a simple equivalence relation and parallel language-internal relations;
2. a set of word-meanings across languages has a simple equivalence relation but diverging language-internal relations;

3. a set of word-meanings across languages has complex equivalence relations but parallel language-internal relations;
4. a set of word-meanings across languages has complex equivalence relations and diverging language-internal relations.

In general we can state that situation (1) is the ideal case. In the case of (4), it may still be that the wordnets exhibit language-specific differences, which have led to similar differences in the equivalence relations. Situation (2) may indicate a mistake or it may indicate that equivalent meanings have been encoded in an alternative way in terms of the language-internal relations. Situation (3) may also indicate a mistake or it may be the case that the meanings are non-equivalent and therefore show different language-internal configurations. Invalid patterns across wordnets can either point to errors in the language-internal relations or errors in the equivalence relations, representing two sides of the same coin.

In Figure 3, we give some examples of these different mismatches. Here we see that *head-1* represents an intermediate level between *human-head-1* and *external-body part-1* in WordNet1.5 which is missing between their Dutch equivalent *lichaamsdeel-1* and *hoofd-1*. While the equivalence relations match, the hyponymy-structure does not (situation 2 above). Furthermore, *kop-1* does not match any synset in WordNet1.5. In the Spanish-English example we see on the other hand that *apéndice-4* and *dedo-1* have complex equivalence relations which are not compatible with the structure of the language-internal relations in the Spanish wordnet and in WordNet1.5 (situation 4 above).

Given the large number of language-internal relations and six types of equivalence relations, the different combinations of mismatches is exponential. It is however possible to differentiate the degree of compatibility of mismatches: some mismatches are more serious than others. We have already discussed some situations of many-to-many matches between synsets and ILI-records. Here we can put some constraints on the differences that may occur, such as parallelism between complex-equivalence relations and the language-internal relations of the involved wordnets. However, the fuzzy-matching of close meaning to multiple records is more difficult to constrain. Another type of fuzziness applies to language-internal relations that are to some extent compatible. In Vossen et al. (this volume) a detailed description is given of these cases.

Instead of trying to prescribe a solution for every situation we have decided to develop a generic tool which makes it possible to compare the wordnets in any way desired.[3] In the next sections we will describe the two main ways of comparing the wordnets that are of greatest importance for their construction.

3.1. SPECIFIC COMPARISON STRATEGY

The objective of multilingual comparison is to learn from structural mismatches across the wordnets. There are two specific goals:

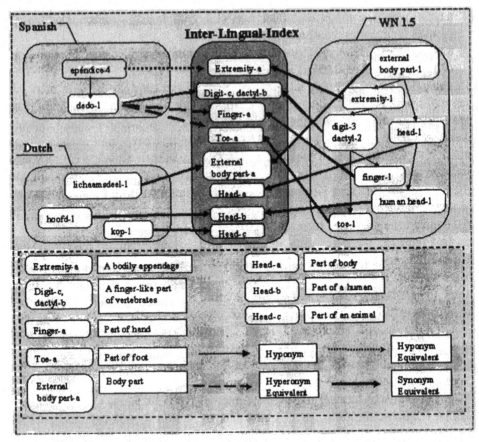

Figure 3. Structural mismatches across wordnets.

1. find alternative classifications for synsets in the Source wordnet from Reference wordnets;
2. find alternative equivalences for synsets in the Source wordnets from Reference wordnets.

When trying to find different or alternative classifications of synsets, we first assume that the equivalence relations are correct. The hypothesis is then that equivalent synsets across wordnets should have hyperonyms that are equivalences as well (assuming the ideal situation 1. described above). It follows that the most important structural mismatch is a difference in hyperonyms across resources. Our experience with comparing hierarchical structures so far has shown that the most common variation within these structures and across languages are (Vossen, 1995):

1. Synsets are classified by another synonymous hyperonym, e.g. *apparatus* or *machine*.
2. Synsets are classified by a wrong hyperonym, e.g. *car* is a kind of *animal*.
3. Synsets are linked to a more general hyperonym, e.g. *car* is an *artifact*.

4. Synsets are classified according to a different conceptualization, e.g. *tricycle* is a *toy* or a *cycle*.

The first situation should not be too much of a problem in our case. Because the relations are already encoded at the synset level (grouping synonymous hypernyms as well) this danger is to a large extent minimalized. In addition, it is possible to look at near synonyms in the Reference wordnet to match hyponymy classifications across wordnets.

In manually created resources, it is seldom the case that a synset is assigned a completely wrong classification (situation 2): i.e. a *car* is not likely classified as an *animal*. As discussed in Vossen et al. (this volume), the main problem for these resources is the incompleteness and inconsistency rather than the logic. However, because our wordnets are partially built using automatic techniques, the last option is not totally unlikely. By selecting the wrong sense of the genus of a definition, a totally wrong class can be assigned.

Situation 3 and 4 are illustrated in Figure 4 below which shows a (hypothetical) matching situation for (sub)hyponyms of *vehicles* in Dutch and Spanish. In both wordnets there is an intermediate level *motorvoertuig* and *vehículo de motor* for *motor vehicle*. In the Spanish wordnet we see that both *automóvil* (car) and *motocicleta* (motorcycle) are linked to this intermediate level. In the Dutch wordnet we see that only *auto* (car) is linked to this level, whereas *motor* (motorcycle) is linked too high up to the higher hyperonym *voertuig* (vehicle). The intermediate level is skipped (situation 3). In the case of the Spanish *triciclo* (tricycle) we see that the Dutch equivalent *driewieler* is linked to the hyperonym *speelgoed* (toy), which expresses a different conceptualization (situation 4), which is not compatible with the Spanish hypernym.

One of the most important reasons for mismatching equivalences is probably the fact that words across languages are translated with closely-related but different words. However, as suggested above, in EWN this danger is already minimized by linking synsets rather than separate words. A more likely situation in our case is the fact that equivalent synsets may be linked to different senses of the same word. As mentioned above, the level of sense-differentiation in WordNet1.5 is very fine-grained. In many cases it is therefore not easy to differentiate between senses in WordNet1.5, as is illustrated by the first two senses of train:

Sense 1

train, railroad train – (a line of railway cars coupled together and drawn by a locomotive)

Sense 2

train – (a connected line of railroad cars behind a locomotive)

In such a case, it is not unlikely that in one wordnet the equivalent is linked to *train* sense 1 and in the other wordnet to sense 2, as is illustrated in Figure 4 below. Because there is still a relation between these mismatches at the word level we call them **near-matches**. In all other cases where synsets across wordnets do not match they represent genuine mismatches where there is no relation. This is illustrated

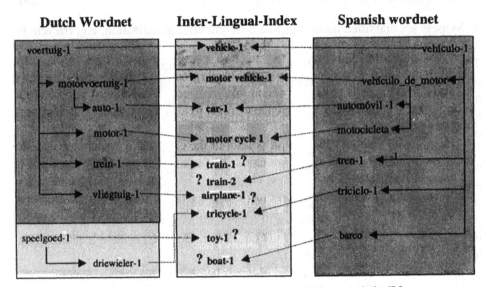

Figure 4. Specific comparison of Dutch and Spanish *vehicles* through the ILI.

below by the ILI-records *airplane* and *boat*, which have no related Spanish and Dutch synset respectively. It may then be the case that the Spanish and Dutch equivalents are linked to other close synsets or that the concepts are not present in the wordnets. It obviously only makes sense to look for these equivalences within a reasonable semantic range of the synsets in the local Source wordnet, which are the *vehicles*.

In the next sections we will describe how the above cases can be extracted in the EuroWordNet database using the generic multilingual interface and the result of comparing 18 semantic clusters across 3 languages.

3.2. GENERIC COMPARISON OPTIONS IN THE EUROWORDNET DATABASE

The EuroWordNet database consists of three components:
- The actual wordnets in Flaim format: an indexing and compression format of Novell.
- Polaris (Louw, 1997): a wordnet editing tool for creating and editing the wordnet databases.
- Periscope (Cuypers and Adriaens, 1997): a graphical database viewer for viewing the wordnet tree-structures.

The Polaris tool is a re-implementation of the Novell ConceptNet toolkit (Díez-Orzas et al., 1995) adapted to the EuroWordNet architecture. Polaris can import new wordnets or wordnet fragments from ASCII files with the correct import format and it creates an indexed EuroWordNet database. Furthermore, it allows a user to edit and add relations in the wordnets and to formulate queries. The Polaris toolkit makes it possible to visualize the semantic relations as a tree-structure that can directly be edited. These trees can be expanded and shrunk by clicking on word-meanings and by specifying so-called TABs indicating the kind and depth of relations that need to be shown. Expanded trees or sub-trees can be stored as a set of synsets, which can be manipulated, saved or loaded. Finally, it is possible to access the ILI or the ontologies, and to switch between the wordnets and ontologies via the ILI. Polaris can be licensed from Linguistic Development in Antwerp. The Periscope program is a public viewer that can be used to look at wordnets created by the Polaris tool and compare them in a graphical interface. Selected trees can be exported to Ascii files. To get to grips with the multilinguality of the database we have developed a specific interface in both programs to deal with the different matching problems:

- A query interface in the wordnet editor **Polaris**, to match sets of synsets across wordnets.
- A graphical interface in **Periscope**, to align parallel wordnets.

Examples of the Periscope viewer have been given above. In the next section we will discuss the comparison options in the Polaris tool.

3.2.1. *Query Interface in the Polaris wordnet editor*

The Polaris query interface presents the results of comparing wordnets in the form of sets of synsets that can be edited. The basic idea is that a particular selection of synsets can be *projected* on another wordnet through the ILI via a special **projection** function. For example, if we take the synsets which are hyponyms and subhyponyms of *vehículo* (vehicle) in Spanish we can first of all generate the set of ILI-records to which they are linked (as EQ_SYNONYM or EQ_NEAR_SYNONYM).[4] Next, we can generate the set of Dutch synsets that are linked to these ILI-records (also as EQ_SYNONYM or EQ_NEAR_SYNONYM). The result of the **projection** function is then: a list with Dutch equivalences that have been recovered by the projection-function, and a list with ILI-records that could not be projected on Dutch. The latter list contains potential gaps in the Dutch wordnet. Taking the above example, this would give the following result:

Expansion of the Spanish wordnet
Spanish (sub)hyponyms of *vehículo*:
    vehículo de motor-1, automóvil-1, motocicleta-1, tren-1, triciclo-1, barco-1
ILI-equivalences of the Spanish *vehicles*:
    motor vehicle-1, car-1, motorcycle-1, train-2, tricycle-1, boat-1

Projection to the Dutch wordnet
Dutch-synsets Projected from Spanish *vehicles*:
    motorvoertuig-1, auto-1, motor-1, driewieler-1
ILI-records for Spanish *vehicles* not projected on Dutch:
    train-2, boat-1

We can now compare the Dutch list of synsets **projected** by the Spanish *vehicles*, with the list of *vehicles* generated by taking the (sub)hyponyms of *voertuig* (vehicle) in the Dutch wordnet directly:

Expansion of the Dutch wordnet

Dutch (sub)hyponyms of *voertuig* (vehicle)   motorvoertuig-1, auto-1, motor-1, vliegtuig-1, trein-1

By applying simple list-operations to the results we will get the following sub-lists:

1. Intersection of Dutch *vehicles* and Spanish projected *vehicles*: motorvoertuig-1, auto-1, motor-1

2. Unique in the Spanish projection: driewieler-1

3. Not-projected Spanish *vehicles*: boat-1, train-2

4. Unique in the Dutch *vehicle* list: vliegtuig-1, trein-1

The intersection of both lists contains matching *vehicles*, classified in a similar way in both wordnets. However, note that we generated the lists by taking the hyponyms at *any* level (including subhyponyms). Because of this we retrieve *motorcycle* in both sets despite the difference in hyponymic level in both wordnets. If we only take the direct hyponyms of *vehicle* this difference will show up. By either taking the specific subtree or the subtree at any depth we can thus focus on different structural mismatches.

The 2nd list then contains synsets that are unique in the Spanish projection. These can be seen as new *vehicles* for the Dutch wordnet. However, the classification of *driewieler* (tricycle) as a *toy* in the Dutch wordnet, may also apply to *triciclo* in the Spanish wordnet, and, perhaps, to other vehicles in both wordnets.

The 3rd and 4th lists contain ILI-records within this semantic scope of *vehicles*, which have not been recovered in the other wordnet. It is then still possible that these synsets represent **near-matches** with other senses of projected ILI-records, as we have discussed above. This can be verified by projecting synsets in a global way to **all** senses of the ILI-records linked to a set of *vehicles*. The projection then takes place on a word level rather than a sense level. This global-projection creates a very large[5] list of ILI-records, many of which cannot be considered as *vehicles* in any way. If we take the ILI-equivalences for the Spanish vehicles above and generate all the senses for all the variants we would get the following list:

```
auto 1;automobile 1;automotive vehicle 1;bicycle 1;bike 1; bike 2;boat
1;boat 2;cable car 1;car 1; car 2;car 3;car 4;car 5;caravan 2;elevator
car 1;gearing 1;gears 1;geartrain 1;gondola 1;gravy boat 1;machine 1;motor
vehicle 1;motorcar 1;motorcycle 1;power train 1;rack 4;railcar 1;railroad
car 1;railroad train 1;railway car 1;roulette wheel 1;sauceboat 1;steering
wheel 1; string 8;train 1;train 2;train 3;train 4;train 5;train 6;train
7;tricycle 1;trike 1;velocipede 1; velocipede 2;wagon train 1;wheel 1;
```

This set includes reasonable senses, such as *train* 1 and 2, but also irrelevant senses such as *train* 6: *long back section of a gown that is drawn along the floor*. By intersecting this incoherent projection with the genuine *vehicles* in Dutch we can

nevertheless filter out the meanings that make sense. In this way we will thus recover the 1st and 2nd sense of *train*, but not *boat* and *airplane*. The latter two then represent genuine mismatches. They can either be:
- translation errors,
- linked to different synsets, which have no overlap at the word level with projected synset members,
- difference in coverage.

This can only be determined by manual inspection.

3.2.2. *Comparing 18 semantic clusters across Spanish, Italian and Dutch*

The following clusters have been examined for the first databases of nouns and verbs, containing between 10,000 and 20,000 synsets per language:
- Dutch wordnet is the Source Wordnet: *Constructions, Comestible, Container, Covering, Feelings, Phenomena*
- Spanish wordnet is the Source Wordnet: *Garment, Place, Furniture, Plant, Cooking, Sounds*
- Italian wordnet is the Source Wordnet: *Animals, Human, Instrument, Vehicle, Movements, Knowledge*

To carry out the comparison, each site has distributed the major hyperonyms that represent the most important tops of these semantic fields, e.g.: {construction-4} in WordNet1.5, {bouwwerk-1} in Dutch, {construzione-1} in Italian and {construcción-4} in Spanish. The comparison then globally consisted of:
- Extract the hyponyms of the Representative hyperonyms in these fields in each wordnet.
- Project the hyponyms of the Reference wordnets to the Source wordnet.
- Compare the projected hyponyms with the hyponyms in the Source wordnet.

The projections in the EuroWordNet database resulted in sets of word meanings (WMs) in the source wordnet related to the same Inter-Lingual-Index concepts.

Table II then gives the overall results of comparing the above clusters in the different source wordnets. The first column for each wordnet gives the total number of synsets in the wordnet fragments that have been compared. The second column gives the number of WMs per cluster linked to the specified hypernyms as hyponyms at any level. The third column gives the number of ILI-records linked to these WMs. The fourth and fifth column give the intersection of the Reference wordnets with the Source wordnet.

The results in Table II are still preliminary because the databases are still in development. At this stage of the project, not all equivalence relations to the ILI have been generated and only part of the total vocabulary has been covered. Obviously, we thus see that the intersections of the WordNet1.5 clusters are the highest (65% average), followed by the Spanish wordnet (34% average), and the Dutch and Italian wordnets (15% average). The lower coverage of the Italian wordnet is due to the fact that the equivalence relations are mainly created by hand, whereas the Dutch and Spanish wordnet generate many equivalences automatically. This

Table II. Comparison results for the first wordnet fragments

	Total of synsets	Word Meanings related to the clusters as hyponyms	The ILI-records related to the WMs in the clusters	Intersection with the Source wordnet	Intersection Percentage of the Source wordnet
WordNet1.5	60,557	16,832	16,832	1272	65%
Dutch wordnet	9,588	3,663	3,312	580	15%
Spanish wordnet	21,179	5,677	5,652	1187	34%
Italian wordnet	24,207	5,406	1,414	286	15%

follows from the low number of ILIs related to the Italian WMs. In the case of Dutch there is a larger set of ILIs but the size of the wordnet fragment is limited (10,000 synsets in total). The comparison clearly shows that a much larger overlap in ILIs is needed to achieve a compatible multilingual resource. This will be the focus of the completion of the wordnets. Note that the total set of synsets aimed at is about 30% of the total set of synsets in WordNet1.5. In this respect, the Spanish and Italian wordnets have already achieved their final size in terms of WMs. The differences in overlap and equivalence relations are partly due to the different approaches followed (see Vossen, this volume). The Spanish wordnet is built by first expanding from WordNet1.5 and only in a later phase by integrating it with a monolingual Spanish resource. The Dutch and Italian wordnets are directly built from monolingual resources, making the mapping to WordNet1.5 more complicated. These mapping problems will show up later for the Spanish wordnet, when it is integrated with the Spanish monolingual resource. Finally, what is not shown in this tables is that 349 cases of near-matches have been found that could be recovered using the projection of all senses of the related ILI-records, as discussed above. In the next section we will discuss how these mismatches can be resolved automatically for all the wordnets.

Note that the lower percentages of intersection for Dutch and Italian do not imply that the clusters are less compatible. It can only imply that a lower proportion of the Reference wordnets is covered. This is obvious since the coverage of Reference wordnets is much higher. To get an impression of the consistency we have inspected the non-overlapping WMs. These WMs can be projected to the Source wordnets but the projected WMs are not part of the clusters of hyponyms: i.e. they are classified differently. Inspection of the non-overlapping WMs has yielded two major conclusions:

- Most mistakes are due to wrong translations, only a few mistakes are due to wrong classifications.
- Alternative classifications occur quite regularly:

constructions:	movable constructions; parts of buildings; institutions
comestibles:	products such as fruits, grain, corn, seeds; drinks; parts of food
containers:	object
covering:	garments; parts of garments
feelings:	stimulus (cause to feel like); more general experiences; attitudes; abilities
phenomena:	process/change/condition; systems; weather conditions; power/force; possibilities; diseases
furniture:	artifact or object
places:	imaginary places; geographic terms; facility/installation (e.g. sports fields); containers
plants:	microorganism; vegetables
sounds:	communicate, breathe
cooking:	creation, change
movement:	sport; natural phenomena

The translation mistakes can be corrected directly in the database but also give feedback on the automatic techniques that have been used to generate the equivalences to the ILI. The alternative classifications have directly been used to extract more consistent classifications across the sites. They represent valuable information to achieve more coherence and consistency across the resources. Partly, they also point to language-specific differences. For example, in Dutch there is no good equivalent for *container* (see Vossen, this volume). Likewise, we see that specific containers are classified in the Dutch wordnet by an alternative hyperonym such as *object*.

4. Adaptation of the Inter-Lingual-Index

As discussed above in section 3, it is possible to find potential areas for revision of the individual wordnets by comparing one wordnet with the other wordnets (including WordNet1.5). These revisions can be done by each site individually but also by revising the ILI-records as such. It is possible to combine an optimalisation of the compatibility of the wordnets with a reduction of the WordNet1.5 sense granularity.

One of the main steps we envisage is the globalization of the matching of meanings with the ILI-synsets (which at present mainly consist of WordNet1.5 sense-distinctions). Typically, many mismatches have to do with differences in the sense-differentiation across the resources. Different lexical resources distinguish different numbers of senses. This is due to the lexicographic criteria that have been applied in the creation of each resource. Especially in WordNet1.5 there appears to be over-differentiation of senses for specific meanings which are often represented by a single meaning in traditional resources (see above: Dutch *schoonmaken* and WordNet *clean*). If we compare the polysemy rate of nouns in WordNet and another resource such as the CRL-LDB (Wilks et al., 1996), and enhanced version of the Longman Dictionary of Contemporary English or LDOCE (Procter, 1978), we obtain the following statistics:

1. monosemic nouns in WordNet which are also monosemic in CRL-LDB: 10046
2. monosemic WordNet synsets which have polysemic CRL-LDB counterparts: 34
3. monosemic CRL-LDB nouns with polysemic WordNet counterparts: 2984

These figures seem to indicate that the granularity of sense distinctions is higher in WordNet than in CRL-LDB. Because of these differences in sense-differentiation across resources and, particularly, the high level of sense differentiation in Word-Net1.5 there is a danger that equivalences across the wordnets are related to different senses of the same word in the ILI. Many cases of these mismatches have been found while determining a shared set of most important meanings in the wordnets (the so-called Base Concepts, see Rodriquez et al. (this volume) for further details). These meanings in the local wordnets have been manually translated to their WordNet1.5 equivalences. The translation often resulted in the selection of different senses of the same words:

- Two project partners have selected the verbal concept *break, damage* (inflict damage upon). This has become a Base Concept.
- A third project partner had selected *break* ("He broke the glass") and *break, bust, cause to break* which has no gloss in WordNet1.5. These have not been selected as Base Concepts. However, the senses are so similar that each matching is equally probable, and the selection of one of these as a base concept must be regarded as arbitrary.

Instead of keeping the extremely-differentiated meanings, one global ILI-record would suffice. A more coarse-grained sense differentiation minimalizes the danger that equivalences across the wordnets are related to different senses of the same word in the ILI.

The high level of polysemy in WordNet also poses problems for NLP applications which depend on semantics. For instance, (cross-language) information retrieval works best with a limited set of senses. The level of ambiguity, and therefore the error rate, rises exponentially when word forms in texts are matched with polysemic WordNet concepts. The situation deteriorates further when the query is expanded by taking in the synonyms of the key word within the synsets (see Gonzalo et al., this volume). NLP applications would also greatly benefit from a more coarse differentiation of the ILI.

In order to account for these diverging mappings from local wordnets onto ILI concepts represented by WordNet1.5 synsets, new ILI records are introduced which constitute a grouping of ILI concepts. These groupings capture lexical regularities or similarities between different senses of words which have not explicitly been indicated within the WordNet structure.

Because the ILI is an unstructured superset of all concepts present in EuroWord-Net (see section 1) we have maximum flexibility to cluster concepts into larger more coarse grained groups. The flexibility would have been greatly reduced if a structured ILI would have impose constraints on the grouping possibilities. From this it follows that the sense grouping is just a relation between concepts in isolation. No obligatory inheritance of the semantic grouping relations applies to hyponyms of grouped concepts. Nevertheless, the semantic regularity defined between the ILI concepts can still serve to indicate potential default sense extensions for hyponyms of concepts in the local wordnets, which are related to sense grouped ILI concepts by means of synonymy. A similar approach has been followed by Hamp and Feldweg (1997), who use a polysemy pointer as a special relational pointer between WordNet based German synsets where strict inheritance is blocked.

Finally, we do not claim that the semantic alternations described by these sense relations are universally applicable to all languages. It may very well be that these regularities are language-specific and we will see below that the database allows for partial linking to subsets of grouped meanings or linking by different forms. This is very much in line with the philosophy behind EuroWordNet which expects the implementation to provide insight into structured language-specific lexicalization patterns and allows flexibility in the encoding of equivalence relations.

Three general types of sense relations have been distinguished: **generalization** for nouns and verbs, **metonymy** for nouns and **diathesis alternations** for verbs. These are described in section 4.1, 4.2 and 4.3 respectively.

4.1. GENERALIZATION

The notion of generalization, from a lexicographical point of view, is not necessarily a systematic relation. The main criterion is that it must be possible to make an ontological generalization over a group of senses which constitutes the lowest common denominator that all senses share. Often it implies a generalization over high-level semantic distinctions such as abstract-concrete and living-non living for nominal ontological classes and verbal semantic subcategorization.

In general, two types of generalization can be distinguished. The first grouping contains members that are more or less equal in ontological status as the following examples show:

> *card 1*: one of a set of small pieces of stiff paper marked in various ways and used for playing games or for telling fortunes;
>
> *card 5*: a sign posted in a public place as an advertisement; "a poster advertised the coming attractions";
>
> *card 6*: formal social introduction;
>
> *card 7*: a record of scores as in golf;

card 8: a list of dishes available at a restaurant.

The common denominator in this case is the fact that all these senses of 'card' denote documents.

give up 6: stop maintaining; of ideas, claims etc.; "He gave up the thought of asking for her hand in marriage"

give up 7: put an end to a state or an activity

The sense distinction in this case is due to difference in semantic preference between the two verb senses.

The second type of generalization reflects a subsumption relation between its members, in that one sense is considered to be underspecified with respect to the other, as in:

child 1: a young person of either sex between infancy and youth; "she writes books for children"; "they're just kids"; " 'tiddler is a British term for youngsters"

child 3: a young male person; "the baby was a boy"; "she made the boy brush his teeth every night"

Here *child 3* is subsumed by *child 1*, which does not specify sex.

4.2. METONYMY

Another typical mismatching problem has to do with the inconsistent representation of instances of regular or systematic polysemy (Apresjan, 1973; Nunberg and Zaenen, 1992; Pustejovsky, 1995). These regular patterns of polysemy allow a systematic ordering of metonymic sense extensions (Copestake, 1995). For instance, *church* may be defined as a *building*, the *service* or both. To model these different types of meaning extension, specific semantic lexical rules may be introduced. Their specificity may increase if necessary, depending on the task of lexical description. Often a metonymic sense extension can be regarded as a derivation of a more basic sense (Ostler and Atkins, 1991). Whenever resources have made different choices for the representation of these regular sense extensions, we may again run into situations where equivalent synsets cannot be linked across wordnets. This problem could be solved by producing relations between classes of regular sense-extensions. A language-specific word meaning linked to *church-building* can thus automatically be linked to another word meaning linked to *church-service,* even though none of the wordnets have both senses.

WordNet1.5 as a general lexicon does have an implicit level of identification of certain types of regular polysemy. An unordered list of regular polysemy types has been created which contains some examples of this phenomenon in the so-called 'cousin' table which is used to produce a grouping on the basis of similarity of meaning (see WordNet database documentation on groups, file groups.7). This cousin table consists of 105 pairs of synsets identifying semantic relations between unrelated branches within WordNet, and is not meant to be exhaustive. The pair members constitute the top nodes of these branches and reflect a number of polysemic regularities such as *organization-building*, *person-social group*, *tree-wood*, *material-product*, *container-quantity* and grinding types (Copestake and Briscoe, 1991) such as *animal-body covering* and *foodstuff-flora*. The lexical relation between each node pair is shared by all descendants of the involved synsets by means of inheritance. This has led to the creation of a 1258 record long table of hyponymic exceptions to the types of semantic relations implicitly contained in the cousin table.

Another attempt at making systematic polysemic patterns in WordNet explicit has been made by (Buitelaar, 1998). Systematic groupings of top level concepts which dominate unrelated branches have been created semi-automatically on the basis of their distribution in WordNet, and form part of the Core Lexical Engine (Pustejovsky, 1995).

It is not a point of discussion here whether these different types of regular polysemy should be individuated in the lexicon or not, and if their explanation/formulation is within the realm of pragmatics or lexical semantics. Nunberg and Zaenen (1992) show that for e.g. grinding operations tests developed by Zwicky and Sadock (1975), which distinguish between vague and ambiguous word usages, imply that grinding licenses one vague 'substance' concept instead of several different senses. A specification of the interpretation can only occur on the basis of pragmatic information or encyclopedic knowledge. This is shown by the acceptability of a sentence like:

My religion forbids me to eat or wear rabbit.

In this example the allowed juxtaposition of the predicates 'eat' and 'wear' causes 'rabbit' to be interpreted as unspecified rabbit stuff.

Specific interpretations for grinding operations and other types of regular polysemy have been encoded as sense distinctions in WordNet, although they do not seem to have been systematically applied. For instance, there are 542 life form-food pairs in WordNet, i.e. words with both a sense under the node life form and a sense under the node food (sometimes with definitions displaying both senses at the same time):

a. buffalo 1:   large shaggy-haired brown bison of N American plains

   buffalo 2:   meat from an American bison

b. mushroom 2:   any of various fleshy fungi of the subdivision Basidiomycota consisting of a cap at the end of a stem arising from an underground mycelium

mushroom 4: fleshy body of any of numerous edible fungi
c. littleneck 2:   a young quahog suitable to be eaten raw

littleneck 1:   a quahog when young and small; frequently eaten raw

Other concepts do not share this sense extension, such as 'bison' and 'dog' which are known to have served as human nutrition on regular occasions.

Within EuroWordNet a first step in grouping noun word senses that display metonymic regularities has been made on the basis of a typology of the noun synset pairs in the WordNet cousins table and regular polysemic types found in the literature. The noun synsets have been grouped under the general header of metonymy, which incorporates the following aspects of systematic polysemy:

- a general notion of involvedness: the senses are related within a typical situation; e.g. social group versus belief, organization versus building:

office   1: where professional or clerical duties are performed; "he rented an office in the new building"

2: an administrative unit of government; "the Central Intelligence Agency"; "the Census Bureau"; "Office of Management and Budget"; "Tennessee Valley Authority"

5: professional or clerical workers in an office; "the whole office was late the morning of the blizzard"

- result:

work   1: activity directed toward making or doing something; "she checked several points needing further work"

2: something produced or accomplished through the effort or activity or agency of a person or thing: "he was indebted to the pioneering work of John Dewey"; "the work of an active imagination"; "erosion is the work of wind or water over time"

- constituent or portion/part vs., whole relations:

drink   1: a serving of a beverage; usually alcoholic

2: any liquid suitable for drinking

4: a liquor or brew containing alcohol; "drink ruined him"

- function:

business 1: a commercial or industrial enterprise and the people who constitute it; "he bought his brothers business"; "a small mom-and-pop business"; "a racially integrated business concern"

2: the activity of providing goods and services involving financial and commercial and industrial aspects; "computers are now widely used in business"

4.3. DIATHESIS ALTERNATIONS AND SEMANTIC PREFERENCE

A third type of regular polysemy in dictionaries is related to the phenomenon of diathesis alternation. Traditional lexical resources often distinguish different meanings for each syntactic pattern that can be associated for a verb, e.g. transitive/intransitive or causative/inchoative usage, even though the core conceptual semantics is not really different. The differentiation is not carried out consistently however, causing again possible mismatches between senses.

In many cases these syntactic patterns can however be predicted from the semantic classification of the meaning. As extensively described in Levin (1993) for English, there are systematic relations between the semantic properties of verbs and their syntactic patterns. This is exemplified by the verbs *hit* and *change*:

a. *hit 1*:   hit a ball (synonym: cause to move by striking)

   hit 2:   come into sudden contact with: "The arrow hit the target"

   hit 3:   deal a blow to; "He hit her hard in the face"

b. *change 1*:   cause to change; make different; cause a transformation; "The advent of the automobile may have altered the growth pattern of the city"; "The discussion has changed my thinking about the issue"

   change 2:   undergo a change; become different in essence; losing one's or its original nature; "She changed completely as she grew older"; "The weather changed last night"

   change 3:   make or become different in some particular way, without permanently losing one's or its former characteristics or essence; "her mood changes in accordance with the weather"; "Prices vary according to the season"

c. *take 1*:   get into one's hands, take physically; "Take a cookie!", "Can you take this bag, please"

   take 27:   have with oneself; have on one's person; "She always takes an umbrella"; "I always carry money"; "She packs a gun when she goes into the mountains"

Differences in arity and the semantic characterization of subcategorized arguments highlight different perspectives on the situation described by the predications, or express semantic notions such as 'causation' and 'result of causation'.

By relating these diathesis alternation patterns to more global ILI-records we will thus be able to link local synsets regardless of whether the verbs in question display dissimilar alternation patterns in different senses, have a number of alternations collapsed in a single sense, or are monosemous.

4.4. PRELIMINARY RESULTS ON POLYSEMY REDUCTION

For the sense grouping task we have first concentrated on the manual grouping of the Base Concepts (1024 synsets in total). The selection of these concepts is described in (Rodriquez et al., this volume). The assumption is that the Base Concepts (BCs) constitute the core vocabulary for the EuroWordNet database and have an anchoring function for any new concepts that will be added. Until now 31 verb and 148 noun sense clusters have been identified. Because work on sense grouping is still ongoing within EuroWordNet only preliminary results can be given here for nouns.

The total number of senses distinguished within WordNet for the 585 polysemous nouns occurring as base concept (BC) synset members is 1052. 786 of these noun senses have actually been clustered into sense groups, which means that sense grouping has been applied to 74 percent of all the senses of the nouns involved. The reduction of 786 senses to 148 sense groups indicates an overall polysemy reduction of 71 percent for the examined BC senses, which is a 14 percent reduction of the polysemy rate of all senses present in WordNet (and therefore the ILI) for the 585 nouns under examination.

To measure the effect of introducing sense-groups for the purpose of comparing the coverage of the different wordnets we have examined sense-groups for cases of regular polysemy between *organisations* and the *constructions* they work in. The following lists the new ILI records which represent sense clusters and the original ILI concepts they consist of:

	new composite ILIs	ILIs clustered by the composite ILIs
construction	6	15
organisation	62	128

The hyponyms of the local representatives of *construction* and *organisation* in each wordnet were projected onto WordNet1.5, before and after the updating of the ILI, as is shown in the following.

Projections of *organisations* to WordNet1.5 (854 synsets in WordNet1.5):

Reference wordnets	Local representatives of organisation	Hyponyms in reference wordnet	Projection to WN15 before ILI update	Projection to WN15 after ILI update	New projections
ES	organización-3	186	186	210	24

IT	gruppo-2	25	15	25	10
NL	organisatie-3	48	53	74	21
Union			222	248	32

Projections of *constructions* to WordNet1.5 (1210 synsets in WordNet1.5):

Reference wordnets	Local representatives of **organisation**	Hyponyms in reference wordnet	Projection to WN15 before ILI update	Projection to WN15 after ILI update	New projections
ES	construccion-4	553	548	561	13
IT	costruzione-1	194	7	10	203
NL	bouwwerk-1	351	195	206	11
Union			666	685	20

The results of this first evaluation indicate that comparison and extension of the wordnets according to patterns of systematic polysemy will lead to more complete and compatible wordnets.

4.5. INTEGRATING SENSE GROUPING INTO THE DATABASE

To accommodate the cases of generalization and metonymy described above, we will add more global records to the ILI that express these grouping relations between other more specific ILI-records. Whenever a local synset is linked to a specific ILI-record it will also be linked to the more global record if present, whereby a special equivalence relation is used. It is then possible to match local synsets, either via direct equivalence relations or via globalized equivalence relations. To achieve this, the structure of the ILI-records has been extended with fields to store the grouped ILI-records and information on the nature of the grouping relation.

When we globalize a meaning we get an ILI-record with a reference to multiple source ILIs and a specification of the globalization relation. In the case of **generalization**, the ILI entry is as follows, where we take the verb "clean" as an example:

ILI-ID	@62475@
Synset	clean,
Polysemy-type	Generalization
Source-references	
Source-id	106221
Word form	clean

POS	VERB
Gloss	(make clean by removing dirt, filth, or unwanted substances from; "Clean the stove!"; "The dentist cleaned my teeth")
Original-ILI-ID	@61238@
Source-id	109110
Word form	clean
POS	VERB
Gloss	(remove unwanted substances from, such as feathers or pits, as of chickens or fruit; "Clean the turkey")
Original-ILI-ID	@61262@
Source-id	881863
Word form	clean
POS	VERB
Gloss	(remove in making clean; "Clean the spots off the rug")
Original-ILI-ID	@66910@
Source-id	881979
Word form	Clean
POS	VERB
Original-ILI-ID	@66911@
Gloss	(as in chemistry)

When we run an update on the ILI-index the program can generate an additional EQ_GENERALIZATION relation for each local-synset which is linked to one of the listed source-wordnets with an EQ_SYNONYM or EQ_NEAR_SYNONYM relation:

Dutch		Spanish	
schoonmaken 1		limpiar 2	
ILI-reference		ILI-reference	
Eq_near_synonym	@61262@	Eq_synonym	@61238@
Eq_near_synonym	@66911@	**Eq_generalization**	**@62475@**
Eq_generalization	**@62475@**		

Here we see that the Dutch wordnet has linked a single sense for *schoonmaken 1* to multiple senses in WN and now has an additional link EQ_GENERALIZATION to the more global ILI-record. The Spanish word *limpiar 2* is linked to a different

WN sense of *clean*. The Dutch and Spanish synsets can now be retrieved as global equivalences via the more global EQ_GENERALIZATION link.

In the case of **metonymy** between *university* as the building and as the institute the structure will look as follows:

ILI-ID	@62489@
Synset	university
Polysemy-type	Metonymy
Source-references	
Source-id	2039764
Word form	university
POS	NOUN
Original-ILI-ID	@12547@
Gloss	(where a seat of higher learning is housed, including administrative and living quarters as well as facilities for research and teaching)
Source-id	5276749
Word form	university
POS	NOUN
Original-ILI-ID	@35629@
Gloss	(the faculty and students of a university);

Here we see a new global ILI-record which relates *university* 1 (the building) and *university* 2 (the institute). There is a new compiled gloss and both senses are referred to in Source-references. In the ILI-synset both meanings are listed. Note that it may also be possible that one of the senses of *university* is missing in WordNet1.5. In that case we can add the missing sense first and next create a global ILI-record where one of the source-references refers to the newly added ILI-record.

When we run an update on the ILI-index the program can again generate an additional EQ_METONYM relation for each local-synset which is linked to one of the listed source-wordnets with an EQ_SYNONYM or EQ_NEAR_SYNONYM relation:

Dutch	Italian	Spanish
universiteit 1 {institution}	universiteit 2 {building}	universidad 1 {institution; building}
ILI-reference	ILI-reference	ILI-reference
Eq_synonym @35629@	Eq_synonym @12547@	Eq_near_synonym @12547@
Eq_metonym @62489@	**Eq_metonym @62489@**	Eq_near_synonym @35629@
universitare 1 {building}		**Eq_metonym @62489@**
ILI-reference		
Eq_synonym @12547@		
Eq_metonym @62489@		

Note that it is not necessary that the metonymy-relation also holds in the local language. In this example only the Dutch wordnet has two senses that parallel the metonymy-relation in the ILI. The relation between these two Dutch senses is now also encoded via the metonymy-equivalence relation with the more global ILI-record. The Italian and Spanish example only list one sense (which may be correct or an omission in their resources). In the case of Spanish there are multiple equivalences of both senses of *university*, whereas the Italian synset is only linked to the *building* sense. The Spanish example is, in fact, equivalent to the new globalized ILI-record. Even though none of the local wordnets has the same differentiation, all four meanings now share the metonymy link and, likewise, can be retrieved in a global way when we look for synsets to the same ILI-record with EQ_METONYM.

In the following example the verb *open* displays an inchoative-causative **diathesis alternation**, which corresponds to an intransitive-transitive distinction:

ILI-ID	@72531@
Synset	open
Polysemy-type	Diathesis
Source-references	
Source-id	00772933
Word form	open, become open, open up
POS	VERB
Original-ILI-ID	@66078@
Gloss	("The door opened")
Source-id	00773597
Word form	open, open up, cause to open
POS	VERB
Original-ILI-ID	@66082@
Gloss	("Mary opened the car door")

Again, it will depend on each language whether the same pattern is encoded in the language-specific structures. Using the global matching we can still retrieve synsets across wordnets linked by a diathesis-relation across languages, regardless of the parallelism in alternation across the languages.

In summary: there will be two references to ILI records for any synsets having an equivalence relation with a specific, i.e. non-generalized ILI concept, and a sense-grouped ILI concept. It is important to note that that the more specific meanings in WordNet1.5 will be preserved by means of their ILI counterparts. This means that finer sense distinctions are always available when needed. A local wordnet builder can thus still link to a specific ILI concept taken from WordNet1.5 and the update function of the database will globalize this reference automatically.

Furthermore, some applications, such as machine translations or language-learning or generation tools, may require these specific meanings.

We can thus query the database for the specific equivalences or for the global equivalences across wordnets, where the latter synsets are related by EQ_GENERALIZATION, EQ_METONYM, EQ_DIATHESIS equivalence relations. This is not any different than querying EQ_NEAR_SYNONYM or HAS_EQ_HYPERONYM relations when examining links with specific ILI concepts. We have shown that most of the restructuring and updating described in this section can be done automatically. Only in cases where we add completely new meanings to the ILI will we have to do an update whereby each site will reconsider the relevant changes.

5. Conclusion

In this paper we discussed the overall design of the EuroWordNet database, the ways in which multilingual relations are expressed and how wordnets can be compared. We argued for a design which uses an unstructured Inter-Lingual-Index or ILI as the interlingua to connect the different wordnets. An unstructured fund of concepts has the following major advantages:

- complex multilingual relations only have to be considered site by site and there will be no need to communicate about concepts and relations from a many-to-many perspective;
- future extensions of the database can take place without re-discussing the ILI structure. The ILI can then be seen as a fund of concepts, which can be used in any way to establish a relation to the other wordnets.

The choice for the design of the database is based on pragmatic considerations. The architecture will allow maximum efficiency for simultaneous multilingual implementation at more than one site, and will offer an empirical view of the problems related to the creation of an inter-lingua by aligning the wordnets, whereby mismatches between 'equivalent' semantic configurations will be revealed. These mismatches may be due to:

- a mistake in the equivalence-relations (inter-lingual links)
- a mistake in the Language Internal Relations
- a language-specific difference in lexicalization

By using the cross language comparison and the tools described in section 3 a particular series of mismatches can provide criteria for selecting which part of the semantic network needs inspection, and may give clues on how to unify diverging semantic configurations. This will constitute the first step towards generating an interlingua on the basis of a set of aligned language-specific semantic networks. Finally, we described how the ILI itself can be improved as a fund of concepts, to provide a better matching of wordnets. By adding globalized synsets and linking the synsets in the wordnets to both the specific meanings and the more global meanings, many potential mismatches due to the inconsistent differentiation of senses in the lexical resources can be recovered. The globalizations are based on ontological generalizations and regular polysemy relations between senses known in the literature. How many of these relations can be extracted semi-automatically from WordNet1.5 is still under investigation.

Notes

[1] Throughout this paper, and also in this example, WordNet1.5 sense numbers may not correspond with the sense numbers generated by the original WordNet1.5 viewer. The version of WordNet1.5 loaded in EuroWordNet is converted from another database which uses different sense numbers. These sense numbers are however still related to the file offset positions that uniquely identify the synsets.

[2] Note that in cases such as *clean* in WordNet1.5, it is not strictly necessary to change the ILI. However, as we will discuss below in section 4, we will nevertheless take some measures to deal with such over-differentiation, so that the matching across synsets will be more consistent.

[3] Finding and classifying the typical mismatches that occur is one of the research goals of EuroWordNet.

[4] In this example the Dutch wordnet is the Source wordnet to be checked and the Spanish wordnet is the Reference wordnet from which we try to infer new information. Obviously, the same strategy can also be applied the other way around with slightly different results.

[5] By just taking all the senses of the Spanish vehicles in the example we would get a list of 17 synsets. However, since we also should consider the senses of the other variants in the synsets the list will even be much bigger than that.

References

Ageno A., F. Ribas, G. Rigau, H. Rodriquez and F. Verdejo. *TGE: Tlinks Generation Environment*. Acquilex II (BRA 7315) Working Paper 7. Polytecnica de Catalunya, Barcelona, 1993.

Alonge, A. *Definition of the Links and Subsets for Verbs*. EuroWordNet Project LE4003, Deliverable D006. University of Amsterdam, Amsterdam, Http: //www.let.uva.nl/~ewn, 1996.

Apresjan, J. "Regular Polysemy". *Linguistics*, 142, 1973.

Bloksma, L., P. Díez-Orzas and P. Vossen. *The User-Requirements and Functional Specification of the EuroWordNet-project*. EuroWordNet deliverable D001, LE2-4003. University of Amsterdam, Amsterdam, Http: //www.let.uva.nl/~ewn, 1996.

Buitelaar, P. *Corelex: Systematic Polysemy and Underspecification*. PhD. Thesis, Department of Computer Science, Brandeis University, 1998.

Climent, S., H. Rodríguez and J. Gonzalo. *Definition of the Links and Subsets for Nouns of the EuroWordNet project*. EuroWordNet Project LE4003, Deliverable D005. University of Amsterdam, Amsterdam, Http: //www.let.uva.nl/~ewn, 1996.

Copeland, C., J. Durand, S. Krauwer and B. Maegaard (eds.). *The Eurotra Formal Specifications*. Luxembourg: Office for Official Publications of the European Community, 1991.

Copestake A. and T. Briscoe. "Lexical Operations in a Unification-based Framework". In *Lexical Semantics and Knowledge Representation*. Ed. J. Pustejovsky and S. Bergler, Association for Computational Linguistics, 1991.

Copestake A., T. Briscoe, P. Vossen, A. Ageno, I. Castellon, F. Ribas, G. Rigau, H. Rodriguez and A. Sanmiotou. "Acquisition of Lexical Translation Relations from MRDs". *Journal of Machine Translation*, 9(3), 1995.

Copestake A. and A. Sanfilippo. *Multilingual Lexical Representation*. Acquilex II (BRA 7315) Working Paper 2. Cambridge University, 1993.

Copestake, A. "Representing Lexical Polysemy". *Proceedings of AAAI*. Stanford: Stanford Spring Symposium, 1995.

Cuypers, I. And G. Adriaens. *Periscope: the EWN Viewer*. EuroWordNet Project LE4003, Deliverable D008d012. University of Amsterdam, Amsterdam. Http: //www.let.uva.nl/~ewn, 1997.

Díez-Orzas P. and I. Cuypers. *The Novell ConceptNet*. Internal Report, Novell Belgium NV, 1995.

Díez Orzas, P., M. Louw and Ph. Forrest. *High Level Design of the EuroWordNet Database*. EuroWordNet Project LE2-4003, Deliverable D007. 1996.

Louw, M. *The Polaris User Manual*. Internal Report, Lermout & Hauspie, 1997.

Levin, B. *English Verb Classes and Alternations, a Preliminary Investigation*. Chicago/London: University of Chicago Press, 1993.

Miller, A., R. Beckwidth, C. Fellbaum, D. Gross, and K. J. Miller. "Introduction to WordNet: An On-line Lexical Database". *International Journal of Lexicography*, 3(4) (1990), 235–244.

Nirenburg, S. (ed.). "Knowledge-based MT". *Special issue Machine Translation*, 4(1 and 2) (1989).

Nunberg, G. and A. Zaenen. "Systematic Polysemy in Lexicology and Lexicography". In *Proceedings of EURALEX'92*. University of Tampere, 1992.

Ostler, N. and S. Atkins. "Predictable Meaning Shift: Some Linguistic Properties of Lexical Implication Rules". In *Lexical Semantics and Knowledge Representation*. Ed. J. Pustejovsky and S. Bergler, Association for Computational Linguistics, 1991.

Peters, W., I. Peters and P. Vossen. "Automatic Sense Clustering in EuroWordNet". *Proceedings of the first LREC Conference*. Granada, 1988.

Procter, P. (ed.). *Longman Dictionary of Contemporary English*. Harlow and London: Longman, 1987.

Pustejovsky, J. *The Generative Lexicon*. Cambridge MA: MIT Press, 1995.

Vossen, P. *Grammatical and Conceptual Individuation in the Lexicon*. PhD. Thesis, University of Amsterdam, IFOTT, Amsterdam, 1995.

Vossen, P. *Right or Wrong: Combining Lexical Resources in the EuroWordNet Project*. In *Proceedings of Euralex-96M*. Eds. M. Gellerstam, J. Jarborg, S. Malmgren, K. Noren, L. Rogstrom and C. R. Papmehl, Goetheborg, 1996, pp. 715–728.

Zwicky, A. and J. Sadock. "Ambiguity Tests and How to Fail Them". In *Syntax and Semantics 4*. Ed. J. Kimball, New York: Academic Press, 1975.